GOLDEN TREASURY OF TEXTS

GOLDEN TREASURY OF TEXTS

FOR EVERY DAY IN THE YEAR

Copyright © 1977 by Christian Herald Association

Revised Edition

Christian Herald Books, Chappaqua, New York 10514

ISBN No. 0-915684-15-2

Library of Congress Catalog Card No. 76-55524

No part of this book may be reproduced or used in any form without the express permission of the publisher in writing.

Manufactured in the United States of America

GOLDEN TREASURY OF TEXTS

A CHRISTIAN HERALD CLASSIC

Introduction

THE GOLDEN TREASURY OF TEXTS FOR EVERY DAY IN THE YEAR is another in the Christian Herald Classics series. This collection of inspirational classics will bring back in a convenient and popular format some of the great works of our Christian heritage. Books in the series will examine many different facets of Christian life, but all will be profoundly biblical in orientation and possess the power to communicate ageless truth because they address the deep and fundamental longings of the human soul for consolation and for hope.

The GOLDEN TREASURY is a daily devotional guide in the style and form we have come to recognize as standard for the type. It was in fact this book which, in large part, established the primacy of the daily devotion format in this country at the turn of the century. Its concise and evocative presentation of biblical themes won wide acceptance. And its three part structure for each daily entry provides an easy scale of steps that lead one from God's Word, to reflection upon that Word, to prayer.

We might call such a design centrifugal. Each daily entry begins with a verse or verses on a common theme from Scripture which provides a focus for the reader's reflection. Next there is a short prose passage which explains, elaborates and expands upon this theme to concentrate and direct our own reflection. Finally, there is a short poetic prayer which leads our thoughts outward from the text to our own lives, to the lives of our loved ones and to the concerns of the world we live in.

This altogether satisfactory format cannot have been accidental. It forms, as it were, a Circle of Devotion—God's Word, Man, Prayer returning to God—which becomes a model for authentic Christian life. Thus we sense that devotional reading is a unique sort of enterprise, one that is emblematic of the Christian's response to life.

Unlike reading for information, the habit of mind in devotional reading is open and receptive, rather than analytical and argumentative. Unlike reading for simple pleasure, the mind is not engaged in an arousal of expectations and desires, rather it is resolved in quietness, calmness. Devotional reading may be regarded as an exercise in "negative capability" in which the mind lets go of self centeredness in preparation for prayer and praise. In devotional reading one finds what one does not seek. One knows what cannot be confirmed by evidence. One is called out to Christian action by a force that is as compelling as it is gentle.

How then should this book be used? Basically it is a tool, a device, for regulating one's own devotional life—in the same fashion that training equipment for physical exercise is used. Many people spend time with this book at a certain hour each day—just before bed, or upon first rising in the morning. But any hour of the day is appropriate, any convenient time when one wants to compose one's thoughts and draw closer to God. The key, just as in physical exercise, is *daily* use. A business man might find that his hurried lunch hour can be transformed into a leisurely feast for the spirit by spending a few quiet moments with this book. Its effect can be physical as well as spiritual, calming one's heart, easing tension and anxiety. A housewife might find a moment to rest in her hectic schedule just after the children are off to school or put down for a nap. The vital rewards of devotion derive from its discipline, regularity and its increasing depth.

In our frantic and clouded world, a time of daily devotion can be a constant shining beacon, a tolling, reassuring bell. May THE GOLDEN TREASURY OF TEXTS FOR EVERY DAY IN THE YEAR be a blessing to your life.

—THE EDITORS

PREFACE.

OGATZKY'S GOLDEN TREASURY has been translated into nearly all European languages, and has obtained an enormous circulation in Germany and Great Britain. In this country very few books, except the "Pilgrim's Progress," have been so largely circulated or so widely read. It will surprise many to learn that more than a century and a half have elapsed since the first publication of this valued volume.

Until the great day of account, it will not be known how many thousands have derived spiritual blessing from its well-known pages. For five or six generations the familiar "Bogatzky" has been in daily use in many a godly household at family worship; in many a quiet chamber the little volume has been a treasured daily monitor; from its pages hundreds of trembling believers have gathered strength and wisdom; from its teachings many an enquiring soul has been led into life and light; and from its consolations many a sorrowing mourner has drawn comfort in tribulation.

PREFACE.

The mission of the book is not yet over. It is hoped and believed that another generation will derive spiritual instruction from a volume which has been richly blest to the one now passing away, as well as to generations which have previously "crossed the flood."

THE PUBLISHER.

THE
GOLDEN TREASURY
OF TEXTS

FOR

EVERY DAY IN THE YEAR.

PUBLISHED BY
THE CHRISTIAN HERALD,
LOUIS KLOPSCH, Proprietor,
BIBLE HOUSE, NEW YORK.

Original title page of the 1895 edition

THE GOLDEN TREASURY.

JANUARY I.

HOSANNA!—Mark xi. 9; Ps. cxviii. 25-29.

A NEW scene of time now begins; put up thy Hosanna, O my soul, that the Lord may save, bless and prosper thee. May He grant thee a "Happy New Year" indeed! For this purpose begin it with a dedication of thyself to God. Thy time, circumstances, and life, are in His hand; with faith and love implore His blessing and protection over thee this ensuing year. Begin this, and every following day with prayer. Let God have thy first thoughts in the morning; the impression they make will not be easily erased by worldly matters. Grace is promised in the use of means; be thou diligent then, and punctual in the performance of them; let thy daily request be for an increasing knowledge of thyself, and of Jesus Christ in His offices; for a sense of pardoning mercy; for a lively, vigorous faith; for communion with the Father and the Son through the Spirit; for true holiness in heart and life; for strength and protection against thy spiritual foes, and for persevering grace to hold out to the end. Pray for the prosperity of Zion: they prosper that love her. Oh, pray for thy friends and relations, begging the Almighty to take them into covenant relation to Himself; for a blessing on thy worldly affairs; for a sanctified use of health or sickness, prosperity or adversity, as God shall please to send. Perhaps, O my soul, this may be the last year of the Lord's patience, and thy pilgrimage. Is thy state safe? Art thou a real believer in Jesus? Is the oil of grace in thy vessel? If so thou art prepared for every emergency.

And now, O soul, another year
Of this world's life is past;
I cannot long continue here,
And this may be the last.

Now a new scene of time begins,
Set out afresh for heaven;
Seek pardon for thy daily sins,
In Christ so freely given.

JANUARY 2.

I will ransom them from the power of the grave; I will redeem them from death: O death, I will be thy plagues; O grave, I will be thy destruction. —Hos. xiii. 14. *Christ having spoiled principalities and powers, He made a show of them openly, triumphing over them in it,* (His cross). —Col. ii. 15. *The sting of death is sin; and the strength of sin is the law. But thanks be to God, who giveth us the victory, through our Lord Jesus Christ.*—1 Cor. xv. 56, 57.

THE world is afraid of a hidden poison where there is none. The real hidden poison is sin, which, the Lord grant me to fear, is everywhere; for it has infected all things, and all places. But, O my dear Saviour, thou being my all-sufficient Preservative and Antidote in all places, oh! dwell in me continually, and, oh! increase my faith, that I may know thee, and enjoy thee more and more! Take away all slavish fears of death and hell from my soul, for thou hast conquered both for me. And, oh! give me the heart that can live on thee by faith every moment, and that can trust thy grace for every blessing. Oh! give me the heart that burns with love to thee, and that can raise its Hosanna in full assurance of the blessed inheritance beyond the grave.

>Hosanna to the Prince of Light
>   That clothed Himself in clay;
>Enter'd the iron gates of death,
>   And tore the bars away.
>
>Death is no more the King of Dread,
>   Since our Immanuel rose;
>He took the tyrant's sting away,
>   And spoil'd our hellish foes.
>
>Now holy triumphs of the soul
>   Shall death itself outbrave,
>Leave dull mortality behind,
>   And fly beyond the grave.

January 3.

But now, O Lord, thou art my Father: we are the clay, and thou our potter; and we all are the work of thy hand.—Isa. lxiv. 8; Dan. iv. 35.

BEING only clay in thy hands, O Lord, as I must not, so I would not, resist thy workings by any means; and I pray and hope thou wilt prepare and perfect me for a meet vessel of grace, in spite of a thousand hindrances. No work of thine comes ever short of its intended perfection; for who can stay thy hand? It is thy own saying, "I will work, and who shall let it?" (Isaiah xliii. 13.)

An artist delights in his own workmanship, and would not leave one single flaw or defect in it designedly (Phil. i. 6). Oh, then look upon me too, thou wise Creator! see how flesh and blood disorder my poor soul, and deliver me from all that may endanger my spiritual life! Knowing thou canst do no less than a human artist, who is ever ready, and exerts his skill to mend and perfect his work, I trust that thou wilt not always suffer these impediments to hinder and disgrace thy work. Nay, such is thy wisdom and power, that out of darkness thou canst bring light; out of sickness, health; and though I am now destitute of strength and life, yet I believe thy work will be finished at last, and glorify the name of its maker (1 Pet. v. 10).

> Finish, Lord, thy new creation!
> Pure, unspotted may we be!
> Let us see our whole salvation
> Perfectly secured by thee.
>
> Changed from glory into glory,
> Till in heaven we take our place,
> Till we cast our crowns before thee,
> Lost in wonder, love, and praise!

JANUARY 4.

David's Prayer :—*Oh that the salvation of Israel were come out of Zion! When the Lord brings back the captivity of His people, Jacob shall rejoice and Israel shall be glad.*—Ps. xvi. 7.

Divine Answer :—*If the Son make you free, ye shall be free indeed.*—John viii. 36. See also verses 31, 32.

NOT as if sin should be utterly destroyed, or entirely dead, and could not stir any more in the heart of believers; for the Scripture speaks of them as having still their lusts and motions of sin (Gal. v. 17); but it imports only, that it has no power either to condemn, or to reign over us; nay, it shall be weakened more and more (Rom. vi. 12, 14); so that Christ reigns in the heart even where sin dwells, in the midst of His enemies (Shorter Catechism, Quest. xxvi.); and it is a dangerous error indeed, to believe that sin is destroyed in the root. If it were so, whence those frequent expressions and exhortations to crucify, withstand, and rule over it? (Gal. v. 24.)

> Now sits our Saviour on His throne,
>   With pity in His eyes;
> He hears the dying prisoners' groan,
>   And listens to their sighs!
>
> He frees the souls condemned to death;
>   And when His saints complain,
> No man shall say that praying breath
>   Was ever spent in vain.
>
> This shall be known when we are dead,
>   And left on long record,
> That ages yet unborn may read,
>   And trust, and praise the Lord;
>
> Then let thy Spirit seal our souls,
>   And mould them to thy will,
> That our weak hearts no more may stray
>   But keep thy precepts still.

January 5.

All that will live godly in Christ Jesus shall suffer persecution.—2 Tim. iii. 12. *The world hath hated them, because they are not of the world.*—John xvii. 14.

The children of God do not love and please the world, and are oftentimes greatly afflicted on account of abounding wickedness, and particularly the profanation of the Lord's name. Now, when you can love the world, and the world can love you, there must be much worldliness in you; for the world loves its own.

Many pretend to be Christians, but they will not endure persecution. Instead of this, they blame others for too much rashness, and not acting prudently enough to avoid the mockings and hatred of the world. Therefore, they propose to take wiser measures; and, in order to do more good, take great care not to be despised and rejected; but under this pretence of wisdom and prudence, very often lie concealed a dangerous love of the world and fear of man. Be thou nobler minded, live as a Christian indeed, and be not ashamed to bear the Cross of Christ. "The disciple is not above his Master." Has eternal love, wisdom and power, endured the contradiction and reproach of sinners? Thou shouldst be wiser than Him indeed if thou couldst escape the reproach and hatred of the world.

> May but His grace my soul renew,
> Let sinners gaze and hate me too!
> The word that saves me does engage
> A sure defence from all their rage.

> God's furnace doth in Zion stand;
> But Zion's God stands by,
> As the refiner views his gold
> With an observant eye.

January 6.

All things are possible to him that believeth.—
Mark ix. 23.

Faith is the principal thing in the Christian religion. It is the spiritual eye, enlightening the mind, directing the feet, and cheering the heart. The whole turns upon it. As our faith is, so is our strength and fruitfulness in good works; but, at the same time, there is nothing more out of our own power than to believe, even after the work of grace has been actually wrought in our hearts; therefore nothing is more needful than to pray for faith as long as we live. May the Lord give and increase it continually! Nothing can be stronger in the universe than the hand of Faith. By this we lay sure hold on our most glorious and Almighty Lord in heaven; and such an inviolable union is established between Christ and a believing soul, that none can separate the one from the other. All the powers of hell and sin avail nothing against it! Faith breaks through the greatest obstacles, removes mountains of difficulties, and has, as it were, a kind of omnipotence in it; "for this is the victory that overcomes the world, even our faith" (1 John v. 4). Nay, it even wrestles with God and prevails (Gen. xxxii. 28). As straw cannot withstand the force of fire, so God, being a wall of fire around His people, the greatest power of our mighty enemies shall be consumed like the stubble. Oh! then, look upon Him steadfastly, my soul, and believe in Him with a simple heart. Wondrous are His ways with His people, and past finding out; but, at last, all their sorrows and strife must come to a triumphant end.

> Oh! let us go from strength to strength,
>   From grace to greater grace!
> From one degree of faith to more,
>   Till we behold thy face!

January 7.

Christ is all, and in all.—Col. iii. 11; Eph. i. 23; Eph. iv. 9, 10.

ALL mankind are Christ's creatures. All conditions are disposed and regulated by His providence. He alone is the source whence all have proceeded, and to Him alone all must return. For a believer to receive and know Christ as his All, is the only means to live truly a life of faith; and when he has done this, it will not be hard to resign all other things. To talk much of Christ, and make frequent use of His name one to another, is commendable, if the heart goes along with the words; but to call upon God the Father with a filial confidence, is also our duty, and does not contradict the apostle's meaning at all; for it is only through Christ we can do it; and, as He says himself, the Father and He are one. Thou art my All, O gracious Lord!—what then can I want? I desire no more than to be put always in mind of this by the animating voice of thy Spirit.

> Let sinners boast of kindred joys,
>   The poor delights of sense;
> 'Tis Christ our inmost thought employs,
>   We draw our comforts thence.
>
> With sweet contentment now we bid
>   Farewell to pleasures here.
> With Christ in God our life is hid,
>   And all its springs are there.
>
> 'Tis now concealed and lodged secure
>   In God's eternal Son.
> From age to age shall it endure,
>   Though to the world unknown.
>
> Jesus, remove whate'er divides
>   Our lingering souls from thee.
> 'Tis fit that where the head resides
>   The members too should be.

JANUARY 8.

They, being ignorant of God's righteousness, and going about to establish their own righteousness, have not submitted themselves unto the righteousness of God. Whosoever believeth on Him shall not be ashamed.—Rom. x. 3, 11.

THE same mistake which proved so fatal to the Jews, proves equally fatal to many who pretend to call themselves *Christians*. Ignorant alike of the Divine character and their own, they build their hope of the favor of God and eternal life upon some works of righteousness which they have done, or intend to do, and reject the righteousness of Christ, in which alone they can be justified and accepted; forgetting this great doctrine of the Gospel, that salvation is "not by works of righteousness which we have done, but according to His mercy He saved us; by the washing of regeneration, and the renewing of the Holy Ghost" (Titus iii. 5). In this mistake the decent and the profane are equally involved; for the worst of mankind fancy themselves possessed of some virtues and good qualities that will entitle them to the Divine favor. The delusion remains till the light of the Holy Ghost darts in, like a sunbeam, upon the mind, and discovers the guilt and pollution that defile the best of us. We then abhor ourselves, and look to the free grace of God in Christ Jesus for pardon and salvation. We have a hope that maketh not ashamed!

> Jesus! thy blood and righteousness
> My beauty are, my glorious dress.
> 'Midst flaming worlds, in these array'd,
> With joy shall I lift up my head.
>
> Bold shall I stand in the great day;
> For who aught to my charge shall lay?
> Fully through these absolved I am,
> From sin and fear, from guilt and shame.

January 9.

I cried with my whole heart; hear me, O Lord: I will keep thy statutes. Great peace have they who love thy law; and nothing shall offend them. I have kept thy precepts and thy testimonies; for all my ways are before thee. I have gone astray like a lost sheep: seek thy servant; for I do not forget thy commandments.—Ps. cxix. 145, 165, 168, 176. *The Lord shall preserve thee from all evil; He shall preserve thy soul.*—Ps. cxxi. 7.

The word of God should be ever connected with prayer; for why is it that many hear and read without being the better? They do not pray in faith for a blessing. We must, like David, pray with the utmost fervor, that we may understand and retain the word of God, and bring forth fruit; for a Christian has nothing so much at heart as that he may always act up to the word and will of God; his prayer is, Lord, let my footsteps be sure, according to thy word; and let nothing contrary to thy law have dominion over me, either in my doctrine or practice! If this prayer be granted, great will be our peace, Jesus Himself will be our peace, and then nothing shall offend us; we shall take heed unto all our ways before God, and so walk before Him as to continue humble, like David, who considered himself as a straying and lost sheep. Lord, we are by nature straying and lost sheep; seek and fetch us back from the error of our ways, and preserve us in thy pasture! Then shall we, with a heart full of gratitude, shew forth the praises of thy glorious name.

> My soul has gone too far astray,
>   My feet too often slip;
> Yet since I've not forgot thy way,
>   Restore thy wandering sheep.

JANUARY 10.

I have waited for thy salvation, O Lord.—
Gen. xlix. 18.

MANY have received comfort from these words in death and waited in faith for their salvation. The thoughtless and impenitent wait only for temporal prosperity in their lives, and therefore cannot expect eternal bliss; but, on the contrary, a dreadful judgment after death. Oh! that they would enter into themselves this very day, that, at the eve of life, they might, like Jacob and Simeon, depart in peace. We will not, therefore, look for any earthly things, but for the Saviour, who is already come, who will grant us His salvation, His aid and deliverance in life and death, and will conduct us safely at last, though we should wait some time for His help. Yes, my Redeemer, they who wait, depend upon, and hope in thee, shall not be ashamed. Grant us only faith and patience, that we may wait on thee from one morning-watch to another; and enduring all things, make the whole course of our lives one perpetual expectation of thy aid; and may we ever abundantly experience thy help and salvation, especially at our latter end.

> Christ's own soft hand shall wipe the tears
>   From every weeping eye;
> And pains and groans, and griefs and fears,
>   And death itself shall die.
>
> How long, dear Saviour, oh! how long,
>   Shall this bright hour delay?
> Fly swiftly round, ye wheels of Time,
>   And bring the welcome day.
>
> Oh! I could break this carnal fence,
>   Drop all my sorrows in the tomb,
> On angel-wings remove from thence,
>   And fly this happy moment home;
> Quit the dark house of mouldering clay,
> And launch into eternal day.

January 11.

For God so loved the world, that He gave His only begotten Son, that whosoever believeth in Him should not perish, but have everlasting life. For God sent not His Son into the world, to condemn the world; but that the world through Him might be saved. He that believeth on Him is not condemned.—John iii. 16-18.

OH! that these truly precious words were ever warmly impressed on our hearts! that they were our last thoughts at night, and the first at our waking in the morning; and that they were improved in such a manner, as to make our dying bed easy in the evening of our life, and to ensure our rising with gladness in the morning of the resurrection! And what more blessed and delightful meditations can I daily dwell upon than to think thus:—God has loved me, even me, when I was His enemy; and so loved me that He gave me His only Son! Bless me with faith in Christ, then Christ is mine, and all things are mine (1 Cor. iii. 21); for "He that spared not His own Son, but delivered Him up for us all, how shall He not with Him also freely give us all things?" (Rom. viii. 32.) He will never suffer a believing soul to perish; He has passed His word for it. It is He that says, "I shall not perish; I shall not be condemned;" but have everlasting life if I believe. This will I build and depend upon to my last moments, as upon an immovable rock. Amen and Amen.

> Oh! for this love let earth and skies
>   With hallelujahs ring!
> And the full choir of human tongues
>   All hallelujahs sing!
>
> "To Him who sits upon the throne,
>   The God whom we adore,
> And to the Lamb that once was slain,
>   Be glory evermore."

January 12.

In Christ we have redemption through His blood, even the forgiveness of sins.—Col. i. 14. *Having forgiven you all trepasses; blotting out the hand-writing of ordinances that was against us, which was contrary to us, and took it out of the way, nailing it to His Cross.*—Col. ii. 13, 14. *Thereford said He, It is finished.*—John xix. 30.

HAST thou, O my soul, felt the weight of thy own guilt and misery, and been enabled, in reality and truth, to lay hold by faith of the blood of CHRIST for thy redemption, and faithfully to devote thyself to Him in heart and life? Then hast thou a sure foundation to go upon. Let it be thy constant care firmly to depend upon these, and such like blessed declarations; look to Jesus for every blessing thou standest in need of. Has Christ brought life and immortality to light?—then look unto Him and live. Is there redemption through His blood, even the forgiveness of sins?—then throw all thy guilt upon His atonement. Has He blotted out the hand-writing of ordinances that was against thee? —then shake off self-righteous dependencies and legal fears also. Did He die for thy sins?—then let His goodness and love lead thee to unfeigned repentance; let the sense of thy sins break thine heart, but encourage thy hope in the Gospel.

'Tis finished—was His latest voice;
 These sacred accents o'er,
He bow'd His head, gave up the ghost,
 And suffered pain no more.

'Tis finished—the Messiah dies
 For sins, but not His own;
The great redemption is complete,
 And Satan's power o'erthrown.

January 13.

David's Prayer:—*Keep me as the apple of the eye; hide me under the shadow of thy wings.*—Ps. xvii. 8.

Divine Answer:—*He shall cover thee with His feathers, and under His wings shalt thou trust: His truth shall be thy shield and buckler.*—Ps. xci. 4.

THERE is none, O Lord, that has more need continually to keep close to thee in prayer and faith; and at the same time none is more unable to do it than I, the least of all thy flock! Oh! that thou wouldst be graciously pleased to incline and enable me to this blessed work! and grant that thy good Spirit, according to His own pleasure, may never suffer me to be faint and backward in the same; Whilst I truly rest my faith under the wings of thy grace, I am sure of defence, power and comfort; but as soon as I wander from thee, I am in danger of losing the comfortable sense of these privileges, and falling into various errors and perplexities. Guide me, O Lord, by thy counsel in this world, and at last receive me into glory! Amen (Ps. lxxiii. 24).

> He that has made his refuge God
> Shall find a most secure abode;
> Shall walk all day beneath His shade,
> And there at night shall rest his head.
>
> Just as a hen protects her brood
> From birds of prey that seek their blood,
> Under her feathers, so the Lord
> Makes His own arm His people's guard.
>
> Thrice happy man! thy Maker's care
> Shall keep thee from the fowler's snare;
> Satan, the fowler, who betrays
> Unguarded souls a thousand ways.
>
> What though a thousand at thy side,
> At thy right hand a thousand died;
> Thy God His chosen people saves
> Amongst the dead, amidst the graves.

January 14.

From that time Jesus began to preach, and to say, Repent; for the kingdom of heaven is at hand. —Matt. iv. 17; iii. 2. *Rend your heart, and not your garments, and turn unto the Lord your God.* —Joel ii. 13.

The kingdom of heaven appertains to those who repent; and the first mark of repentance is poverty of spirit; whence Jesus saith (Matt. v. 3), "Blessed are the poor in spirit, for theirs is the kingdom of heaven." John preached repentance; Jesus preaches it here, and so did His apostles afterward. This true repentance is necessary for all; and the beginning of it is to acknowledge ourselves poor miserable sinners, depraved by nature, and totally void of any righteousness or worth of our own—to confess our nakedness—to drop all the fig-leaves of vain excuses and false comforts—to lay open our poverty and wants before God—to accuse ourselves, and plead guilty of all our sins, but seek mercy from Christ. If we do this we are blessed, and the kingdom of heaven is ours. This poverty of spirit is both the first and last foundation laid in the heart; for the faithful are more and more grounded in poverty of spirit the nearer they approach to their consummation. "I dwell, saith He whose name is holy, with him who is of a contrite and humble spirit, to revive the spirit of the humble, and the heart of the contrite ones" (Isa. lvii. 15).

> Pure are the joys above the sky,
> And all the region peace;
> No wanton lips, nor envious eye,
> Can see or taste the bliss.
>
> These holy gates forever bar
> Pollution, sin, and shame;
> None shall obtain admittance there
> But followers of the Lamb.

January 15.

Pray without ceasing.—1 Thess. v. 17. *Men ought always to pray, and not to faint.*—Luke xviii. 1. *Continuing instant in prayer.*—Rom. xii. 12.

If we have not got grace enough, it is because we do not pray enough; for most true it is, we need not strive to move God to compassion, and extort, as it were, the blessings from Him by our prayers, which He has promised. Very far from it. He is every minute communicating himself to us; in every word He holds forth Christ and every good thing to us; but we must always have a soul hungering after Christ, and by incessant prayer stretch out the hand of Faith to receive Him. This is chiefly to be understood of the inward desires and groanings of our spirit; but we must not omit to pour out our supplications daily, as often as we can, by words, else our secret mental prayers at last may become so secret, as to cease perhaps entirely. We must always remember that we are dependent on God for every good; without Him we can do nothing. Let us feel that dependence at all times, and we shall always be in the spirit of prayer. Nor let us cease praying till we have received a full answer to our prayers. "Ye people, pour out your heart before Him: God is a refuge for us" (Ps. lxii. 8).

> Holy Father, lend an ear
> Whilst I sue in Jesu's name;
> Surely thou wilt kindly bear,
> Since I bring no human claim;
> Let me for adoption stay,
> Only give me power to pray.
>
> Grant me comfort or deny;
> Visit, or from me depart,
> Only let thy Spirit cry
> Abba, Father, in my heart!
> Abba, Father, would I say,
> Only give me power to pray.

JANUARY 16.

Abide in me.—John xv. 4. *Lord, to whom shall we go? thou hast the words of eternal life.* —John vi. 68. *It is good for me to draw near to God. I have put my trust in the Lord God.* —Ps. lxxiii. 28.

To abide in Christ, who is our righteousness and strength, and not to be moved from Him, is the very life and power of Christianity. We do this when our thoughts are going out after Him, our hearts cleaving to Him, and our minds stayed upon Him. Now, to know Christ, and thus to abide in Him, as our righteousness, brings peace and joy; which joy in the Lord is certainly followed with strength to overcome sin and the world, which believers renounce the more readily, as they have found something better in Christ. May the Lord give me grace likewise immovably to abide in Him! May He strengthen me with might in the inner man, even with the might of the Holy Spirit, that I may not only abide in Christ, but may abide with Him for evermore in the New Jerusalem which is above.

> Christ is my light, my life, my care,
>   My blessed hope, my heav'nly prize
> Dearer than all my passions are,
>   My limbs, my bowels, or my eyes.
>
> The strings that twine about my heart,
>   Tortures and racks may tear them off;
> But they can never, never part
>   With their dear hold of Christ my love.
>
> My God, and can a humble child,
>   That loves thee with a flame so high,
> Be ever from thy face exil'd,
>   Without the pity of thine eye?
>
> Impossible! for thine own hands
>   Have tied my heart so fast to thee,
> And in thy book thy promise stands,
>   That where thou art thy friends must be.

January 17.

Christ has redeemed us from the curse of the law, being made a curse for us; for it is written, Cursed is every one that hangeth on a tree; that the blessing of Abraham might come on the Gentiles through Jesus Christ, that we might receive the promise of the Spirit through faith.—Gal. iii. 13, 14.

The spirit of sanctification is the gift of Christ. "Elect according to the foreknowledge of God the Father, through sanctification of the Spirit, unto obedience and sprinkling of the blood of Christ" (1 Peter i. 2). Consequently there is a great difference between moral actions done by our own strength, and true sanctification of the spirit. The latter cannot take place before the soul truly receives Christ, and abides in Him as its only propitiation, righteousness and peace; for He being first made to us of God our righteousness, will then be made our sanctification likewise (1 Cor. i. 30); and the kingdom, work, and image of God, will go on best when we trust least to our own strength. Sanctification is now become a more easy task, since Christ lives and works in us, and we, in a child-like temper, live henceforth to Him who died for us. Let me always be as a little child—as a new-born babe, with a heart hungry for the sweet milk of the Word of God, without malice, without guile, without hypocrisies, and envies, and all evil speakings (1 Pet. ii. 1, 2).

> The law commands and makes us know
> What duties to our God we owe;
> But 'tis the Gospel must reveal
> Where lies the strength to do His will.
>
> The law discovers guilt and sin,
> And shows how vile our hearts have been;
> Only the Gospel can express
> Forgiving love and cleansing grace.

January 18.

Christ is the end of the law for righteousness to every one that believeth.—Rom. x. 4. See Rom. viii. 1-17.

WHERE the law ends Christ begins. The law ends with representative sacrifices. Christ begins with the real offering. The law is our schoolmaster to lead us unto Christ. It cannot save us; but it leaves us at His door, where alone salvation is to be found (Gal. iii. 24). The law calls for a perfect righteousness, which, in ourselves, never will be found; but all its demands were fulfilled by our surety. Every true believer finds that righteousness in Christ which he stands in need of, and is enabled, through the Spirit, to rest upon it for sanctification. He faithfully endeavors to obey the law, as the great rule of his duty both to God and man; yet is so sensible of his own manifold defects, that he would utterly despair if he could not look up unto Jesus, and say, "Thou shalt answer for me, O Lord, my God!"

>Lord, when my thoughts with wonder roll
>O'er the sharp sorrows of thy soul,
>And read my Maker's broken laws,
>Repair'd and honored by thy cross;
>
>When I behold death, hell, and sin,
>Vanquish'd by that dear blood of thine,
>And see the Man that groaned and died
>Sit glorious by His Father's side,
>
>My passions rise and soar above;
>I'm wing'd with faith and fir'd with love.
>Fain would I reach eternal things,
>And learn the notes that Gabriel sings.
>
>But my heart fails, my tongue complains,
>For want of their immortal strains;
>And in such humble notes as these
>Must fall below thy victories.

January 23.

The more they afflicted them, the more they multiplied and grew. And the children of Israel sighed by reason of the bondage, and they cried; and their cry came up to God, by reason of the bondage. And God looked upon the children of Israel, and God had respect unto them.—Exod. i. 12, and ii. 23, 25.

The more we are oppressed by our spiritual and temporal enemies, the more will the kingdom of God increase in and through us. And when distress and dangers oppress us most, God hastens to our aid, and makes our necessity itself the means of our relief; for the ways of God are always wonderful. It was in extreme distress when the children of the Israelites were cast into the river; but this was the means of preserving Moses, their intended deliverer. When Moses came, they were not relieved immediately, for their calamities increased. This is God's method. But they cried the more to God, and He relieved them by signs and wonders. After this, their distress was greater than ever at the Red Sea; for after God has shown His glory in assisting us, He can still send greater trials. But when they were beset on all sides by distress and death, then came the most glorious succor of all, and their enemies perished in the Red Sea. Lord, suffer us not to despair in any extremity; but enable us to believe and experience, that the greater our distress, the nearer and more glorious will be thy aid, and all our enemies will be consumed as stubble before the devouring flame.

> What sinners value I resign;
> Lord, 'tis enough that thou art mine.
> I shall behold thy blissful face,
> And stand complete in righteousness.

January 24.

Herein is love, not that we loved God, but that He loved us, and sent His Son to be the propitiation for our sins: We love Him, because He first loved us.—1 John iv. 10, 19. *He that loveth me shall be loved of my Father, and I will love him, and will manifest myself to him. We will come unto him, and make our abode with him.*—John xiv. 21, 23.

OH! what a glorious promise! what manner of love is this! Lord, I would not change my cross and sufferings, much less my love, for the love and honors of the world. Only make it more known to me how great thy love is, and how much thou hast forgiven me, that I may love thee much again, and be thereby still better purged from the inordinate love of temporal things. It is my earnest desire that the gates of my heart should be opened to none but thee, that thou alone mayest dwell in me. Shed thy love abroad in my heart, quicken and renew all the faculties of my mind and body, and work everything in and for me, that thy love may be my life, and the keeping of thy law my joy!

> Love Divine, all love excelling;
>   Joy of heaven to earth come down;
> Fix in us thy humble dwelling,
>   All thy faithful mercies crown.
>
> Oh! for this love let rocks and hills
>   Their lasting silence break,
> And all harmonious human tongues,
>   The Saviour's praises speak!
>
> Breathe, oh! breathe thy loving Spirit
>   Into every troubled breast;
> Let us all in thee inherit,
>   Let us find thy promised rest.

JANUARY 25.

Wherefore we labor, that, whether present or absent, we may be accepted of Him.—2 Cor. v. 9.

THIS indeed is the true disposition of a soul espoused to Christ. She has but one care, which is to please Him in all things. And this desire to do His will is, as it were, the ring and seal of her Bridegroom; which she may look upon, even in the absence of all spiritual joy, as a token for good that she is His spouse. Ought not then, this day, O my soul, to be a new wedding day with Christ? He is desirous that thou shouldst be betrothed unto Him even now, and waits only for thy consent. Hearken, O daughter! consider, and incline thine ear; be no longer married to the world. Forget thine own people and thy father's house, and take Him alone for thy husband; so shall the King greatly desire thy beauty. Wilt thou give the refusal to this glorious and loving Saviour? I hope not. Give it rather to the world, and resolutely say, I have done with thee, O poor world! I break the bonds of my former love; my eyes and feet shall henceforth only be directed to the blessed and eternal city of the new Jerusalem, where my heavenly Bridegroom resides. And, oh! what need I have to be duly prepared, dressed, and beautified against His coming, and the time of His taking me home to Himself! Lord Jesus, keep me longing for thine appearance—for the happy day when I shall go with thee to glory.

> If Christ is ours, we may despise
> All rage, though hell against us rise
> His love experienc'd will impart
> Immortal transport to thy heart!

January 26.

Let us therefore come boldly unto the throne of grace, that we may obtain mercy, and find grace to help in time of need.—Heb. iv. 16.

OH! that we were all so wise as to prepare and provide ourselves in due time with the right armor of faith, before the time of need, and hour of death approach. Come, my reader, let us begin now, and go directly to the gate of mercy, lest we should come too late and be undone. Behold the encouragement of Christ:—"I am the door," says He, "and the way" (John x. 9; chap. xiv. 6). Now, by this door you may find the entrance into the heart and favor of God, Christ himself sitting on a mercy seat to receive and welcome the vilest of sinners. And there is no drawing near to God but through Him, and clothed in the righteousness of our only Redeemer, Mediator, and Advocate. He is Alpha and Omega, the beginning and the end; nay, the very all in all to believers. With Christ they can never part; and He can never part with them (Col. iii. 10, 11).

>Of Him who did salvation bring,
>I could forever think and sing!
>Arise, ye guilty, He'll forgive!
>Arise, ye poor, He will relieve!

>Ask but His grace, and, lo! 'tis giv'n;
>Ask, and He turns your hell to heav'n;
>Though sin and sorrow wound my soul,
>Jesus, thy balm can make it whole!

>Guide thou, O Lord, guide thou my course,
>And draw me on with thy sweet force;
>Still make me walk, still make me tend,
>By thee, my way, to God my end.

January 27.

God commendeth His love toward us, in that while we were yet sinners, Christ died for us. Much more then, being now justified by His blood, we shall be saved from wrath through Him: for if, when we were enemies, we were reconciled to God by the death of His Son; much more, being reconciled, we shall be saved by His life.—Rom. v. 8-10.

Here we have much more reason to cry out than Moses had (Deut. xxxiii. 3), "The Lord loved the people;" but here I must beseech thee too, O Lord, that the infinite gift of thy Son may appear to me greater and greater every day; and that thy love, shining out in His redemption, may go on so to increase in my soul, as to disperse all clouds of darkness, unbelief, and hard thoughts of thy goodness. Whenever this slanderous spirit tries to lift up his head, grant that my faith and love may be quickened and strengthened in such a manner as heartily to praise thy great love in spite of all his suggestions; this is the chief desire which I offer unto thee in all my prayers, night and day. The want of faith and love, I am sensible, is still my greatest want; my soul is like a large empty vessel, but I pray thee to fill it speedily, notwithstanding any opposition that may be made by my unrenewed part.

> Come, guilty souls, and flee away,
> Like dove to Jesu's wounds;
> This is the welcome gospel-day,
> Wherein free grace abounds.

> God loved the world, and gave His Son
> To drink the cup of wrath;
> And Jesus says, He'll cast out none
> That come to Him by faith.

January 28.

For even hereunto were ye called; because Christ also suffered for us, leaving us an example, that ye should follow His steps.—1 Pet. ii. 21.

To believe in Christ for justification, is but one-half of the duty of faith; it respects Christ only as He died and suffered for us, as He made atonement for our sins, peace with God, and reconciliation for us, and as our righteousness; unto these ends He is, indeed, primarily and principally proposed unto us in the Gospel; and with respect unto them, we are exhorted to receive Him, and to believe in Him; but this is not all that is required of us; Christ in the Gospel is proposed unto us as our pattern and example of holiness; and as it is a cursed imagination, that the whole end of His life and death was to exemplify and confirm the doctrine of holiness, which He preached, so to neglect His being our example in considering Him by faith unto that end, and laboring after conformity to Him, is evil and pernicious; wherefore, let us be much in contemplation of what He was, what He did, how in all instances of duties and trials He carried himself, until a glorious image of His perfect holiness is implanted in our minds, and we are made like unto Him thereby. And let us always bear in mind, that ye were called to a state of suffering when ye were called to be Christians, for the world cannot endure the yoke of Christ.

> Oh! let me walk with Christ below,
>   His holy footsteps trace,
> And daily taking up His cross,
>   Be nourish'd by His grace.
>
> So shall my walk be close with **God**,
>   Calm and serene my frame;
> So purer light shall mark the road
>   That leads me to the Lamb.

January 19.

But the dove found no rest for the sole of her foot, and she returned unto Noah into the ark. Then he put forth his hand, and took her, and pulled her in unto him into the ark.—Gen. viii. 9.

THAT dove-like spirit communicated to the soul in regeneration, can find no rest for the sole of its foot until it bring us to Jesus, who is the great ark of the covenant. Many, on their first awakening from sin, apply themselves to very hard works and rigorous duties, thereby expecting to find rest for their wounded consciences. But though the right and diligent use of all the means of grace is absolutely required, yet great care must be taken not to quiet ourselves by that only. We should not place any confidence at all in our own doings, but only look for rest through the blood of Christ. To be found in Him justified and accepted would soon fill our hearts with peace, nay, encourage and enable us to do good works, and in the doing of good, we must always cherish a meek and grateful spirit, knowing that all is of the infinite grace of God.

In vain the trembling conscience seeks
   Some solid ground for rest;
With long despair the spirit breaks,
   Till we apply to Christ.

Just as we see the lonesome dove
   Bemoan her widowed state,
Wand'ring she flies thro' all the grove,
   And mourns her loving mate;—

Just so our thoughts from thing to thing
   In restless circles rove;
Just so we droop and hang the wing,
   When Jesus hides His love!

While Jesus shines with quickening grace,
   We sing and mount on high;
But if a frown becloud His face,
   We faint, and tire, and die!

JANUARY 20.

By this shall all men know that ye are my disciples, if ye have love one to another.—John xiii. 35. Forbearing one anothe rin love; endeavoring to keep the unity of the Spirit in the bond of peace. Let not the sun go down upon your wrath; but be kind one to another, tender-hearted, forgiving one another, even as God, for Christ's sake, hath forgiven you.—Eph. iv. 2, 3, 26, 32.

EVERY member of the mystical body of Christ should labor for the comfort and edification of the whole, and the honor of the Head. He that would live a quiet life and keep the unity of the Spirit in the bond of peace, must be as backward to take offence as to give it. He must live in love, and full of love. Humble Christians never affect singularity, nor pretend to have the preference one of another. They rather study to be of one mind, and strive not about words, lest the general harmony subsisting between them and the edification of souls shall be hindered. Whoever judges and blames everything, and can never agree in words and notions, or join in devotion with other experienced Christians, is puffed up with self-conceit, and is in the way to make a dangerous shipwreck; for "pride comes before a fall."

> Nor diff'rent food, nor diff'rent dress,
> Compose the kingdom of our Lord;
> But peace, and joy, and righteousness,
> Faith, and obedience to His Word.
>
> When weaker Christians we despise
> We do the Gospel mighty wrong;
> For God, the gracious and the wise,
> Receives the feeble with the strong.
>
> Let pride and wrath be banished hence,
> Meekness and love our souls pursue;
> Nor shall our practice give offence
> To saints, the Gentile, or the Jew.

January 21.

While the bridegroom tarried, they all slumbered and slept.—Matt. xxv. 5.

Oh! that I may be roused out of my slumber, and be watchful and ready against the coming of my Bridegroom! How many are there that set out in good earnest in their way to heaven, and run well for some time, but at last are lulled to rest, and are entangled again with a false notion of liberty! Even the wise virgins fell asleep. Let this be a warning to me, O Lord! Set thou a guard before my eyes, ears, and other faculties, lest the world should again enter through these avenues of the heart. If the spark be not speedily extinguished, it will soon break out into a flame. Thus sin is of a progressive nature, and its venom spreads very quickly and very wide, unless it be stopped and opposed in time. Watch, therefore, over this unsteady heart of mine, O thou keeper of Israel, that as soon as it begins to wander from thee, I may be alarmed to flee from sin as from a serpent. Give me grace to look upon every hour as my last, so that, being ever wisely upon my guard, I may meet thee with joy when my time is run out, whenever it shall please thee to call me hence. And let my going out and my coming in be guided by thy Spirit, so that every day may bring me nearer to thyself.

> The fearful soul that tires and faints,
>   And walks the ways of God no more,
> Though number'd once among the saints,
>   Now makes his own destruction sure.
>
> Lord, let not all my hopes be vain;
>   Create my heart entirely new;
> Which hypocrites could ne'er attain,
>   Which false apostates never knew.

January 22.

But while men slept, his enemy came and sowed tares among the wheat.—Matt. xiii. 25.

No wonder that Christians lose their power and strength, if the enemy of souls find them asleep. How soon may he gain an advantage from without, if a strict guard is not kept within! Though Satan seems to sleep sometimes, and we should, by all appearance, be in no great danger, it is only his stratagem to make us careless. He never fails to be vigilant, and watch his opportunity, that he may offer us battle with advantage; and who knows but he may gain the victory by those very sins to which, perhaps, we, for many years, had hardly any temptation. Oh! how cunningly does he work! how enticing is the world! even in lawful things, very often the most dangerous snares lie hidden. A single word that we hear may be able to disturb our peace. One unguarded look is sometimes enough to infatuate our hearts. There is danger on all sides. Unless the Lord open our eyes, and preserve us on all occasions, each of us, even the best, may still be overcome and deadly hurt by sin and the world. Satan is particularly busy to sift the godly most of all; and having catched them in his net, triumphs exceedingly over them. O Lord, suffer me never to fall asleep again!

> Help me to watch and pray,
>   And on thyself rely!
> And let me ne'er my trust betray,
>   Lest I forever die!
>
> Quick as the apple of an eye,
>   O God, my conscience make
> Awake my soul when sin is nigh,
>   And keep it still awake.

January 23.

The more they afflicted them, the more they multiplied and grew. And the children of Israel sighed by reason of the bondage, and they cried; and their cry came up to God, by reason of the bondage. And God looked upon the children of Israel, and God had respect unto them.—Exod. i. 12, and ii. 23, 25.

The more we are oppressed by our spiritual and temporal enemies, the more will the kingdom of God increase in and through us. And when distress and dangers oppress us most, God hastens to our aid, and makes our necessity itself the means of our relief; for the ways of God are always wonderful. It was in extreme distress when the children of the Israelites were cast into the river; but this was the means of preserving Moses, their intended deliverer. When Moses came, they were not relieved immediately, for their calamities increased. This is God's method. But they cried the more to God, and He relieved them by signs and wonders. After this, their distress was greater than ever at the Red Sea; for after God has shown His glory in assisting us, He can still send greater trials. But when they were beset on all sides by distress and death, then came the most glorious succor of all, and their enemies perished in the Red Sea. Lord, suffer us not to despair in any extremity; but enable us to believe and experience, that the greater our distress, the nearer and more glorious will be thy aid, and all our enemies will be consumed as stubble before the devouring flame.

> What sinners value I resign;
> Lord, 'tis enough that thou art mine.
> I shall behold thy blissful face,
> And stand complete in righteousness.

January 24.

Herein is love, not that we loved God, but that He loved us, and sent His Son to be the propitiation for our sins: We love Him, because He first loved us.—1 John iv. 10, 19. *He that loveth me shall be loved of my Father, and I will love him, and will manifest myself to him. We will come unto him, and make our abode with him.*—John xiv. 21, 23.

OH! what a glorious promise! what manner of love is this! Lord, I would not change my cross and sufferings, much less my love, for the love and honors of the world. Only make it more known to me how great thy love is, and how much thou hast forgiven me, that I may love thee much again, and be thereby still better purged from the inordinate love of temporal things. It is my earnest desire that the gates of my heart should be opened to none but thee, that thou alone mayest dwell in me. Shed thy love abroad in my heart, quicken and renew all the faculties of my mind and body, and work everything in and for me, that thy love may be my life, and the keeping of thy law my joy!

> Love Divine, all love excelling;
> Joy of heaven to earth come down;
> Fix in us thy humble dwelling.
> All thy faithful mercies crown.
>
> Oh! for this love let rocks and hills
> Their lasting silence break,
> And all harmonious human tongues,
> The Saviour's praises speak!
>
> Breathe, oh! breathe thy loving Spirit
> Into every troubled breast;
> Let us all in thee inherit,
> Let us find thy promised rest.

JANUARY 25.

Wherefore we labor, that, whether present or absent, we may be accepted of Him.—2 Cor. v. 9.

THIS indeed is the true disposition of a soul espoused to Christ. She has but one care, which is to please Him in all things. And this desire to do His will is, as it were, the ring and seal of her Bridegroom; which she may look upon, even in the absence of all spiritual joy, as a token for good that she is His spouse. Ought not then, this day, O my soul, to be a new wedding day with Christ? He is desirous that thou shouldst be betrothed unto Him even now, and waits only for thy consent. Hearken, O daughter! consider, and incline thine ear; be no longer married to the world. Forget thine own people and thy father's house, and take Him alone for thy husband; so shall the King greatly desire thy beauty. Wilt thou give the refusal to this glorious and loving Saviour? I hope not. Give it rather to the world, and resolutely say, I have done with thee, O poor world! I break the bonds of my former love; my eyes and feet shall henceforth only be directed to the blessed and eternal city of the new Jerusalem, where my heavenly Bridegroom resides. And, oh! what need I have to be duly prepared, dressed, and beautified against His coming, and the time of His taking me home to Himself! Lord Jesus, keep me longing for thine appearance—for the happy day when I shall go with thee to glory.

> If Christ is ours, we may despise
> All rage, though hell against us rise
> His love experienc'd will impart
> Immortal transport to thy heart!

JANUARY 26.

Let us therefore come boldly unto the throne of grace, that we may obtain mercy, and find grace to help in time of need.—Heb. iv. 16.

OH! that we were all so wise as to prepare and provide ourselves in due time with the right armor of faith, before the time of need, and hour of death approach. Come, my reader, let us begin now, and go directly to the gate of mercy, lest we should come too late and be undone. Behold the encouragement of Christ:—"I am the door," says He, "and the way" (John x. 9; chap. xiv. 6). Now, by this door you may find the entrance into the heart and favor of God, Christ himself sitting on a mercy seat to receive and welcome the vilest of sinners. And there is no drawing near to God but through Him, and clothed in the righteousness of our only Redeemer, Mediator, and Advocate. He is Alpha and Omega, the beginning and the end; nay, the very all in all to believers. With Christ they can never part; and He can never part with them (Col. iii. 10, 11).

> Of Him who did salvation bring,
> I could forever think and sing!
> Arise, ye guilty, He'll forgive!
> Arise, ye poor, He will relieve!
>
> Ask but His grace, and, lo! 'tis giv'n;
> Ask, and He turns your hell to heav'n;
> Though sin and sorrow wound my soul,
> Jesus, thy balm can make it whole!
>
> Guide thou, O Lord, guide thou my course,
> And draw me on with thy sweet force;
> Still make me walk, still make me tend,
> By thee, my way, to God my end.

January 27.

God commendeth His love toward us, in that while we were yet sinners, Christ died for us. Much more then, being now justified by His blood, we shall be saved from wrath through Him: for if, when we were enemies, we were reconciled to God by the death of His Son; much more, being reconciled, we shall be saved by His life.—Rom. v. 8-10.

Here we have much more reason to cry out than Moses had (Deut. xxxiii. 3), "The Lord loved the people;" but here I must beseech thee too, O Lord, that the infinite gift of thy Son may appear to me greater and greater every day; and that thy love, shining out in His redemption, may go on so to increase in my soul, as to disperse all clouds of darkness, unbelief, and hard thoughts of thy goodness. Whenever this slanderous spirit tries to lift up his head, grant that my faith and love may be quickened and strengthened in such a manner as heartily to praise thy great love in spite of all his suggestions; this is the chief desire which I offer unto thee in all my prayers, night and day. The want of faith and love, I am sensible, is still my greatest want; my soul is like a large empty vessel, but I pray thee to fill it speedily, notwithstanding any opposition that may be made by my unrenewed part.

> Come, guilty souls, and flee away,
>   Like dove to Jesu's wounds;
> This is the welcome gospel-day,
>   Wherein free grace abounds.

> God loved the world, and gave His Son
>   To drink the cup of wrath;
> And Jesus says, He'll cast out none
>   That come to Him by faith.

JANUARY 28.

For even hereunto were ye called; because Christ also suffered for us, leaving us an example, that ye should follow His steps.—1 Pet. ii. 21.

To believe in Christ for justification, is but one-half of the duty of faith; it respects Christ only as He died and suffered for us, as He made atonement for our sins, peace with God, and reconciliation for us, and as our righteousness; unto these ends He is, indeed, primarily and principally proposed unto us in the Gospel; and with respect unto them, we are exhorted to receive Him, and to believe in Him; but this is not all that is required of us; Christ in the Gospel is proposed unto us as our pattern and example of holiness; and as it is a cursed imagination, that the whole end of His life and death was to exemplify and confirm the doctrine of holiness, which He preached, so to neglect His being our example in considering Him by faith unto that end, and laboring after conformity to Him, is evil and pernicious; wherefore, let us be much in contemplation of what He was, what He did, how in all instances of duties and trials He carried himself, until a glorious image of His perfect holiness is implanted in our minds, and we are made like unto Him thereby. And let us always bear in mind, that ye were called to a state of suffering when ye were called to be Christians, for the world cannot endure the yoke of Christ.

> Oh! let me walk with Christ below,
>   His holy footsteps trace,
> And daily taking up His cross,
>   Be nourish'd by His grace.
>
> So shall my walk be close with God,
>   Calm and serene my frame;
> So purer light shall mark the road
>   That leads me to the Lamb.

January 29.

The Gospel is made known to all nations for the obedience of faith.—Rom. xvi. 26.

The obedience of faith here spoken of, is the same thing as believing the report of the Gospel (Rom. x. 16). A hearty submission to the righteousness of God, even to Christ, who is the end of the law for righteousness to every one who believeth,—this is the obedience of faith, strictly speaking, by which we give glory to God, take full shame to ourselves, renounce all that nature is proud of, and are brought to rest, for our justification and acceptance with God, on that alone which has satisfied His law and justice. However slightly we may be disposed to pass over this, it is a high point of obedience, not easily brought about in such a creature as man, and needing an effectual light and energy from above. It is taught purely from above; and he who would learn it, must seek it by much prayer continually; for in vain shall we strive to obey God in other things, until we learn to obey Him in this. Careless reader, see to it that you learn your need of Christ. Awakened and distressed sinner! seek not to heal yourself by forced obedience; learn the obedience of faith, that you may be purged in your conscience from dead works to serve God. Self-despairing sinner! obey the gospel-call of God to your soul, and live. Believer! let your fruit be to holiness.

> Within us, Lord, thy Spirit place,
>   Conveying health, and peace, and pow'r;
> And let us daily grow in grace,
>   That we may love and serve thee more.
>
> Oh! may thy Spirit seal our souls,
>   And mould them to thy will,
> That our weak hearts no more may stray,
>   But keep thy precepts still.

JANUARY 30.

Come unto me, all ye that labor and are heavy laden, and I will give you rest.—Matt. xi. 28.

This is a free invitation to every weary and heavy-laden sinner, made by Him who alone is able to take away the load and guilt of sin. Every person under the pressure of sin, not only may, but must come to Jesus, thus laden with guilt, if he hopes to succeed for pardon! While we endeavor to prepare our way for our holy qualifications, we rather fill it with stumbling-blocks, whereby our souls are hindered from attaining to the salvation of Christ! Christ would have us to believe on Him, who justifies the ungodly, and therefore He doth not require us to be godly before we believe: He came as a physician for the sick, and doth not expect they should recover their health in the least degree before they come to Him. The vilest sinners are fitly prepared and qualified for this design, which is to shew forth the exceeding riches of His grace, pardoning of our sins, and saving us freely (Eph. ii. 5, 9). It is no affront to Christ, or slighting or contemning the justice and holiness of God, to come to God while we are polluted sinners; but rather it is an affronting and contemning the saving grace, merit, and fulness of Jesus, if we endeavor to make ourselves righteous and holy before we receive Christ Himself, and all holiness and righteousness in Him by faith.

> How long the time since Christ began
> To call in vain on me!
> Deaf to His warning voice I ran
> Through paths of vanity.
>
> But could I hear Him once again,
> As I have heard of old,
> Methinks He should not call in vain
> His wanderer to the fold.

January 31.

The kingdom of heaven is like unto a merchant-man seeking goodly pearls; who, when he had found one pearl of great price, went and sold all that he had, and bought it.—Matt. xiii. 45, 46.

BLESSED are they to whom the Gospel has made known the unsearchable riches of Christ! He is that one pearl of great price, in comparison of whom all other goodly things that men desire are worthless. Without Him we are poor and miserable, though we abound in all manner of worldly store; but if we have found Him, and discovered the excellency of His name, we are in possession of a treasure that makes us rich indeed, and have reason to be content with our portion, though stripped of every earthly comfort; for the Father gives grace and glory, even eternal life, in His Son Jesus Christ; and he that hath the Son of God hath life. O my soul! thou, like the merchantman, hast been seeking goodly pearls, and eagerly looking here and there for happiness all thy days! Hast thou at length been enlightened to perceive where true joys are to be found? Then wilt thou be willing to sell all in order to win Christ, and be found in Him: if there is anything that thou art unwilling to part with for His sake, thou knowest not His value—thou art not worthy of Him!

> Long did my soul in Jesu's form
>   No comeliness or beauty see,
> His sacred name, by others priz'd,
>   Was tasteless still, and dead to me.
>
> Thanks to the Author of all grace!
>   That shew'd me wretched, naked, poor;
> That sweetly led me to the Rock
>   Where all salvation stands secure.
>
> Glad I forsook my righteous pride,
>   My moral tarnish'd sinful dress;
> Exchang'd my dross away for Christ,
>   And found the robe of righteousness.

Blessed are the poor in spirit; for theirs is the Kingdom of Heaven.

———

Blessed are they which are persecuted for righteousness' sake; for theirs is the Kingdom of Heaven.—Matt. v. 3, 10.

———:o:———

In Him was life; and the life was the Light of men.—John i. 4.

———

Then spake Jesus—I am the Light of the world; he that followeth Me shall not walk in darkness; but shall have the light of life.—John viii. 12.

February 1.

God, who commanded the light to shine out of darkness, hath shined in our hearts, to give the light of the knowledge of the glory of God in the face of Jesus Christ.—2 Cor. iv. 6.

WITHOUT this saving knowledge we have no God, no Christ, no grace, no faith, no union with Christ, no actual justification, pardon of sin, peace, nor eternal life. But whoever has found Christ, the pearl of great price, the treasure hid, has found matter of great rejoicing; for he was poor before, and this treasure enricheth him; he was naked before, but finding this treasure, he is gloriously clothed; he was forced before to feed upon husks, but now he feeds on the bread of life; he was far in debt before, but now he sees the debt is paid, that he is justified from all things, and pardoned for ever; he saw he was a child of wrath before, but now he is become a child of God; that he was a captive, and in chains before, but now he is set at liberty; condemned before, but now he sees there is no condemnation to him, nor to any one that is in Christ Jesus; that he was a fool before, but now he is made wise unto salvation. Reader, canst thou set thy seal to the truth and power of such experience? Then thou art wise indeed; if not, thou hast much to learn : apply with speed, and remember, it is God alone that gives this light and knowledge. Take heed unto the sure word of prophecy, as unto a light that shineth in a dark place, until the day dawn, and the day-star arise in your hearts (2 Peter i. 19).

> Father of love and grace,
>   Thy light to me impart;
> Reflected from thy dear Son's face,
>   And beaming on my heart.

February 2.

This is His commandment, that we should believe on the name of His Son Jesus Christ.—1 John iii. 23. *For God sent His only-begotten Son into the world, that we might live through Him.*—1 John iv. 9.

The Father breaks forth, as it were, through the whole Scripture in high praises of His Son; He calls out from heaven, "This is my beloved Son, in whom I am well pleased, hear ye Him" (Matt. xvii. 5). Nothing, therefore, can be more agreeable to Him than to receive this His Son, and to believe His report (John xvi. 27); and on doing this we shall have life; but by omitting it, we look upon Him as a liar. Unbelief, therefore, which refuses to accept of this great gift, is no doubt the greatest of all sins. O Lord, teach me this, and grant me faith.

"Why art thou so backward, O my poor soul, to believe, like the rest of God's children, in Christ? Hast thou not as good a right to do it as they have? Who can dispute with thee this privilege? It is the express will of the Father; nay, He even commands thee to do it. Has he not given His only Son, by an act of inconceivable love, to die for thee, to the very end that thou shouldst live? Oh! what a pleasing thing will it be to Him, to put thy whole trust upon this His well-beloved Son! This would be the joy of His heart more than anything else; therefore delay no longer to receive what His love has offered thee, but firmly believe that the Father loves thee as well as the Son."

> Author of faith, to thee I lift
> My weary longing eyes;
> Oh! let me now receive that **gift**,—
> My soul without it dies!

FEBRUARY 3.

Worthy is the Lamb that was slain to receive power, and riches, and wisdom, and strength and honor, and glory, and blessing.—Rev. v. 12. *Thou art worthy, O Lord, to receive glory, and honor, and power.*—Rev. iv. 11.

O LORD, how mean and slight notions have I often of thy great power! By these I am discouraged, and thou art robbed of thy praise. Grant, therefore, that though I would always be duly abased and convinced of my vileness, in such a manner as never to ascribe any good to myself, or think myself worthy of the least thing in the way of merit, for at the best I am but an unprofitable servant, yet thy grace and power may, at the same time, appear to me abundantly greater than all my sins, so that I may have always encouragement enough to believe in and praise thy holy name. And grant that the delusive pleasures of this world may never twine so closely round my heart that thy glory and thy praise do not always occupy my song.

> Come let us join our cheerful songs
>   With angels round the throne;
> Ten thousand thousand are their tongues,
>   But all their joys are one.
>
> "Worthy the Lamb that died," they cry,
>   "To be exalted thus!"
> "Worthy the Lamb," our lips reply,
>   "For He was slain for us!"
>
> Let all that dwell above the sky,
>   In air, in earth, and seas,
> Conspire to lift His glories high,
>   And speak His endless praise.
>
> The whole creation join in one,
>   To bless the sacred name
> Of Him that sits upon the throne
>   And to adore the Lamb.

February 4.

My soul shall be satisfied as with marrow and fatness, and my mouth shall praise thee with joyful lips.—Ps. lxiii. 5. *Alleluia! for the Lord God Omnipotent reigneth. Let us be glad and rejoice, and give honor to Him; for the marriage of the Lamb is come.*—Rev. xix. 6, 7.

WHAT tends not to thy glory, O Lord, and is not thy own work, whatever appearance it may have, is not really good and profitable. Preserve and assist me, therefore, to do all things as of thee, in thy sight, and to thy honor. May my soul be ever magnifying thy name, O my dear Redeemer and Bridegroom, and my whole conversation be directed to thy praise! Grant that my heart and mouth may be ever full of thy great mercies, and overflow continually with thanksgiving, and that in thy worship I may enjoy such a full sensation of spiritual comfort and joy, that no desire shall be left unsatisfied.

>My God, my King, thy various praise
>Demands thanksgiving all my days;
>Oh! let thy grace employ my tongue
>Till death and glory raise the song!

>Grant, Lord, that ev'ry hour may bear
>Some thankful tribute to thine ear;
>And ev'ry setting sun may see
>New works of duty done for thee!

>Thy faithfulness endures the same;
>Thy bounty flows an endless stream;
>Thy mercy swift, thine anger slow;
>But dreadful to the stubborn foe.

>And who can speak thy wondrous deeds!
>Thy greatness all our thoughts exceeds
>Vast and unsearchable thy ways!
>Vast and immortal be thy praise.

FEBRUARY 5.

David's Prayer :—*Forsake not the works of thine own hands.*—Ps. cxxxviii. 8.
Divine Answer :—*He who hath begun a good work in you, will perform it until the day of Jesus Christ.*—Phil. i. 6.

THE right way to grow in grace is to give up thyself wholly to thy heavenly Father, who knoweth all thy wants and has engaged to supply them. Then labor diligently to walk with Christ, and carefully cherish the new life, which, be it ever so weak and little now, in comparison to the old man, will increase and gradually outgrow him, as a new skin does the old. May the Lord only give us grace to watch against the opposite extreme, so as never to be lulled into a false rest, or a lukewarm spirit, but to be ever diligently and seriously employed in crucifying the flesh, and using all the means of grace !—then we need not be anxiously troubled for the growing of the work of God in our souls, for " He which hath begun a good work in you, will perform it unto the day of Jesus Christ ;" that is, till Christ shall come to call you home to glory in the happy mansions He has prepared above the sky.

> My soul lies cleaving to the dust;
>   Lord, give me life divine;
> From vain desires and every lust
>   Turn off these eyes of mine.
>
> I need the influence of thy grace
>   To speed me in thy way.
> Lest I should loiter in my race,
>   Or turn my feet astray.
>
> Are not thy mercies sov'reign still,
>   And thou a faithful God?
> Wilt thou not grant me warmer zeal
>   To run the heavenly road?

February 6.

The fashion of this world passeth away.—
1 Cor. vii. 31.

As long as we feed on the husks of the world, and are in love with it, we are neither willing nor able to taste the comforts of the love of God; but when sin and the world are become an abomination to us, and we desire to be rid of them, and seek diligently unto Jesus Christ for the help of His grace, and the benefit of His blood, we are then in a right way to receive the love of God, and every blessing of salvation; and though we are chastened by the Lord, yet He is not angry with us, but does it to embitter sin and the world more and more to us, and to make us loathe them, that we may not be condemned with the world; but that we may be kept from the evil that is in the world (John xvii. 15).

> Let worldly minds the world pursue,
>   It has no charms for me;
> Once I admir'd its trifles too,
>   But grace has set me free.
>
> Its pleasures now no longer please,
>   No more content afford;
> Far from my heart be joys like these,
>   Now I have known the Lord.
>
> As by the light of op'ning day
>   The stars are all conceal'd,
> So earthly pleasures fade away
>   When Jesus is reveal'd.
>
> Now, Lord, I would be thine alone,
>   And wholly live to thee,
> But may I hope that thou wilt own
>   A worthless worm like me?
>
> Yes; though of sinners I'm the worst
>   I cannot doubt thy will;
> For if thou hadst not lov'd me first,
>   I had refus'd thee still.

February 7.

Thine is the kingdom, and the power, and the glory, forever. Amen.—Matt. vi. 13. *They cast their crowns before the throne, saying, Thou art worthy, O Lord, to receive glory, and honor, and power.*—Rev. iv. 10, 11.

One that is really poor in spirit, though he hath practiced the duties of the Christian life ever so long, and ever so diligently, always thinks himself to have received but a very little portion of Christ, and the work of sanctification hardly to be begun in his soul. So far is he from believing he has already attained it, that after all his best actions, he counts himself not worthy to be called by the name of a grateful son. He is never pleased with himself. No degree of holiness will satisfy his soul. He seeks and finds no rest or comfort but in the infinite mercy of God, and in the pardon of his sins by faith, though he does not divide Christ, but receives Him in all His offices, and gives himself entirely up to Him, without reserve, to be more and more sanctified and perfected; and in this state he is safe indeed, he is prepared for death, and has no reason to be anxiously afraid, though earnestly desirous of higher degrees of sanctification.

> Forever hallow'd be thy name
>   By all beneath the skies;
> And may thy kingdom still advance,
>   Till grace to glory rise.
>
> A grateful homage may we yield,
>   With hearts resigned to thee;
> And as in heaven thy will is done,
>   On earth so let it be.
>
> For thine the pow'r, the kingdom thine;
>   All glory's due to thee;
> Thine from eternity they were,
>   And thine shall ever be.

February 8.

He hath made with me an everlasting covenant, ordered in all things, and sure; for this is all my salvation, and all my desire.—2 Sam. xxiii. 5.
I have made a covenant with my chosen.—Ps. lxxxix. 3.

This was David's plea and confidence when, with eternity full before him, he was just going to make his appearance before an infinitely pure God. This must be our plea also if ever we would obtain the approbation of our judge. After a life of the most eminent holiness, the best of men will have reason to cry out, "Enter not into judgment with thy servant, O Lord!" It is true, indeed, the believer will discover some evidences of grace, just to shew the child of God, and no more, but all so imperfect, that he dares not ground his expectations on them. Here the covenant of grace steps in to his relief, wherein he sees ample provision made for the security of his eternal interest; for the covenant is made with Christ and His seed. It is an everlasting covenant, not only made before time, but extending its beneficial effects through the ages of eternity. It is ordered in all things; therefore nothing can be wanting in it, either to promote the glory of God, or the salvation of believers. It is sure also; depending on no conditions, requiring nothing but what it gives, conferring its blessings freely, and making them sure to all the seed, being established upon better promises. Happy souls, who are interested in this well-ordered covenant! May it be all my salvation, and all my desire!

> Thy word is truth, thy promise sure,
>   Hence faith and hope abide;
> True faith in Jesus will endure;
>   Nought can from Christ divide!

February 9.

I will pray the Father, and He shall give you another Comforter, that He may abide with you forever; even the Spirit of Truth; whom the world cannot receive, because it seeth Him not, neither knoweth Him: but ye know Him; for He dwelleth with you, and shall be in you.—John xiv. 16, 17.

When God designed the great and glorious work of recovering fallen man, and the saving of sinners, "to the praise of the glory of His grace," He appointed, in His infinite wisdom, two great means thereof; the one was the giving of His Son for them; and the other was the giving of His Spirit unto them. And hereby was way made for the manifestation of the glory of the whole blessed Trinity, which is the utmost end of all the works of God. Hereby were the love, grace and wisdom of the Father, in the design and contrivance of the whole; the love, grace and condescension of the Son, in the execution, purchase and procurement of grace and salvation for sinners; with the love, grace and power of the Holy Spirit, in the effectual application of all unto the souls of men, made gloriously conspicuous. To these heads may all the promises of God be reduced. Happy for the Church that the Spirit is to abide with it for ever; and awful to think that the unconverted world neither can receive nor know the Spirit.

> Holy Spirit, heav'nly Dove,
> Bringing peace, and bringing love,
> Take me, and possess me whole;
> Form the Saviour in my soul.
>
> Be my true and constant Guide;
> In my fainting heart abide;
> All the grace of God reveal,
> And each precious promise seal.

February 10.

Godly sorrow worketh repentance to salvation not to be repented of; but the sorrow of the world worketh death.—2 Cor. vii. 10.

There is a sorrow which has the breach of God's holy law for its object, called *godly*, because it is produced by the Spirit of God discovering the evil of sin, and the plague and corruption of our own hearts, and deeply humbling us under a sense of sin, producing evangelical repentance, and leading the soul to cry to the Lord Jesus Christ for pardon and salvation; the Holy Spirit at the same time enabling us to believe in Him, and rest upon His person, blood and righteousness, for redemption and salvation: which repentance will never be repented of. But sorrow arising from the love of this world, worketh death,—death eternal! Lord Jesus, grant me to feel more of this godly sorrow for sin, and to rejoice more in thee as my Saviour!

> Father, thy long-lost child receive;
>   Saviour, thy purchase own;
> Blest Comforter, with peace and joy,
>   Thy waiting creature own.
>
> Return, my roving heart, return,
>   And life's vain shadows choose no more;
> Seek out some solitude to mourn,
>   And thy forsaken God implore.
>
> O thou great God, whose piercing eye
>   Distinctly marks each deep retreat,
> In these sequestered hours draw nigh,
>   And let me here thy presence meet.
>
> Through all the windings of my heart,
>   My search let heavenly wisdom guide
> And still its beams unerring dart,
>   Till all be known and purified.
>
> Then let the visits of thy love
>   My inmost soul be called to share,
> Till every grace combine to prove,
>   That God has fixed His dwelling there.

February 11.

Light is sown for the righteous, and gladness for the upright in heart.—Ps. xcvii. 11. *Unto the upright there ariseth light in the darkness; he is gracious, full of compassion, and righteous.*—Ps. cxii. 4. *Cast not away therefore your confidence, which has great recompense of reward; for ye have need of patience, etc. For yet a little while, and He that shall come will come, and will not tarry.*—Heb. x. 35-37; Isa. lviii. 10-12.

This shews that believers are subject to many changes of joy and sorrow. In a state of gladness, therefore, we have reason to fear; and in the hours of trouble and sadness, to entertain good hopes. Thus we shall always be able to keep the happy medium between the extremes of levity and despair. Before a man has a true sense of his own miseries, the complaints and infirmities of the saints are often a stumbling-block; but afterward they will administer to him great comfort. This is the reason that God has revealed them in Scripture; for the complaints of His elect children give more comfort than all their most heroic actions. Grant, O Lord, that whether sorrowing or rejoicing, I may have the light of the Holy Spirit to direct me.

> Alas! it swells my sorrows high
>   To see my blessed Jesus frown;
> My spirits shrink, my comforts die,
>   And all the springs of life are down.
>
> Yet why, my soul, why these complaints?
>   Still while He frowns His bowels move;
> Still on His heart He bears His saints,
>   And feels their sorrows and His love.

FEBRUARY 12.

I find a law, that when I would do good, evil is present with me.—Rom. vii. 21. *For the flesh lusteth against the Spirit, and the Spirit against the flesh: and these are contrary the one to the other; so that ye cannot do the things that ye would.*—Gal. v. 17.

O MY soul! thou art always striving, yet sin is always stirring: thou fearest the truth of grace, because thou findest the working of sin; but it will be always thus; thou canst not come out of Egypt, but Amalek will lay wait in the way; the flesh will be sure to trouble thee, although it be never able to conquer thee. He therefore that sits down, and is at rest in sin, it is a sign that Satan is there, the strong man, because his kingdom is in peace; but where there is any work of Christ, there will be always war with sin. Sin was the womb of death, and only death must be the tomb of sin. God would have my soul humbled; therefore, though He hath broken my prison, yet He hath left the chain upon my feet. God would have my graces exercised; therefore, though He hath translated me into the kingdom of life, yet He hath left the Canaanite in the land. God would have my faith exercised; therefore, Goliath still shews himself in the field, that so I might go out to him "in the name of the Lord." I will betake me to the strength of Christ; and though I cannot help the rebelling power of sin, yet through grace I will labor to prevent the ruling power of it. God grant me of that strength according to my daily need!

> Though sin will in believers dwell
>   Till death the inmates part;
> O Jesus, save me from this hell
>   Which lurks within my heart!

February 13.

God was in Christ, reconciling the world unto Himself, not imputing their trespasses unto them; for He has made Him to be sin for us who knew no sin, that we might be made the righteousness of God in Him.—2 Cor. v. 19, 21.

WHAT a glorious statement for the contrite sinner, "God is in Christ!" And how employed? "Reconciling the world unto himself." But how? By "not imputing their trespasses unto them." And how can the justice of God do this? By making "Him to be sin for us who knew no sin;" and all "that we might be made the righteousness of God in Him." May not the Christian, then, live at perfect peace? He may. Yet it highly concerns believers, who desire to keep a constant peace in their bosoms, to be ever sensible of their spiritual poverty, and to feed and rest wholly on the all-sufficient atonement and righteousness of Jesus Christ. Disquiet of mind and laziness of soul, often proceed from self-righteousness and not looking to Christ for everything, but trusting secretly to something in ourselves.

> Jesus, thou art my righteousness,
>   For all my sins were thine.
> Thy death has bought of God my peace,
>   Thy life has made Him mine!
>
> Forever here my rest shall be,
>   Close to thy bleeding side!
> 'Tis all my hope, and all my plea;
>   For me the Saviour died!
>
> My dying Saviour and my God,
>   Fountain for guilt and sin;
> Sprinkle me ever with thy blood,
>   And cleanse and keep me clean.

February 14.

Nevertheless I am continually with thee; thou hast holden me by my right hand. Thou shalt guide me with thy counsel, and afterward receive me to glory. Whom have I in heaven but thee? and there is none upon earth that I desire beside thee. My flesh and my heart faileth; but God is the strength of my heart, and my portion forever.—Ps. lxxiii. 23-26.

BABES in religion not only long for Christ, but for sensible communion with Him; and very often they are indulged with it, that they may be weaned from the world. But those of fuller age, who have their senses more exercised, are thankful they can trust Him when they do not see Him, and can follow Him when they feel no comfort; relying more upon the word and covenant of God than on sweet sensations, which, though ever precious and desirable, are oft withdrawn in times of trouble and temptation. Bestow thy grace, thou blessed Jesus, upon my poor soul, that by faith I may lay hold on thee, and esteem thee as my chief joy, my sure portion, and exceeding great reward.

> How oft have sin and Satan strove
>   To rend my heart from thee, my God!
> But everlasting is thy love,
>   And Jesus seals it with His blood.
>
> In just temptations sharp and strong
>   My soul to this dear refuge flies;
> Hope is my anchor, firm and strong,
>   While tempests blow and billows rise.
>
> The Gospel bears my spirit up,
>   A faithful and unchanging God
> Lays the foundation of my hope
>   In oaths, and promises, and blood.

February 15.

There is a river, the streams whereof shall make glad the city of God. God is in the midst of her; she shall not be moved.—Ps. xlvi. 4, 5. *Ye are of God, little children, and have overcome them; because greater is He that is in you, than he that is in the world.*—1 John iv. 4; Ps. cx. 5; Zech. ii. 5.

TRUE Christians, in a right spirit, still are subject to temptations from within and without; but watching unto prayer, they do not fall by them. On the contrary, as temptations are great helps to discover their hidden infirmities, and stir them up to be more cautious, serious and faithful, they are followed and rewarded with great and glorious victories. Temptations are not indeed joyous in themselves, but are attended with good fruit and blessed effects in the faithful. Hence St. James bids us count it all joy when we fall into divers temptations. What reason have we then to be afraid of temptations, since every one carries a new blessing along with it?

>Jesus, lover of my soul,
> Let me to thy bosom fly,
>While the nearer waters roll,
> While the tempest still is nigh.
>
>Hide me, O my Saviour! hide,
> Till the storm of life is past.
>Safe into the haven guide!
> Oh! receive my soul at last!
>
>Other refuge have I none;
> Hangs my helpless soul on thee;
>Leave, oh! leave me not alone!
> Still support and comfort me.
>
>All my trust on thee is stay'd,
> All my help from thee I bring,
>Cover my defenceless head
> With the shadow of thy wing.

February 16.

Let not sin reign in your mortal body, that ye should obey it in the lusts thereof.—Rom. vi. 12. *Resist the devil, and he will flee from you.*—James iv. 7.

O my soul, how awful is thy state by nature and practice! Sin hath gained a dominion over thee; its influence is universal over the soul and body and over every son and daughter of Adam: it hath brought death on the body, and subjected the soul to everlasting misery; its authority is unjust, and its power cruel and destructive. Lord Jesus, let me adore thine effectual grace, that it hath in any measure delivered me from its power, and assist my poor heart in opposing and rejecting every temptation to obey it in the lusts thereof; let thy precious blood effectually secure me from the guilt of sin in this life, and the punishment of it in another! O my soul, if thou art a faithful follower of Jesus, though Satan received a deadly wound when Christ was crucified for us, yet his malice is still the same; thou hast a thousand enemies, and the devil is the leader of them all. O may I with the deepest humility, look to Jesus, rest upon Jesus, and derive daily strength from Him to resist the devil, and, finally, to come off conqueror, and more than conqueror, through Him that loved me. Amen.

> Oh! that thou would the heavens rend,
>   In majesty come down,
> Stretch out thine arm Omnipotent,
>   And seize me for thine own!
>
> What though I cannot break my chain,
>   Or e'er throw off my load,
> The things impossible to men
>   Are possible to God.

February 17.

Though we have known Christ after the flesh, yet now henceforth know we Him no more.—2 Cor. v. 16. *It is the Spirit that quickeneth; the flesh profiteth nothing: the words that I speak unto you, they are spirit, and they are life.*—John vi. 63.

What is it to know Christ after the flesh? It is to content ourselves with carnal views of His person, character and kingdom. This was the case with all those who followed Him not on account of His miracles and doctrines, but for the loaves and fishes. Alas! are there not too many who wish to know Christ for carnal, worldly interest, and not that they may be saved from a proud rebellious heart, and an ungodly life? O my soul, let me see to it, that my seeking after Christ may not be carnal, but spiritual; worldly interest is too apt, it may be feared, to influence both private professors and even public preachers. True believers can say that henceforth this carnal knowledge of Christ is not their pursuit. Where the spirit of Jesus regenerates the heart, and we are brought to a spiritual and experimental knowledge of Christ, we shall love Him, rejoice in Him, humbly submit to His will in all things, and daily pray to be more and more like Him. O thou dear and precious Jesus! grant that this may be more and more my experience till I shall know thee in all thy holiness and glory, for ever and ever!

> Is there a thing beneath the sun
> That strives with thee, my heart, to share?
> Ah! tear it thence, and reign alone
> The Lord of every motion there,
> Then shall my heart from earth be free
> When it hath found repose in thee.

February 18.

The Lord preserves the simple: I was brought low, and He helped me.—Ps. cxvi. 6.

He who walks in godly simplicity and humility, accounting his own infirmities always the greatest, will best be preserved from being puffed up and sifted by the enemy of souls; and, truly, nothing should humble us more than justification by free grace. The more we consider and carefully cherish that, the more this simple, child-like, quiet temper will increase; for since there is nothing in ourselves which can be depended upon, but all must be freely received from Christ, this, at the same time cutting off all vain boasting, brings us low, settles our peace in Christ, who is our All, and is sure enough to be rested upon. It is only from thee, O my dear Saviour, I can learn true simplicity! Teach me, therefore, to turn mine eyes, not upon others, but upon myself. Humble me to the uttermost, and fashion me after thy own mind, that I may be careful to avoid every thing that is contrary to love. Keep me, O my Light, from all self-independence and self-conceit, bridle my carnal reason, and pull down all vain imaginations! Grant that my eye may be fixed only upon that one thing needful which lasts eternally; and that in all my words, deeds and gestures, I may always resemble the simplicity, innocence, fidelity and love of a little child (Matt. xviii. 3).

> Rich grace, free grace most sweetly calls,
>   Directly come who will;
> Just as you are, for Christ receives
>   Poor helpless sinners still.
>
> 'Tis grace each day that feeds our souls;
>   Grace keeps us inly poor;
> And oh! that nothing else but grace
>   May rule forever more.

FEBRUARY 19.

The Lord is my Shepherd, I shall not want.—Ps.
xxiii. 1. He says it Himself:—*I am come that
they might have life, and that they might have it
more abundantly. I give unto them eternal life;
and they shall never perish, neither shall any
pluck them out of my hand.*—John x. 10, 28.

Is the Lord Jesus thy Shepherd? Has He called
thee out of the wilderness? called thy heart from
the love of sin and the world, and brought thee
unto His fold and pastures? brought thee into a
close attendance on His ordinances? And does He
feed and refresh thy soul with His word? Canst
thou distinguish the Shepherd's voice from the
voice of an hireling? And does thy heart cleave
to the Shepherd in faith and love, adoring His
person and approving His laws, as well as admiring
His doctrines? Then fear not, the Lord is with
thee; Jesus is thy Shepherd, thou shalt want nothing that is really good. Follow thy Shepherd till
He bring thee to glory!

> The Lord's my Shepherd, I'll not want.
>   He makes me down to lie
> In pastures green: He leadeth me
>   The quiet waters by.
>
> My soul He doth restore again;
>   And me to walk doth make
> Within the paths of righteousness,
>   Even for His own name's sake.
>
> Yea, though I walk in death's dark vale,
>   Yet will I fear none ill;
> For thou art with me; and thy rod
>   And staff me comfort still.
>
> My table thou hast furnished
>   In presence of my foes;
> My head thou dost with oil anoint,
>   And my cup overflows.
>
> Goodness and mercy all my life
>   Shall surely follow me:
> And in God's house for evermore
>   My dwelling place shall be.

February 20.

The everlasting Gospel.—Rev. xiv. 6. *And upbraideth them with their unbelief and hardness of heart, because they believed not.*—Mark xvi. 14.

The Gospel is properly called "Glad Tidings," for these reasons: We are polluted with the filth of sin; in it is opened a fountain for sin and uncleanness. The way to heaven is blocked up by our sins; it reveals "a new and living way through the flesh of Christ." We are imprisoned debtors by multiplied transgressions; it shews that a price, the most inestimable, has been paid to discharge us. We have by nature hard, strong and impenitent hearts; in it is promised a heart of flesh. We can of ourselves do nothing; it shews that through Christ we can do all things! We feel that we are liable to err and backslide; it declares that God will scourge us till we return to Him, but not take His loving-kindness from us. We know that we are liable to many calamities; it teaches us that they shall all work together for our good. We see that we are dying creatures; by it we are assured that we have a Forerunner in heaven, and an eternal habitation with God in glory. Lord, send abroad and bless this Gospel. Make bare thine own holy arm, and let the people be willing in the day of thy power. Oh! let the world adoring see triumphs of mercy wrought by thee.

  Salvation, oh! Salvation,
   The joyful sound proclaim,
  Till each remotest nation,
   Has learned Messiah's name.

  Salvation! let the echo fly,
   The spacious earth around;
  And all the armies of the sky
   Conspire to raise the sound.

February 21.

They profess that they know God, but in works they deny Him.—Tit. i. 16; Jude 4; 2 Tim. iii. 5.

There is a profession of a special kind, which, in its own nature, is exposed to reproach in the world: "they that will live godly in Christ Jesus shall suffer persecution." There is a being in Christ, and not living godly; for there are branches in the vine by profession, that bring forth no fruit; men that have not in them the mind that was in Christ Jesus, which torments the men of the earth; but they that will live godly—that is, engage in a profession that shall, on all occasions, and in all instances, manifest the power of it, they shall suffer persecution. We see many every day keep up a profession; but such a profession as will not provoke the world. Now this is to be ashamed of the Gospel—to be ashamed of the power and glory of it, to be ashamed of the Author of it. No man can put Jesus Christ to greater shame than by professing the Gospel without shewing the power of it (Phil. iii. 18; Rev. xi. 10). There can be no more vile and sordid hypocrisy, than for any to pretend unto inward habitual sanctification, while their lives are barren in the fruits of righteousness and obedience. Reader, of all dangers in profession, beware of a customary, traditional, or doctrinal owning of Gospel truths, without an experimental acquaintance with the reality and efficacy of them; for all such will have their portion where is "wailing and gnashing of teeth!"

> O fairest pearl of price,
>   Thy riches let me see,
> And freely sacrifice
>   The world's esteem for thee!
> For thee I would count all things loss,
> And only glory in thy cross.

FEBRUARY 22.

I will put enmity between thee and the woman, and between thy seed and her seed; it shall bruise thy head, and thou shall bruise his heel.—Gen. iii. 15. See Gal. iv. 4-6; Col. ii. 14, 15; and Heb. ii. 14.

By "the seed of the woman" is to be understood Christ the Saviour; not excluding His friends and followers in every age of the world. This prediction of a Saviour signifies to our first parents these *four* things: 1. That the promised Saviour was not to be the man's, but the woman's seed, or born of a virgin. 2. That He was to be a man by that expression, "Thou shalt bruise his heel." 3. That He should break the head of the serpent, or destroy his power and dominion over mankind, and punish him, and all his votaries with an utter destruction; and, 4. That in order to our Saviour's doing so, He must have His own heel, or human nature, that lowest part of His mediatory person, bruised by the serpent, or persecuted and put to death by the devil and his emissaries. This was the first intimation of a Saviour that was made to the world; it was made to the serpent for his immediate confusion; made in the presence of our first parents, and before their sentence was pronounced, to inspire them with the hope of pardon and life, and with a sense of the distinguishing mercy of God, who, before he denounced so much as any temporal punishment, animated them with the hope of eternal redemption.

> Arise, arise, thou woman's seed.
>   And bruise the serpent in my heart;
> Employ thy vengeance on his head,
>   And deadly strokes each day impart.

February 23.

The Lord do that which seemeth Him good.—2 Sam. x. 12. *Thy will be done.*—Luke xxii. 42.

A CHRISTIAN still feels the motion of self-will, and, consequently, of sin in his heart. And if it be asked, How can Christ and sin dwell together in one heart? the answer is: As a king and rebels in in one kingdom or town; He does not agree or correspond with them, but subdues them, and maintains peace. But where self-will has the dominion, there is nothing but trouble and confusion; for unsanctified passions, and a bad conscience, not only are inward torments, but often occasion perplexity and damage in our worldly affairs; whereas, in the blood of Christ, we have a good conscience, abundance of peace, and can be contented and happy in the most indifferent outward circumstances.

Take heed, therefore, O my dear Christian, never to be led by thy own spirit, were it even in such things as seem to bring glory to God, if it is not of His own appointment. Our hearts sometimes are very deceitfully desirous of what pleases ourselves, while we pretend to seek God's glory; and were we not crossed in these our designs, they would prove a great burden to our life. Blessed is he who not only prays with his lips, but is heartily willing also that nothing but the will of the Lord should be done in everything. It is God alone that understands what may be good or dangerous to our spiritual or temporal circumstances. We being often blinded, or drawn by our lusts, are too much inclined to choose at random what would be perhaps most detrimental.

> Saviour, to my heart be near,
> Exercise the shepherd's care;
> Guard my weakness by thy grace,
> Let me feel a constant peace.

February 24.

The Lord will regard the prayer of the destitute, and not despise their prayer.—Ps. cii. 17. *They looked unto Him and were lightened; their faces were not ashamed.*—Ps. xxxiv. 5. See also instance of the woman of Canaan, Matt. xv. 21-28; what Christ says, Luke xi. 5-13; xviii. 1-8; likewise of a tossed vessel, Matt. viii. 24-27.

The load of outward and inward affliction is not always prayed away with a few words, or in a few days. Sometimes it is necessary even to wrestle with God, and be very instant too; how else could faith and patience be exercised? If, therefore, the trials be sharp and lasting, it is not to weaken our faith, but to stir us up to be more instantly zealous in prayer, and the right use of the word of God; and by this means to be so much more gloriously delivered and strengthened in faith; for whatever God sends upon us, it is not for the lessening, but for the increase of our faith. "Blessed is the man that endureth temptation; for when he is tried, he shall receive the crown of life, which the Lord hath promised to them that love Him" (James i. 12).

> God is our refuge and our strength,
>   In straits a present aid;
> Therefore, although the earth remove,
>   We will not be afraid;
>
> Though hills amidst the seas be cast;
>   Though waters roaring make,
> And troubled be; yea, though the hills
>   By swelling seas do shake.
>
> A river is, whose streams do glad
>   The city of our God;
> The holy place, wherein the Lord
>   Most High hath His abode.
>
> God in the midst of her doth dwell;
>   Nothing shall her remove;
> The Lord to her an helper will,
>   And that right early prove.

February 25.

I dwell in the high and holy place, with him also that is of a contrite and humble spirit, to revive the spirit of the humble, and to revive the heart of the contrite ones. For I will not contend for ever, neither will I be always wroth; for the spirit should fail before me, and the souls which I have made.—Isa. lvii. 15, 16.

How sweet are all God's promises, and what a cheering hope do they impart! "I dwell with him that is of a contrite and humble spirit." Oh! how consoling are these words to the broken heart and to the wounded spirit; to the spirit wounded on account of sin! How unbounded the joy of the true believer! God doth dwell with him. Yet to insist too much upon the sensible joy of faith, might make weak souls weaker still. Many a sincere Christian's heart is like a bottle of a very narrow passage, which can receive the dew of a heavenly comfort only by little drops. But dost thou feel thyself quite naked, and void of all good? Christ will surely cover thee with the robe of righteousness. Go entirely out of thyself, looking only to Him for everything; and whatever gifts of joy, peace and holiness may be given thee, be very thankful for them, yet trust not in them, but in Christ alone. This will make thee pure and keep thy heart at rest.

> The man who walks with God in truth,
>   And ev'ry guile disdains,
> Who hates to lift oppression's rod,
>   And scorns its shameful gains;
>
> His dwelling, 'midst the strength of rocks,
>   Shall ever stand secure;
> His Father will provide his bread,
>   His water shall be sure.

February 26.

Lord, by thy favor thou hast made my mountain to stand strong; thou didst hide thy face, and I was troubled.—Ps. xxx. 7. See also civ. 29-31.

See, my soul, in this verse, a picture of thine own experience; how much art thou and David alike! When I look up to heaven, how often do I see the sun both shine and set! When I look down into myself, how often do I see my comforts rise and fall! One while I am upon Mount Tabor, and have a glance of heaven; another while I lie in the valley of Bochim weeping, because I have lost sight of my heavenly country. Joshua's long day is many times turned into Paul's sad night. When God would quicken my affections, He gives me a glance of heaven, that so I may be in love with what I see. When I begin to bless myself, and rest in my happy privileges, He draws a veil over the bright vision, that I may rest in nothing but Himself, nor loathe what I so greatly love. He suffers my happiness here to be imperfect, that so I may be pressing on to that place where I shall be perfectly happy for ever. Lord, when thou shewest thyself, let me love thee; when my mountain stands strong, let me praise thee; when thou withdrawest thyself, let me follow thee; when thy countenance is hid, let me still believe that thou lovest me; under all my changes here, let my soul be always breathing, panting, longing and reaching after thee, till I shall so perfectly enjoy thee, that I may never lose thee more. But bound up in the bundle of life, when life closes, my soul may wing its way to dwell with thee for ever. Amen.

> Lord, guide me in this Christian race,
> And keep my mind intent on thee;
> Rejoicing when I see thy face,
> And trusting when I cannot see.

FEBRUARY 27.

Satan hath desired to have you, that he may sift you as wheat; but I have prayed for thee, that thy faith fail not.—Luke xxii. 31, 32. *Yet shall not the least grain fall upon the earth.*—Amos ix. 9. *For I will keep thee from the hour of temptation.*—Rev. iii. 10.

SOMETIMES we may imagine ourselves to be Divinely convinced of the will of God, both by seeming outward providences and inward persuasions of faith; and yet it is possible that the siftings of Satan are at the bottom; however, the Lord will overrule him at last, and order all things to the best for His people. May the Lord make us watchful against our own spirit, and against the evil one, especially when he is transformed into an angel of light, that it may not be in his power to sift us so as to gain an advantage over us, by our listening to his inward suggestions, or yielding to his subtle temptations! And, O my soul, what a precious truth is this for thee, "I have prayed for thee, that thy faith fail not!" Remember who He is that prays for thee. It is Christ. Thou hast still the same intercessor, who is now at God's right hand. He has the same merits to plead now that He had when upon earth. Wilt thou despise his prayer? Pause, my soul; hast thou ever asked for this prayer? Thou hast need of it. Turn even now to Christ and plead for it. Plead in earnest and thou shalt get it.

> In vain the baffled prince of hell
>   His cursed project tries;
> We that were doom'd his endless slaves,
>   Are rais'd above the skies.
>
> Oh! may my Jesus guard me safe
>   From ev'ry ill design;
> And to His heav'nly kingdom keep
>   This feeble soul of mine.

February 28.

Whose adorning, let it not be that outward adorning of plaiting the hair, and of wearing of gold, etc.; but let it be the hidden man of the heart, in that which is not corruptible, even the ornament of a meek and quiet spirit, which is in the sight of God of great price.—1 Pet. iii. 3, 4. *In rest shall ye be saved; in quietness and in confidence shall be your strength.*—Isa. xxx. 15.

A Christian's best accoutrements and festival clothes, in which he daily celebrates his Sabbath, is called (Col. iii. 10, 12, 14), "The new man, bowels of mercies, kindness, humbleness of mind, meekness, long-suffering, and, above all, charity." These are our true ornaments, and we should seek to be dressed in them.—Reader, what dost thou adorn most?—thy body or thy soul! "O thou meek and quiet Lamb of God, justly I blush before thee, when I consider my impatience, though I am never innocent like thee! I humbly beseech thee to forgive me these transgressions, since thou hast made sufficient atonement for all by thy meritorious silence; but deliver me from this choleric, hot and peevish temper also; and give me grace, in all inward and outward troubles, to have the long-forbearing mind which was in thee! Make me daily more and more like a lamb, that on all occasions, grievous or joyful, I may be duly composed, and shew that excellent heavenly ornament of a meek and quiet spirit, not in many words, but in reality and power. Amen."

> Giver of concord, Prince of Peace,
>   Meek, lamb-like Son of God,
> Bid our unruly passions cease,
>   And quench them with thy blood.

(*Leap Year.*)—FEBRUARY 29.

Behold these three years I come seeking fruit on this fig-tree, and find none, etc.—Luke xiii. 7-9.

Thou fruitless fig-tree, thou barren professor, dost thou hear this, and not tremble? God is come seeking fruit;—will thy bare profession, thy knowledge of the principles of religion, satisfy the great God? Will the notions of truth in thy head, thy talking and disputing, thy hearing the word preached, thy commending or censuring sermons and preachers, just as thou art in the mood, will this serve thy turn?—and wilt thou thus endeavor to ward off the heart-searching God? Know thou, God is come to seek for fruit, and for good fruit from thee;—not the fruit of good words only, but the fruit of good works; not the fruit of talking well, but of walking well, the fruits of holiness in life and conversation:—fruit short of this God will not regard. If thy conscience be awakened, look to thy merciful High Priest, consider well His intercession for such a barren soul as thou art: "Lord, let it alone," etc. Father, let this man live one year longer;—oh! turn away from this thine anger! I will yet see what may be done. I will take other methods,—I will try what corrections may do;—perhaps the rod may work more upon him than my word has hitherto done, and may tend to make his barren heart fruitful; I will also stir up my servants to awaken him by a more sharp and searching manner; and if these new efforts be blessed to him, all shall yet be well, thy grace magnified, and his soul saved; if not, then thou shalt cut him down.

> If under means of grace no fruits of grace appear,
> It is a dreadful case! tho' God may long forbear,
> At length He'll strike the threaten'd blow,
> And lay the barren fig-tree low.

MARCH 1.

I live by the faith of the Son of God.—Gal. ii. 20;
2 Cor. v. 15; read also 1 Thess. v. 10, and 1
Peter iv. 2.

In spiritual things we are too often living upon self; we seek in frames, forms, creatures and animal life, that inward peace and stability of mind which is only to be found in the Redeemer. Outward duties are well in their places; they are to be performed, but not to be trusted in; they are as the scaffold to the building,—a mean for carrying on the work, but not the work itself. When favored with the gracious presence of Jesus, they are blessings; without it, they are nothing. The whole dependence must be on Jesus. He being the way, the truth, and the life, without Him prayers, praises, rights and ordinances, are carcasses without a soul. This is the case with every external service that is destitute of the presence and blessing of the Holy Spirit, who alone imparts communion of heart, and a quickening of the soul in faith, and in love to Jesus, and often a delightful view of that which is behind the veil of outward ordinances, such as no carnal eye can behold,—a purely spiritual discovery of the Lord in His goodness, beauty, grandeur and glory. Oh! may the Spirit be poured out on my soul, and by the faith which He imparts may I get a foretaste of the joys of the heavenly state! Amen.

> I wish, as faithful Christians do,
>   Dear Lord, to live to thee;
> And by my words and walk to shew
>   That thou hast died for me.
>
> Oh! grant me, through thy precious blood
>   Thy Gospel thus to grace;
> Renew my heart, O Lamb of God,
>   Thus shall thy works thee praise.

March 2.

Broad is the way that leadeth to destruction, and many there be which go in thereat; but narrow is the way which leadeth unto life, and few there be that find it.—Matt. vii. 13, 14; read also Luke xiii. 24.

This sounds too harsh in the ears of the old man, who would not have the Law made use of in these Gospel times, either to the converted or unconverted; and yet to the old man, the Law, and not the Gospel, properly belongs. St. Paul, the great preacher of the Gospel, made use of the Law to rouse unconverted Felix from his security (Acts xxiv. 25), and to warn the converted Romans from falling into it again (Rom. viii. 13).

Which way dost thou walk? Examine thyself. Is it in the narrow way? Art thou quite sure of it? Venture not to go on any farther at random. It is matter of great consequence; if thou wilt be safe, try better for it; thou mayest easily be deceived. Alas! thou art surely in the broad way to destruction, if thou still lovest and art conformed to the world. Art thou but indifferent with regard to the things of God, relishing more the vanities, pleasures, companies, treasures and honors of this world?—thou art not in the good narrow way that leads unto life. Oh! consider this well, and stop short before it is too late, and thou drop into the bottomless pit of perdition! Nothing renders this way either narrow or difficult but sin. Leave off thy sin, and thou mayest not only find the way, but abide, walk and persevere in it till the end.

> Strait is the way, the door is strait,
>   That leads to joys on high;
> 'Tis but a few that find the gate,
>   While crowds mistake and die!

MARCH 3.

Aaron shall bear the names of the children of Israel in the breastplate of judgment upon his heart, when he goeth into the holy place, for a memorial before the Lord continually; and thou shalt put into the breastplate of judgment the Urim and Thummim, — namely, light and integrity. — Exod. xxviii. 29, 30.

Now am I, saith the believer, for ever in gracious remembrance with God, since my great high priest and advocate, Christ Jesus, bears my name continually before Him on His heart. Whenever I am troubled about my sins, His powerful mediation will surely obtain mercy for all my transgressions, and supply my wants abundantly! God not denying Him anything, I can through Him continually be heard, and obtain grace: for He makes perpetual intercession for me in heaven, by which all my prayers, at all times, and even now, are sanctified, and presented to the Father, who heareth Him always. Oh! who would not send up his petition to heaven in faith? Yet, O my soul, is thy prayer the prayer of faith? Dost thou offer it believing that thou shalt receive? and dost thou with anxious expectation look for the answer! Ah! consider well, dost thou not pray, aud then think thy work is done? Prayers without the longing desire are no prayers at all. Let not such be thine.

>Now may our joyful tongues
> Cur Maker's honor sing;
>Jesus, the priest, receives our songs,
> And bears them to the King.
>
>Before His Father's eye
> Our humble suit He moves;
>The Father lays His thunders by,
> And looks, and smiles, and loves.

March 4.

If any man will come after me, let him deny himself, and take up his cross daily, and follow me.
—Luke ix. 23; see also Matt. x. 38; Mark viii. 34; and Luke xiv. 27.

Doing this, all the rest will be easy. If we know that we are nothing, are unworthy of everything, and having nothing of our own, we can lose nothing. We have no property, since we are but stewards of the Lord. We have no honor or shame of our own, after the manner of the world; this being our only honor, if God be glorified; and our only shame, if He be dishonored by us. The glory of God we must have at heart, and in His cause be like lions; but in our own cause like lambs. Therefore, when we are crossed in things which do not concern the glory of God and the real good of our neighbor, but our own interest, and are unwilling to suffer anything, we shall miscarry and be involved in greater troubles; but denying ourselves, we shall lose only a good deal of vexation; and instead of this, receive Christ, with all His spiritual and temporal blessings, as far as we want them; which alone can make us cheerful and happy. But whoever desires to please the world, seeking himself and his own glory, cannot be a follower of Christ. And how will it be with him in the hour of death and judgment? By this every one, learned or unlearned, may try themselves: whom do they please?—God or the world?

> Jesus, I my cross have taken,
>   All to leave, and follow thee;
> Naked, poor, despised, forsaken,
>   Thou, from hence, my all shall be.
>
> Perish every fond ambition,
>   All I've sought, or hoped, or known,
> Yet how rich is my condition,
>   God and heaven are still my own!

MARCH 5.

Unto you therefore which believe He is precious.—
1 Pet. ii. 7.

READER, put these following questions to thine own heart, as in the presence of God: if thou canst answer them affirmatively, doubt not thy real interest in Him, and in His great salvation:—Is the Lord Jesus Christ precious to me, as He is to all that believe? Once He was to me without form or comeliness, and I saw no beauty in Him; is He now to me the chief of ten thousands, yea, altogether lovely? Do I behold an infinite amiableness and glory in His person, a transcendent excellency in His righteousness, an inexhausted fullness in His grace, and a heaven of happiness in His love? Do I esteem Him above every name, love Him above every creature and thing, and value an interest in Him before ten thousand worlds? Is the language of my soul, "None but Christ, none but Christ! Whom have I in heaven but thee? and there is none upon earth that I desire besides thee?" Is all the world, all that is admired in it, esteemed by me as dung, and beheld with the greatest contempt, when compared with a glorious Christ, the ravishing sweetness of His love, and the unsearchable riches of His grace? Do I wish nothing so ardently, seek nothing so diligently, and rejoice in nothing so greatly, as to win Christ, and be found in Him? Be this my portion!—and I can say, I want, I wish, I ask no more!

> In vain I seek for rest
>   In all created good!
> It leaves me yet unblest,
>   And makes me pant for God.
> And sure at rest I cannot be,
> Until my heart find rest in thee!

March 6.

Upon thy right hand did stand the queen in gold of Ophir. The King's daughter is all glorious within; her clothing is of wrought gold. Hearken, O daughter, and consider, and incline thine ear; forget also thine own people, and thy father's house; so shall the King greatly desire thy beauty; for He is thy Lord, and worship thou Him.— Ps. xlv. 9-11, 13.

OBSERVE, O my soul, that thy celestial Bridegroom does not require any ornament, merit, worthiness, or beauty of thine own! No; He will wash thee himself with His blood, He will adorn thee, and make thee truly amiable to himself and to His Father. Oh! sweet and eternal truth: "He has loved us and washed us from our sins in His own blood." And being clothed with His righteousness, we have more than angelic beauty. If we have received the Spirit of Adoption, let us cleave to Christ alone, love Him above all things, and walk in His commandments. This is not only our duty, but a needful evidence of our sonship.

> The King of saints, how fair His face,
> Adorn'd with majesty and grace!
> He comes with blessings from above,
> And wins the nations to His love!
>
> At His right hand our eyes behold
> The queen arrayed in purest gold;
> The world admires her heav'nly dress,
> Her robe of joy and righteousness.
>
> He forms her beauties like His own;
> He calls and seats her near His throne;
> Fair stranger, let thine heart forget
> The idols of thy native state.
>
> So shall the King the more rejoice
> In thee, the favorite of His choice;
> Let Him be lov'd, and yet ador'd,
> For He's thy Maker and thy Lord.

MARCH 7.

They that are Christ's have crucified the flesh with the affections and lusts.—Gal. v. 24; Rom. vi. 6. See also Gal. ii. 20.

ALTHOUGH the flesh be alive still, and frequently stir, yet it cannot fulfill its desires when it is fastened to the cross;—with the crucifying of the flesh we have to do as long as we live. This is the cross we are to take up daily, and which either prevents many outward crosses, or at least yields great comfort under them. The cross being an extraordinary good mean to experience the sweetness of the word of God, O my soul! thou must always be ready and prepared for it, O my soul! And if none come from without, take care to break thy own will in everything. Painful and hard as this may seem to be at first, yet it will certainly very soon grow easier, and be matter of real joy. Blessing and peace will attend thy ways and steps, and thou shalt glorify God for having been resigned and guided, not by thy own, but by His good-will and pleasure. Self-will, on the other hand, creates nothing but vexation, trouble, and uneasiness. It is punished by itself, deprives us of real blessings, and therefore deserves, and is best to be broken and crucified in its first motions. Then help me, by pouring the Holy Spirit into my heart, to crucify the flesh with the vile affections and lusts thereof.

> Still I feel a fleshy part,
> Much corruption in my heart;
> Oh! I'm very vile indeed!
> Of thy blood I sure have need!
>
> Break, oh! break this heart of stone,
> Form it for thy use alone;
> Bid each vanity depart;
> Build thy temple in my heart.

MARCH 8.

The Lord has respect unto Abel, etc.—Gen. iv. 4, 5.

HERE are two brothers, each bringing an oblation to the Lord. Cain, as a husbandman, brought of the produce of the ground he cultivated; Abel, as a shepherd, some of the firstlings of the flock, with the fat of them; consequently both believed that there was a God that made the world, and was to be worshiped; and yet one was accepted and the other rejected. Cain's sacrifice was wholly eucharistical, or a thank-offering to God for the blessings of His providence. Abel's was not only of the eucharistic, but of the expiatory kind; and while it was an expression of gratitude for the blessings of Providence, it was also typical of the atonement by Christ, and expressive of His hope of redemption through Him; but what made the chief difference between them was, that Cain presented his offering while his heart was withheld, and without faith in Christ, so was of the wicked one. Abel brought forth his person and sacrifice an offering to the Lord: he presented his oblation, and performed the other parts of worship with faith in God, and the promised Saviour, and with sincerity, humility, and love. Thus God had respect to him and his offering; accepted first his person as justified, then his offering; but neither the person nor offering of Cain was accepted. Reader, mark the difference; by this Abel speaks to thee: Art thou in a state of acceptance with God? Is thy whole dependence for pardon and life on Christ? Dost thou obey from a principle of love? Then thou shalt be blessed with righteous Abel here and for ever.

> Oh! that the Lord would guide my ways,
>   To keep His statutes still;
> Oh! that my God would grant me grace
>   To know and do His will!

MARCH 9.

On that day shall the priests make an atonement for you, to cleanse you, that ye may be clean from all your sins before the Lord. It shall be a Sabbath of rest unto you, and ye shall afflict your souls by a statute for ever. The life of the flesh is in the blood; and I have given it to you upon the altar, to make an atonement for your souls, for it is the blood that maketh an atonement for the soul.
—Lev. xvi. 30, 31; and xvii. 11.

OUR great day of atonement is that on which Christ shed His blood for us on the cross, and thereby made atonement for us. Now, if it was necessary for the Israelites to afflict their souls, and chastise their bodies on the great day of atonement, how much more ought we to pray for humility and repentance, as the evidence of our interest in the propitiation made by Christ Jesus! And as they abstained from all labor on that day, when the high-priest alone was employed, so should we abstain from all our sinful works, and particularly from all self-sufficiency of righteousness, and seek our salvation only in the meritorious blood of atonement shed by our High-priest; for the life of our souls is in the blood of Jesus. O my Redeemer, may I, with an afflicted soul, ever seek my atonement, life, and salvation, in thy blood and death! and may I lie down and rise up in a comfortable hope that I am pardoned through thy blood, thy Spirit bearing witness of it to my conscience!

> Father, God, who seest in me
> Only sin and misery;
> See thine own anointed One!
> Look on thy beloved Son!
>
> Hear His blood's prevailing cry;
> Let thy bowels then reply;
> Then, through Him, the sinner see;
> Then, in Jesus, look on me!

MARCH 10.

By the grace of God I am what I am.—1 Cor. xv. 10.

BE this my motto, both as to my natural and spiritual life;—how else could I have existed at all? Had not foreknowledge planned, and wisdom contrived, and power put every atom together, and fixed my scene of action, I had never been here. Nor is this God of grace less to be seen in every motion of my soul toward Him; had not every spring been in Him, this table on which I lean had felt as much bias towards Him as I. The first check of conscience, the first thrill of fear, the first view of guilt, the first tear of penitence, were all His own; the first drawings of the Spirit, the first sight of Christ, the first dawn of hope, were all His own; every succeeding step in the path of duty, every attainment in grace, every victory over the world and sin, every evidence and token of the safety of my everlasting state, and every sweet interval of communion I have had with Him, were still all His own; and the last labor of love, the last act of faith and conquest over sin, death and hell, together with an admission into eternal glory, must and shall be all His own likewise. The spring is love; the mean is Christ; the footing firm; "the headstone shall be brought forth with shoutings, crying, Grace, grace unto it!" and grace shall be crowned with everlasting glory.

> Whate'er I am, whate'er I hope,
>   Proceeds from bounty of rich grace;
> Grace makes and holds my body up,
>   And heals my spirit's sickly face.
>
> Grace taught me first the heavenly road,
>   Grace led me on the heavenly way,
> And grace, the boundless grace of God!
>   Shall lodge me in eternity.

March 11.

The love of Christ constraineth us, because we thus judge, that if one died for all, then were all dead; and that He died for all, that they who live, should not henceforth live unto themselves, but unto Him who died for them, and rose again.
—2 Cor. v. 14, 15.

If we have the love of God shed abroad in our hearts, it will cause us to love God intensely, and to love and labor for the salvation of men. And as God so loved the world as to give His Son for it, and as Christ so loved the world as to give His life for it, so we, influenced by the very same love, will desire to spend and be spent for the glory of God, and the salvation of immortal souls. And if the love and power of Christ constrain us, we must needs be meditating and relying on Him and His death. This will cut off all workings of our own, and make room for Christ to work everything in us, and through us. O Lord, may thy love on the cross fire my frozen heart also; that I may now begin to love and praise thee purely and fervently, and to offer my whole life up to thee as an entire sacrifice of love.

> Now, sinners dry your tears,
>   Let hopeless sorrows cease;
> Bow to the sceptre of Christ's love,
>   And take the offer'd peace.
>
> Lord, we obey thy call;
>   We lay an humble claim
> To the salvation thou hast brought,
>   And love and praise thy name.
>
> Raise your triumphant songs
>   To an immortal tune;
> Let the wide earth resound the deeds
>   Celestial grace has done.
>
> Sing how eternal love
>   Its chief Beloved chose,
> And bade Him raise our wretched race
>   From sin's destructive woes.

MARCH 12.

Whatsoever thy hand findeth to do, do it with thy might; for there is no work, nor device, nor knowledge, nor wisdom, in the grave, whither thou goest.—Eccles. ix. 10.

THE business of life is to glorify God, and to work out our own salvation; all other concerns are subordinate to these; "the time is short; as the tree falleth, so it lieth;" and where death strikes down, there God lays out either for mercy or misery; so that I may compare it to the Red Sea; if I go in an Israelite, my landing shall be in glory, and my rejoicing in triumph, to see all mine enemies dead upon the seashore; but if I go in an Egyptian—if I be on this side of the cloud, on this side the covenant, and go in hardened among the troops of Pharaoh, justice shall return in its full strength, and an inundation of judgment shall overflow my soul for ever. Or I may compare death to the sleep of the ten virgins, of whom it is said, "They all slumbered and slept;" we shall all fall into this sleep. Now, if I lie down with the wise, I shall go in with the Bridegroom; but if I sleep with the foolish, without oil in my lamp, without grace in my soul, I have closed the gates of mercy upon me for ever! I see then this life is the time wherein I must go forth to meet the Lord; this is the hour wherein I must do my work; and the day wherein I must be judged, according to my works, is at hand. I know not how soon I may fall into this sleep; therefore, Lord, grant that I may live every day in thy sight, as I desire to appear at the last day in thy presence.

> Awake, my sluggish soul,
>   The heavenly race to run;
> Believe and pray, and speed thy way
>   For night is drawing on.

March 13.

Sin is a reproach to any people.—Prov. xiv. 34.

Be not deceived, therefore, with false notions of faith. Where there is true faith, no sin has dominion. Sin will be ever stirring, often raging, and sometimes prevailing; but never reigning where true faith is. A believer, through a strong and sudden temptation, may be captivated by sin, but he is no willing captive; he hates sin, and prays and watches against it; and as faith increases, his power over sin increases too, and the image of God waxes brighter in his heart. A man having no feeling of the desperate wickedness of his heart, may imagine he has faith enough; but being once convinced of that, he soon perceives that it is the hardest thing in the world to believe; it requires the same power by which Christ was raised from the dead. St. Paul most emphatically describes it with six remarkable words (Eph. i. 19, 20). How then can any man think it an easy matter to believe? Oh! the dreadful blindness and security which all the world runs into! May the Lord open their eyes!

> Lord, how secure my conscience was,
>   And felt no inward dread!
> I was alive without the law,
>   And thought my sins were dead.
>
> My hopes of heaven were firm and bright;
>   But since the precept came
> With a convincing pow'r and light,
>   I find how vile I am!
>
> I'm like a helpless captive, sold
>   Under the pow'r of sin;
> I cannot do the good I would,
>   Nor keep my conscience clean.
>
> My God, I cry with every breath
>   For thy kind pow'r to save,
> To break the yoke of sin and death,
>   And thus redeem the slave!

March 14.

At the commandment of the Lord the children of Israel journeyed, and at the commandment of the Lord they pitched; and in the place where the cloud abode, there the children of Israel pitched their tents. And when the cloud tarried long upon the tabernacle many days, then the children of Israel kept the charge of the Lord, and journeyed not.—Numb. ix. 17-19.

Thus the spiritual Israelites; they ought not to undertake anything from their own will, lest confusion and disappointment should encompass every path. The unconverted are full of their own will; how should they succeed! They are bewildered here, and run into perdition eternally. Sometimes the faithful may, with a good design, when they are engaged in a good work, outrun the will of God, and not wait for His counsel. And yet the Israelites journeyed not, though the cloud tarried many days, and they might imagine they were losing time on their journey. Oh! my God, grant that in all things, even in my best works, I may be guided by thine eye, and wait for thy counsel with a resigned temper. May I speak or be silent, work or rest, when and as thou wilt. Then shall my ways be blest, and thou wilt never leave me nor forsake me. And may I remember that God guides the way of His saints by a merciful dispensation of His providence; and in that dispensation He proportions the burden to the back that is to bear it; and that He "tempers even the blast to the shorn lamb."

> My God, the steps of pious men
>   Are ordered by thy will;
> Tho' they should fall, they rise again,
>   Thy hand supports them still!

MARCH 15.

In Him was life; and the life was the light of men.—John i. 4. *And this is the record, that God hath given to us eternal life; and this life is in His Son.*—1 John v. 11. *I am the light of the world; he that followeth me shall not walk in darkness, but shall have the light of life.*—John viii. 12.

WHATEVER notional knowledge men may have of Divine truths, as they are doctrinally proposed in the Scripture, yet if they know them not in their respect unto the person of Christ, as the foundation of the counsels of God; if they discern not how they proceed from Him, and centre in Him, they will bring no saving spiritual light unto their understandings; for all spiritual life and light is in Him, and from Him alone. The difference between believers and unbelievers as to knowledge, is not so much in the matter of their knowledge, as in the manner of knowing. Unbelievers, some of them, may know more, and be able to say more of God, His perfections and will, than many believers; but they know nothing as they ought, nothing in a right manner, nothing spiritually and savingly, nothing with a holy, heavenly light. The excellency of a believer is not that he hath large apprehensions of things, but that what he doth apprehend, which may, perhaps, be very little, he sees it in the light of the Spirit of God, in a saving, soul-transforming light. And this is that which gives us communion with God, and not prying thoughts, or curious-raised notions. In this knowledge, Lord, give me to increase every day!

> Dear Lord, anoint my head and heart,
> And light and life bestow on me;
> Light that will Gospel truth impart,
> And life to make me live to thee!

March 16.

We then that are strong ought to bear the infirmities of the weak, and not to please ourselves.—Rom. xv. 1. *Considering thyself, lest thou also be tempted.*—Gal. vi. 1. *Who art thou that judgest another man's servant.*—Rom. xiv. 4.

EXTRAORDINARY quickenings and strengthenings, being often followed by particular temptations, conflicts and sufferings, require a particular watchfulness, if we would be earnest not to provoke the Lord to visit us with sore punishments for our carelessness. Fear, therefore; rejoice with trembling; and as a needful means to secure thyself from falling, temper thy joy with true humility and gentleness toward the faults of others. Be never so high-minded, O man, at the miscarriages of others, as to think thou wouldst not do so should it happen to be thy case; for if God does not hold thee up himself, thou wilt surely make greater mistakes. Therefore, thou hadst better not look upon others, but upon thyself; and for fear of falling, be continually watchful in prayer. A great many would not have fallen so deep had they been truly humble, and more charitable in judging of others. He who exalteth himself above others, and does not bear with the weak, is sometimes humbled and debased under the very weakest of all. Bear, therefore, since God bears with thee; and he that bears most with others, shews the greatest strength.

> Jesus, Lord, we look to thee;
> Let us in thy name agree;
> Each to each unite, endear,
> Come and spread thy banner here.
>
> Make us of one heart and mind,
> Courteous, pitiful, and kind,
> Lowly, meek in thought and word,
> Altogether like our Lord.

March 17.

Thou art my rock and my fortress; therefore, for thy name's sake, lead me and guide me.—Ps. xxxi. 3. *They shall come with weeping, and with supplications will I lead them: I will cause them to walk by the rivers of waters in a straight way, wherein they shall not stumble; for I am a father to Israel.*—Jer. xxxi. 9.

He that comes in this manner will certainly be led of God. Now, O Lord, I am blind, and heartily desire to be directed by thee alone in all my ways and steps, in great and in little things. Suffer me never to follow my own spirit and natural inclinations, whatever good appearance they may have. Be pleased to cross them continually whenever they are contrary to thy will. Often have I been deceived by false appearances already; my zeal has not always been according to knowledge; I have put natural passion in the place thereof, and thought I was contending for the faith once delivered to the saints, and have afterward found it no better than the effects of a party spirit. Be then a father to me, O Lord, and instruct thy waiting child in all necessary truths, and lead me in all thy righteous ways!

> Thou art my portion, O my God!
>   And Christ my living way;
> Incline my heart to keep thy word,
>   And on my Christ to stay.
>
> I would be always wholly thine;
>   Oh! save thy servant, Lord!
> Thou art my shield, my hiding-place;
>   My hope is in thy word.
>
> Thou hast inclined this heart of mine
>   Thy statutes to fulfill;
> And thus, till mortal life shall end,
>   Would I perform thy will!

March 18.

Thou wilt keep him in perfect peace whose mind is stayed on thee; because he trusteth in thee. Trust ye in the Lord for ever; for in the Lord Jehovah, is everlasting strength.—Isa. xxvi. 3, 4. *Let him take hold of my strength, that he may make peace with me; and he shall make peace with me.*—Chap. xxvii. 5.

LET us get the Divine favor, and we will be at peace, and have happiness in our own souls, and then shall good come unto us. The peace which God gives is a peace of unutterable happiness. In it is contained all the blessings of the Gospel of Christ. Let us search well our own hearts, and see if we have that peace; and let us do it now, for we know not what a day may bring forth. But to enjoy this undisturbed peace, great care must be taken that we do not look and depend upon anything in ourselves, since all is but imperfect, and ever will be so. We are to trust only in the Lamb of God which takes away the sin of the world, to feed our souls continually on this Gospel of peace, and be ever seeking Him by diligent prayer, watchful, faithful, quiet and humble; for we never lose anything of our peace, except it is stolen by some pride or other unguarded affection.

> Hence from my soul, sad thoughts, begone,
>   And leave me to my joys;
> My tongue shall triumph in my God,
>   And make a joyful noise.
>
> Darkness and doubts had veiled my mind,
>   And drown'd my head in tears,
> Till sovereign grace, with shining rays,
>   Dispell'd my gloomy fears.
>
> Oh! what immortal joys I felt,
>   And raptures all Divine,
> When Jesus told me I was His,
>   And my Beloved mine!

MARCH 19.

Thy Maker is thy husband; the Lord of Hosts is His name. The ransomed of the Lord shall return, and come to Zion with songs, and everlasting joy upon their heads.—Isa. liv. 5; xxxv. 10.

WHEN Cyrus took the king of Armenia, and his son Tigranes, and their wives, and children prisoners, and, upon their humble submission, beyond all hope, gave them their liberty and their lives—in their return home, as they were all commending Cyrus—some for his personage, some for his power, some for his clemency, Tigranes asked his wife, "What thinkest thou of Cyrus? is he not a comely and a proper man, of a majestic presence"—"Truly," said she, "I know not what manner of man he is; I never looked upon him." "Why," said he, "where were thine eyes all the while? upon whom didst thou look?"—"I fixed mine eyes," said she, "all the while upon him (meaning her husband) who, in my hearing, offered to Cyrus to lay down his life for my ransom." Thus, if any question the devout soul—once indeed captivated by the world, but now enamored of Christ, her heavenly Bridegroom—whether she is not charmed with the riches, pleasures, and gayeties of the world?—her answer is, that her eyes and her heart are now fixed on a nobler object, even on Him who not only made an offer, like Tigranes, to die in her stead, but actually laid down His life to ransom her; and as her dear Bridegroom is now in heaven, her looks are after Him, and she can esteem nothing on earth in comparison of Him.

> Sweet the moments, rich in blessing,
>   Which before the cross I spend;
> Life, and health, and peace possessing,
>   From the sinner's dying Friend.

March 20.

Thou shalt have no inheritance in their land, neither shalt thou have any part among them: I am thy part and thine inheritance.—Numb. xviii. 20.

Whoever loves and possesses the Lord Jesus, finds unspeakably more delight, honor and riches in Him, than in all other things. He is the precious burden of their cares. All is willingly denied for His sake, and this denial springs from faith. Now, O Lord, thou art the All I need to make me happy, —the only inheritance that can supply my every want; and to draw near to thee is my greatest joy! I desire to love thee evermore, and to shew that love by keeping thy commandments; and I pray that a sweet sense of thy love to me may become my daily portion, and my only bosom treasure; and that I may be enabled to adopt the language of the Psalmist as my own, "Whom have I in heaven but thee? and there is none upon the earth that I desire besides thee; thou art the strength of my heart and my portion for ever" (Ps. lxxiii. 25, 26).

> Beset with snares on ev'ry hand,
> In life's uncertain path I stand;
> Saviour Divine! diffuse thy light,
> To guide my doubtful footsteps right.
>
> Engage this roving, treach'rous heart,
> Great God, to choose the better part;
> To scorn the trifles of a day
> For joys that none can take away.
>
> Then let the wildest storms arise,
> Let tempests mingle earth and skies;
> No fatal shipwreck shall I fear,
> But all my treasure with me bear.
>
> If thou, my Jesus, still art nigh,
> Cheerful I live and cheerful die;
> Secure when mortal comforts flee,
> To find ten thousand worlds in thee!

MARCH 21.

Likewise the Spirit also helpeth our infirmities, for we know not what we should pray for as we ought; but the Spirit itself maketh intercession for us.—Rom. viii. 26.

"GOD is a Spirit; and they that worship Him, must worship Him in spirit and in truth." God hath many worshipers on particular occasions, who cannot be called spiritual worshipers. Take, for instance, the prayers of wicked men under their convictions, or their fears, troubles and dangers, and the prayers of believers:—the former is merely an outcry that distressed nature makes to the God of it, and as such alone it considers him; but the other is the voice of the Spirit of Adoption, addressing itself from the hearts of believers unto God as a father. Woe to professors of the Gospel, who shall be seduced to believe, that all they have to do with God consists in their attendance upon moral virtue; it is fit for them so to do who, being weary of Christianity, have a mind to turn Pagans; but "our fellowship is with the Father and His Son Jesus Christ," under the promised working and intercession of the Spirit; for by them alone are the love of the Father, and the fruits of the mediation of the Son communicated unto us, without which we have no interest or comfort in them; and by the influences of the Spirit alone we are enabled to make any acceptable returns of obedience to God. To exclude the internal operations of the Holy Ghost, is to destroy the Gospel.

> Spirit of wisdom, grace, and pow'r!
> Of prayer and faith the quick'ning spring!
> With Father, Son, we thee adore,
> And Holy, holy, holy, sing!

March 22.

Now they strive to obtain a corruptible crown, but we an incorruptible.—1 Cor. ix. 25. *For he that overcometh shall inherit all things.*—Rev. xxi. 7.

To be only an almost Christian, is a very hard thing; but to be a Christian altogether, makes all easy and pleasant; and such as desire to have the whole Christ, His whole salvation, and all this is His, must needs give themselves up to Him, not only in part, but wholly, according to that fundamental and most reasonable rule, "All for all;" and as far as we deny Him anything, we make ourselves unhappy; but the more we are resigned to Him, the more we are fit to enjoy Him and His spiritual blessings.

Many would sooner be persuaded to follow Christ, if it was allowed to serve Him by halves, and reserve some things to themselves. But what could that profit them? Christ will not be bargained with; and nothing is more dangerous than the dividing our hearts between Him and the world, or waiting from time to time for a more convenient season to break through. Thus you may live many years, and be neither cold nor hot; and so at last be spewed out of the Lord's mouth. Consider this well, O ye double-minded, luke-warm souls! Christianity requires great striving, and overcoming all things, even our most favorite and darling lusts. Rouse, therefore, thy drowsy heart—spare thyself no longer—rise above the trifles of this world—fight the good fight of faith, and lay hold on eternal life, whereunto thou art called.

Take away my darling sin; make me willing to be clean;
Make me willing to receive what thy goodness waits to give!
Force me, Lord, with all to part; tear all idols from my heart;
Let thy pow'r on me be shewn; take away the heart of stone.

MARCH 23.

A new commandment I give unto you, That ye love one another; as I have loved you, that ye also love one another.—John. xiii. 34.

It is a precept of the Levitical law, "Thou shalt love thy neighbor as thyself" (Lev. xix. 18). But this commandment of Christ's was something more than the Mosaic precept. It is added, "as I have loved you." Christ loved His neighbor MORE than himself, for He laid down His life for men. And in this He calls upon all His disciples to imitate Him. But this is not the only one of His commandments that enjoins brotherly love; all the commandments of God are commandments of love, tending to our real good and great happiness; far from being grievous to those who have faith and love, the practice thereof is life and peace. The world may think it a grievous burden; but this is a great mistake indeed. Sin is grievous. In hatred, envy, anger, revenge, pride, there is nothing but torment and slavery; but in love there is a sweet rest and pleasure. Thus a sinner always punishes himself, and is robbed of great peace and blessing, by transgressing the commandments of God.

> Saviour, look down with pitying eyes,
>   Our jarring wills control;
> Let cordial, kind affections rise,
>   And harmonize the soul.
>
> Subdue in us the carnal mind,
>   Its enmity destroy;
> With cords of love th' old Adam bind,
>   And melt him into joy.
>
> Us into closest union draw,
>   And in our inward parts
> Let kindness sweetly write her law;
>   Let love command our hearts.

March 24.

One thing is needful, etc.—Luke x. 42.

We must not pretend to serve God with only going to church and doing other acts of outward devotion; whilst we are dead and cold, our religion is vain. Who first, by faith, seeks grace from the words of Christ, like Mary, is served by Christ; and this constrains him to serve Christ and his neighbor readily again. It is almost impossible for such to go on in haughtiness, envy, hatred and disobedience. Grace and faith will resist it, and make them lowly, gentle, willing, obedient, active, without relying on any works of their own. He that obtains Christ, the one thing needful, receives with Him all the rest, and has no more need to be troubled about many things. He being our All, we may always live happily; whereas the children of this world must always be cumbered and divided between fears and hopes about their fate. In vanity we shall never find this good part; neither is there any salvation in the works of the law. Faith alone takes hold of it; and whoever withdraws his heart and senses from the noise and bustle of this world, who quickly looks for salvation through the blood and righteousness of Christ, will certainly find it his better part.

>The one thing needful, that good part
>That Mary chose with all her heart,
>I would pursue with heart and mind,
>And seek unwearied till I find.
>
>O Lord, my God, to thee I pray,
>Teach me to know and find the way
>How I may have my sins forgiv'n,
>And safe and surely get to heaven.
>
>Hidden in Christ the treasure lies,
>That goodly pearl of so great price;
>No other way but Christ there is
>To endless happiness and bliss.

March 25.

Purge me with hyssop, and I shall be clean. Hide thy face from my sins, and blot out all mine iniquities.—Ps. li. 7, 9. *Though your sins be as scarlet, they shall be as white as snow.*—Isa. i. 18.

Let us ever have our sins before our faces (Ps. li. 3). Let us remember that the eye of God is constantly upon us; and that, as He looketh not on the outward, but on the inward parts, His purity and His justice will be highly incensed. With a just horror, then, of our transgressions, let us beg God to turn away His face from them—to blot them all out as a thick cloud. Let us come and do this freely, and let us come daily. We must not keep away from Christ on account of our stumblings and manifold faults. This would cast us under the law again, and bind us under condemnation; but we should humble ourselves directly before God, and seek earnestly for pardon through the blood of Christ. The longer we delay this, the worse our cause will grow; and the sooner it is done, the sooner we shall have forgiveness. The Lord not imputing those sins to us which are sincerely repented of, our soul returns to its rest again; and, instead of falling into carnal security (as some may think), it will rather strengthen our faith, and make us more watchful. Hasten, therefore, and come as soon and as well as thou canst. He will receive thee if thou canst but creep.

O Lord, I fall before thy face;
My only refuge is thy grace!
No bleeding beast, nor flood, nor sea,
Can wash the dismal stain away.

Jesus, my God, thy blood alone
Has pow'r sufficient to atone;
Thy blood can make me white as snow;
No Jewish type could cleanse me so.

March 26.

Christian's Prayer:—*Deliver us from evil.*—Matt. vi. 13.

Divine Answer:—*Fear not; for I have redeemed thee; I have called thee by thy name; thou art mine. When thou passest through the waters, I will be with thee; and through the rivers, they shall not overflow thee. When thou walkest through the fire, thou shalt not be burnt; neither shall the flame kindle upon thee.*—Isa. xliii. 1, 2. *Christ has, by His own blood, once entered into the holy place, having obtained eternal redemption for us.*—Heb. ix. 12.

THIS precious redemption is the foundation of our present deliverance, and will finally produce an everlasting deliverance from all evil. He who hates and detests not only the evil of punishment, but of sin itself, and, consequently, pants after Jesus, both for His love and for His likeness—such a one hath faith already, and sin has lost its dominion over him. And though he may be tempted with it severely, yet he is under the law no more; for the reigning power of sin being broke, the law has lost its condemning power also; we are delivered from the power of the evil one, and we may be sure of a continual, nay, eternal redemption. We may often feel the evil, but by prayer and watchfulness be as often delivered from it also.

> Thy solemn vows are on me, Lord;
>   Thou shalt receive my praise!
> I'll sing, "How faithful is thy word!
>   How righteous all thy ways!"
>
> Thou hast secured my soul from death,
>   Oh! set thy prisoner free!
> That heart, and hand, and life, and breath,
>   May be employed for thee!
>
> Assist me while I wander here,
>   Amidst a world of cares;
> Incline my heart to pray with love,
>   And then accept my prayers.

March 27.

Stir up the gift of God, which is in thee.—2 Tim. i. 6; Ps. liii. 3; 2 Sam. vii. 18, 28.

How can this be done? Answer: By looking as well upon thy own great poverty and wants, as upon the riches of grace which is in Christ for thee, and so drawing near to God through Him in faith; but it is not enough to do this once for all, or now and then only. It is to be thy daily work. One day's omission may greatly hurt thy soul. Especially the morning hours are very proper for this purpose. These must directly be laid hold on to converse with God in prayer, before we meddle with anything else in our business, though ever so needful and important, for fear of being entangled and distracted perhaps the whole day; and to gather the whole strength, draw as near to Christ as possible, and even wrestle with Him, as if it were the last time! Pour out thy whole heart before Him—not giving over too soon; but be instant in thy supplications, at least with continual inward groaning, till thy heart burn within thee, and thou feel the quickening influence of His grace and Spirit. Then great care is to be taken to preserve this blessing and strength in a quiet and well-composed mind, examining thyself frequently, especially at nights, how the day has been spent; and be not put off with a slight answer.

> I'll lift my hands, I'll raise my voice,
>   While I have breath to pray or praise
> This work shall make my heart rejoice,
>   And spend the remnant of my days.
>
> Of Him who did salvation bring,
>   I could for ever think and sing;
> When with His name I'm charm'd in song,
>   I wish myself all ear and song.

March 28.

For every one that useth milk is unskilful in the word of righteousness; for he is a babe.—Heb. v. 13.

The Apostle, with some severity of expression, tells the Hebrews, or converted Jews, to whom he wrote, that instead of being capable of strong meat, or attaining to the perfection of Christian doctrine, and being skilful in the word of righteousness, they chose to continue babes in knowledge; and, like children, had all their work to begin again. It is, therefore, a matter of the greatest importance to know what that word of righteousness is, in which they were unskilful, not having their senses exercised to discern between good and evil, truth and error. Let it only be observed, that they were looking back to the law, and consequently in danger of returning to it for justification, and thus falling from the doctrine of grace. The design of this epistle was to keep them steadfast in the faith; and it will appear at once, that the righteousness which they were ignorant of, or ready to reject, is that of Christ, "who, by one offering," the finishing act of His obedience, "hath perfected for ever them that are sanctified" (Heb. x. 14). How many, at all times, who have the name and appearance of well-grown Christians, are just such babes as the Hebrews were, and have the same need to be told that they are unskilful in the word, reason, or ground of a justifying righteousness, and exhorted to go on to perfection in Christian doctrine, as well as to further degrees of Christian holiness!

> Lord, I unskilful am,
>   A babe in knowledge yet!
> I sip the milk of thy sweet Word,
>   But ask for stronger meat.

MARCH 29.

For our Gospel came not unto you in word only, but also in power.—1 Thes. i. 5.

By the Gospel, the Son of God and Divine truths are revealed to us; and by the Spirit they are revealed in us. External revelation by the Word, and internal by the Spirit, are both necessary to salvation. Though Paul was separated from his mother's womb to be called by the grace of God, yet he had not an inward revelation of Jesus Christ in his heart till he heard the external word of Christ with his ear saying, "Saul, Saul, why persecutest thou me?" (Acts xi. 4). Hence learn to prize both the outward testimony of the Word, and the inward testimony of the Spirit. The Gospel is a revelation of Jesus Christ, without which we could never have known that our sins are atoned for by the blood, our persons justified by the righteousness, and our souls everlastingly saved by the work of Christ; but is this knowledge all that is necessary to salvation? No! persons may attain a notion of these things in the head, and understand somewhat of them, and yet the heart be without precious faith in Christ, destitute of the love of Christ, and of any saving hope in Him. Professor, look well to it; many have said, Lord, Lord, and have heard Christ preach in their streets, who little expected to meet with this rebuff from Him, "I know not whence ye are; depart, ye workers of iniquity!" Many heard the Gospel preached in Thessalonica; but they alone were blessed to whom it came "with power, and in the Holy Ghost, and with much assurance."

> The Gospel is like sun and shower,
> If once the Spirit seals the word,
> It comes with truth, and comes with power,
> And will both light and life afford.

MARCH 30.

To reveal His Son in me.—Gal. i. 16. *Flesh and blood hath not revealed it unto thee, but my Father which is in heaven.*—Matt. xvi. 17.

HENCE begins our spiritual life; a life proceeding from God, and holding communion with God, and tending to the glory of God; the honor and happiness of our souls ariseth from this revealing of Christ in us. Oh! for the reviving comfort of this while we consider it! To reveal Christ in us, is to make such a clear discovery of the matchless charms and glory of His person to our souls, as we never saw before; so that our hearts are enamored with Him, we choose Him, love Him, delight in Him, and cleave to Him in all His offices and characters; for by the eye of our soul we then behold His glory—the glory as of the only-begotten of the Father, full of grace and truth to us miserable sinners; hence He is the only-beloved of our souls. Without this revelation of Jesus Christ in us, alas! what is all outward profession? No more than mere talk, dry formality and heavy drudgery. O my soul! O my dear friends! be not content to live without a constant revelation of Christ to your souls! This makes the conscience peaceful, the heart heavenly, and the soul happy. This inspires love, subdues lust, captivates the affections, makes the whole man happy in God, and creates heaven in the soul. If Christ be within the heart, all will be right and well without in the life. If you believe Christ as revealed in the Word, this blessed promise is for you: "I will manifest myself unto him" (John xiv. 21).

> Great God, thy Scriptures will impart
> The Saviour to my list'ning ear;
> Yet, oh! reveal Him in mine heart!
> And let me feel His presence there!

March 31.

The blood of Jesus cleanseth us from all sin.—
1 John i. 7.

WHATEVER we do of ourselves, in answer to our convictions, is a covering, not a cleansing; and if we die in this condition, unwashed, uncleansed, unpurified, it is utterly impossible that we should be admitted into the blessed presence of the holy God (Rev. xxi. 7). Let no man deceive you with vain words. It is not the doing a few good works, it is not an outward profession of religion, that will give you an access with joy unto God. Unless you are washed from your actual transgressions in the blood of Christ, and cleansed from the pollution of your nature by the Spirit of God, you shall not inherit the kingdom of God; yea, without this washing you will be a horrible sight unto saints and angels—to yourselves, and to one another, when the shame of your nakedness shall be made to appear. If, therefore, you would not perish, and that eternally; if you would not perish as base defiled creatures, an abhorring unto all flesh, then, when your pride, and your wealth, and your beauty, and your ornaments, and your duties, will stand you in no stead, look out betimes after that only way of purifying and cleansing your souls which God hath ordained: "Without shedding of blood there is no remission" (Heb. ix. 22). "The blood of Jesus cleanseth from all sin." "Ye were not redeemed with corruptible things; but with the precious blood of Christ, as of a lamb without blemish and without spot" (1 Peter i. 18, 19).

> No works of ours, the most or best,
>   Can wash a conscience clean;
> The blood of Christ, our great High Priest,
>   Will only cleanse from sin!

Ye were not redeemed with corruptible things, as silver and gold, but with the precious Blood of Christ, as of a Lamb without blemish and without spot.—1 Peter i. 18, 19.

Behold the Lamb of God, which taketh away the sin of the world.—John i. 29.

—:o:—

It shall come to pass, when I bring a cloud over the earth, that the bow shall be seen in the cloud.

And the bow shall be in the cloud; and I will look upon it, that I may remember the everlasting covenant between God and every living creature of all flesh that is upon the earth.—Gen. ix. 14, 16.

APRIL 1.

I do set my bow in the cloud, and it shall be for a token of a covenant between me and the earth.— Gen. ix. 13.

THE rainbow is a token of the covenant of preservation made with Noah, and with all the creatures of the earth; it is fixed and sure; it may be considered also as an emblem of the covenant of grace (Isa. liv. 9, 10); or rather, it may be an emblem of Christ Himself (Rev. x. 1) as appears in many particulars. When we are apt to fear being overwhelmed by the rain, Jehovah shews this seal of His promise that we shall not. Thus He removes our fears, when we weep for sin, and are afraid of a flood of wrath, by reminding us of the Covenant of Grace established in Jesus. The thicker the cloud, afterward the brighter the bow in the cloud; so when afflictions abound, consolations do much more abound. The bow appears when one part of the sky is clear; which intimates mercy remembered in the midst of wrath. The rainbow is caused by the refraction of the beams of the sun; so all the glory of the Covenant of Grace and the significancy of the seals, are derived from Christ, the Sun of Righteousness. The bow speaks terror; but this is without string or arrow, is directed upward, and not to the earth. God looks upon the bow to remember His covenant; so should we, that we may be mindful of the Covenant of Grace with faith and thankfulness.

> Christ's open arms like rainbows stand,
> To grasp and save a guilty land;
> Oh! take me, Lord, within thy bow,
> And all its glories sweetly shew.
>
> My darkened mind with light divine,
> Irradiate from that bow of thine;
> And may my soul thy covenant keep,
> And heaven's eternal glories reap.

April 2.

God forbid that I should glory, save in the cross of our Lord Jesus Christ, by whom the world is crucified unto me, and I unto the world.—Gal. vi. 14.

WHATEVER others may do, or whatever they may exult or glory in, God forbid that I should exult, except in the cross of our Lord Jesus Christ, and in the grand doctrine of justification and sanctification through Him. And what else could I exult or glory in? for a true believer has nothing to glory in but Christ alone. Even in his very best performances he will be often deeply humbled and cry out, "Lord, enter not into judgment!"—and well he may; for the ground of our glory, comfort and salvation is not in works, but in Christ, and the free grace of God; who, for His Son's sake, lays nothing to our charge, but daily covers and richly pardons all our iniquities. And thus believers, walking steadily, might always be kept in solid peace; for the Cross of Christ is a solid and unshaken foundation.

> When I survey the wondrous cross
> On which the Prince of Glory died,
> My richest gain I count but loss,
> And pour contempt on all my pride.
>
> Forbid it, Lord, that I should boast,
> Save in the cross of Christ my God:
> All the vain things that charm me most,
> I sacrifice them to His blood.
>
> His dying crimson, like a robe,
> Spreads o'er His body on the tree;
> Then I am dead to all the globe,
> And all the globe is dead to me.
>
> Were the whole realm of nature mine,
> That were a present far too small;
> Love so amazing, so Divine,
> Demands my soul, my life, my all.

APRIL 3.

Purifying their hearts by faith.—Acts xv. 9.

By faith in the Son of God we get an interest in His great and glorious salvation; we are justified by faith; we have peace with God by faith. This is an excellent grace, which brings us out of a state of slavery and sin, into the liberty of the sons and daughters of God, and will issue in everlasting salvation. Faith purifies the heart of man, naturally vicious, and unites us to Christ, the root of all holiness. Now, reader, examine yourself whether you be in the faith. Try the tree by its fruits. Ask yourself these questions: Has my faith a purifying influence on my heart? Does the view of Christ dying for my sins make me die unto them? Has my faith in Christ, as wounded for my transgressions, and bruised for my iniquities, made me bitterly lament them, sincerely hate them, and seek the death of every one of them? Though there may be still sin in me, is there none allowed? Is there none, no, not one; no, not that sin which does most easily beset me, which I desire to be spared and excused in? Do I rather look upon all sin as the enemy of Christ and my own soul, and, as such, do I hate it with a perfect hatred? Am I praying fervently for Divine grace to subdue it? and in the strength of that grace, do I maintain a constant and vigorous war with it, determined never to give it any rest in my heart, never to cease my conflict with it, till I have gained the complete and everlasting victory? Then thou art upright, go on and prosper!

> That faith to me, O Lord, impart,
>   Which, while it bringeth peace,
> Will daily purify my heart,
>   And bring in holiness.

APRIL 4.

He shall cause them that come of Jacob to take root. Israel shall blossom and bud, and fill the face of the world with fruit.—Isa. xxvii. 6. *They shall again take root downward, and bear fruit upward.*—Chap. xxxvii. 31. *They shall bring forth fruit in old age; they shall be fat and flourishing.*—Ps. xcii. 14. *Her leaf shall be green, and shall not be careful in the year of drought, neither shall cease from yielding fruit.*—Jer. xvii. 8.

The evangelical Christians look upon themselves as barren trees, ever crying out, "Oh! my leanness! my leanness!" Even before the judgment-seat of Christ, they acknowledged no fruits, nor will plead them, though they have been fruitful (Matt. xxv. 37-39). The reason is, they are poor in spirit, and are not pleased with their fruits, but only with Christ. Grant, O Lord, that I may earnestly seek to bring forth fruits, and may grow in fruitfulness as I grow in years, and never cease from yielding fruit; hereby proving myself to be a tree of the Lord's planting, whose leaf is green, and whose branches are flourishing and fruitful! Yet bless me also with deep poverty of spirit, that I may see myself still nothing, having nothing of my own to glory in, or to justify me; and thus esteem Christ my All, and rest upon Him wholly.

> Lord, 'tis a pleasant thing to stand
> In gardens planted by thy hand.
> Let me within thy courts be seen,
> Like a young cedar, fresh and green.
>
> There grow thy saints in faith and love,
> Blest with thy influence from above.
> Time, that doth all things else impair,
> Still makes them flourish strong and fair.
>
> Laden with fruits of age, they shew
> The Lord is holy, just, and true.
> None that attend His gates shall find
> A God unfaithful or unkind!

APRIL 5.

The breaker is come up before them; they have broken up, and have passed through the gate; and their King (as the Author and Finisher of faith) *shall pass before them, and the Lord on the head of them.*—Micah ii. 13. *Be of good cheer, I have overcome the world.*—John xvi. 33; Heb. xii. 1, 2.

SOMETIMES the enemy seems to get an advantage over us; but the battle is not over yet. At last thou shalt have the victory, and carry the day for all that. In hard struggles remember the power of Christ, who, in His resurrection, broke through everything. With Him thou canst also break through, and be more than conqueror. Yea, in every conflict, if thy faith be firm, thou canst be sure of victory beforehand; for faith engages Christ's power, and His power ensureth victory. It is as impossible for thine enemies to keep thee always in bonds, as it was impossible that Christ could be kept in the grave by the stone, seal and keepers. Nay, the greater their force is, the more glorious will be the victory of Christ over them.

> Hosanna to our conq'ring King
>   The Prince of Darkness flies.
> His troops rush headlong down to hell,
>   Like lightning from the skies.
>
> There, bound in chains, the lions roar,
>   And fright the rescued sheep;
> But heavy bars confine their power
>   And malice to the deep.
>
> Hosanna to our conqu'ring King
>   All hail, incarnate love!
> Ten thousand songs and glories wait
>   To crown thy head above!
>
> Thy vict'ries and thy deathless fame
>   Thro' the wide world shall run,
> And everlasting ages sing
>   The triumphs thou hast won.

April 6.

Can two walk together except they be agreed?
—Amos iii. 3.

They must be agreed in heart, in affection, in will, in their inclinations and pursuits, or they cannot walk together in any mutual confidence and comfortable communion. "What communion hath light with darkness? and what concord hath Christ with Belial? or what part hath he that believeth with an infidel?" (2 Cor. vi. 15). We cannot walk with Jesus without a living union with Him, a hearty love to Him, and a holy delight in Him; nor can He walk with us on any other principles. We cannot walk with each other without mutual love. A living union with Jesus, cemented and sealed by His Holy spirit, is the only bond of union and agreement between Christians, whereby they can walk together, to the honor of God and their own benefit. Alas! how much it is to be lamented that those who, through grace, are thus united, should be so visibly shy of each other, because they differ in lesser matters. O my dear Saviour! help me to be more agreed with thee, and to walk more closely with thee, and in more real affection and love with all those who are really thine, to the praise and glory of thy grace! Amen and Amen!

> May the grace of Christ our Saviour,
> And the Father's boundless love,
> With the Holy Spirit's favor,
> Rest upon us from above!
>
> Thus shall we abide in union
> With each other and the Lord,
> And possess in sweet communion,
> Joys which earth cannot afford.
>
> Love is the golden chain that binds
> The happy souls above,
> And he's an heir of heaven who finds
> His bosom glow with love.

APRIL 7.

Let your moderation be known unto all men,—Phil. iv. 5; *for Charity* (that is, love) *edifieth.*—1 Cor. viii. 1.

IF thou rebukest others, and wouldst have them to be like thee, thou oughtest to examine thyself first, whether it flows from a blind party-zeal, impatience and self-will, or from a true principle of love; and whether thou art also much in prayer for them, both before and after. He who lays the long-sufferings of the Son of God truly to heart, and considers how gently He has treated him, and still treats him like the weakest child, must needs be moderate also toward all men, and think, "If nobody would bear with others, surely I must." Lord, give me the right spirit of meekness, to shew all lenity to my fellow-Christians, to bear with their infirmities and weaknesses, and in everything to ascribe the blame to my own wicked and perverse heart. Keep me, O Lord, from pride and vain conceit, that stirreth up to boldness in the works of the flesh, and that engendereth strife. Let the meek and the lowly mind of the holy child Jesus dwell in me: and through it let my moderation be known unto all men; for charity edifieth.

> Watch o'er my lips, and guard them, Lord,
> From ev'ry rash and heedless word;
> Nor let my feet incline to tread
> The guilty path where sinners lead.
>
> Oh! may the righteous, when I stray,
> Smite and reprove my wand'ring way;
> Their gentle words, like ointment shed,
> Shall never bruise, but cheer my head!
>
> When I behold them pressed with grief,
> I'll cry to Heav'n for their relief;
> And by my warm petitions prove
> How much I prize their faithful love.

April 8.

David's Prayer:—*Put thou my tears into thy bottle; are they not in thy book?*—Ps. lvi. 8.

Divine Answer:—*They that sow in tears shall reap in joy. He that goeth forth and weepeth, bearing precious seed, shall doubtless come again with rejoicing, bringing his sheaves with him.*—Ps. cxxvi. 5, 6.

BELIEVER, if thou art now reaping in joy, if thou hast a heart full of gladness and art singing hymns of triumph, be thankful, for few have attained to such a state of assurance and happiness; but remember that this work belongs more to the next world than the present. Here weeping and rejoicing follow each other—weeping for thy sad subjection to sin, Satan, the world and the flesh—rejoicing for the victories Christ is giving thee over them. However strong be thy faith, sorrow will oft find a lodging in thy bosom; for there is no retreat from the field of battle; and thine enemies will not leave thee while thou hast a breath to draw. Let this be a check to impatience. Let it humble thee in the sight of the Holy One of Israel, the Lord thy Redeemer. It is indeed needful to be humbled under a sense of thy misery so as to sigh, groan and weep often; and this is the true seed for eternity. This is the precious seed which the Lord requires you to bear, and which going forth bearing while engaged in the Christian warfare, you shall return from the field of battle, ladened with a rich harvest of glory, into Immanuel's peaceful land. Not a single tear or groan will be lost; they are all in the book of the Lord.

> Let those who sow in sadness, wait
>   Till the fair harvest come;
> They shall confess their sheaves are great,
>   And shout the blessings home.

APRIL 9.

The Lord hath heard my supplication. He will be a refuge for the oppressed, a refuge in times of trouble. And they that know thy name will trust in thee; for thou, Lord, hast not forsaken them that seek thee. The needy shall not always be forgotten: the expectation of the poor shall not perish for ever.—Ps. vi. 9; ix. 9, 10, 18. See also Ps. iii. 4; xxxi. 1, 7; xci. 14, 15; xii. 5.

WHOEVER would receive comfort from these words, must first be sensible of his poverty and misery, and shew it by confessing his sins, and feeling nothing in himself but helplessness and unworthiness. He must come with all his poverty to a rich Saviour, and daily entreat His mercy, carefully remembering that the Lord has promised to supply all our wants, however great our poverty and misery may be; therefore, beware of unbelief, and do not suspect the Lord's kindness, but seek to Him, and hope in Him, and expect all good things from Him; assuring thyself that neither thy hope, nor thy prayer, nor a single sigh of thine will be lost. O my God! grant me faith to say, The Lord heareth my supplication! the Lord receiveth my prayer! Praised be God, who hath not rejected my prayer, nor turned away His goodness from me, but is my protector and hope.

> My best desires are faint and few,
>   I fain would strive for more;
> But when I cry, "My strength renew,"
>   Seem weaker than before.
>
> Thy saints are comforted, I know,
>   And love thy house of prayer;
> I therefore go where others go,
>   But find no comfort there.
>
> Oh! make this heart rejoice or ache,
>   Decide this doubt for me,
> And if it be not broken, break,
>   And heal it if it be.

APRIL 10.

Christian's Prayer :—*Lead us not into temptation.*—Matt. vi. 13.

Divine Answer :—*God is faithful, who will not suffer you to be tempted above what ye are able; but will with the temptation also make a way to escape, that ye may be able to bear it.*—1 Cor. x. 13. Ps. lxvii. 3.

THE nearer to heaven, the higher the mountains, the deeper the valleys, and the sharper the conflicts. But be not discouraged; it is only for the trial of our faith. God gives also more strength, carries us through all, as He has done from the beginning, and suffers none to be ashamed who trust in Him. Sometimes we may seem to be tempted above measure, and are afraid of being confounded; but far from it. It is quite impossible we should. Here thou hast the plain words of the Lord. Take hold on them, and wait His time; for since the world stood, none have been confounded in anything who have waited for His promise; and surely He will not make thee the first instance of the failure of His Word. By no means (Phil. i. 10; Isa. liv. 10), "Rather shall the mountains depart, and the hills be removed, says the Lord, that hath mercy on thee."

> Our God, how firm His promise stands,
>   E'en when He hides His face!
> He trusts in our Redeemer's hands
>   His glory and His grace.
>
> Then why, my soul, these sad complaints,
>   Since Christ and we are one?
> Thy God is faithful to His saints;
>   Is faithful to His Son.
>
> Beneath His smiles my heart has lived,
>   And part of heaven possest.
> Oh! praise His name for grace received,
>   And trust Him for the rest.

APRIL 11.

David's Prayer:—*Oh! satisfy us early with thy mercy.*—Ps. xc. 14.
God's Answer:—*Open thy mouth wide, and I will fill it.*—Ps. xxxi. 10. *For my people shall be satisfied with my goodness.*—Jer. xxxi. 14. *The river of God is full of water.*—Ps. lxv. 9. *With joy shall ye draw water out of the wells of salvation.*—Isa. xii. 3. *This is the Fountain opened for sin and for uncleanness.*—Zech. xiii. 1.

O MY soul, keep close to the Gospel. There only is a fullness to supply all thy wants—food for the hungry, and raiment for the naked soul; and everything in plenty. Whoever will may come and be fed and clothed, without money, and without price. Therefore let not the law hinder thee from eating and drinking, rejoicing and adorning thyself in a Gospel manner. The law, as one justly observes, brings in a great bill, but nothing wherewith to discharge it. It sets the soul a-working, but so as to neglect the proper nourishment necessary for it. No wonder, therefore, that she is destitute of sufficient strength—that she faints, and never comes to the right mark. There is no such thing as making amends by the law. We must go directly to Christ, and receive first the grace and strength required, out of His fullness, by faith.

> Let ev'ry mortal ear attend,
>   And ev'ry heart rejoice;
> The trumpet of the Gospel sounds
>   With an inviting voice.
>
> Rivers of love and mercy here
>   In a rich ocean join;
> Salvation in abundance flows,
>   Like floods of milk and wine.
>
> Dear God, the treasures of thy love
>   Are everlasting mines;
> Deep as our helpless mis'ries are,
>   And boundless as our sins.

April 12.

Fear not, daughter of Zion.—John xii. 15. *But greatly rejoice and shout, O daughter of Jerusalem, behold thy King comes unto thee; He is just, and having salvation.*—Zech. ix. 9. *The King of Israel, even the Lord, is in the midst of thee; thou shalt not see evil any more.*—Zeph. iii. 15. See also Isa. liv. 12; Jer. xv. 19.

THOUGH Satan be endeavoring to bind his chains fast about thee—though thy heart quake and be ready to fail for the many sins that encompass it— though destruction and death be in thy way, yet fear not—"Behold thy King cometh;" trust Him, He will restrain, He will defend. How strong soever thine inward enemies—thy corruptions—may be now, fear not, and be not discouraged. Thy King is bound, by His office, love and promise, to help thee with strength to overcome. Even the hardships of a Christian work together for His good in this world, and brighten His crown of glory in the world to come. Too oft, instead of casting and laying a burden upon the Lord by faith at once, we parley with temptation and undertake to heal ourselves by a thousand false contrivances, the effect of which is, to make a conflict long that might have been short (2 Chron. xvi. 7–9). Lord, give me grace to be watchful, and to keep on the armor of faith, that as I pass from conflict to conflict, I may pass on conquering and to conquer, daily pressing forward and experiencing Jesus every hour, my mighty King and Saviour.

> Rejoice, the Lord is King,
>   Your Lord and King adore,
> Mortals, give thanks and sing,
>   And triumph evermore.
> He sits at God's right hand,
>   Till all His foes submit,
> And bow to His command,
>   And fall beneath His feet.

APRIL 13.

Thou shalt not be afraid of them; but shalt well remember what the Lord thy God did unto Pharaoh, and all Egypt.—Deut. vii. 18. *Be ye not terrified because of them, for the Lord your God is He that goes with you, to fight for you against your enemies, to save you.*—Chap. xx. 3, 4. *Hitherto shalt thou come, and no farther, and here shall thy proud waves be stayed.*—Job xxxviii. 11.

The Lord on high is mightier than the noise of many waters; yea, than the mighty waves of the sea (Ps. xciii. 4). He controls the strength of nations, and the most powerful empires are as grasshoppers in His sight. Those, therefore, who trust in Him have nothing to fear. Shall we not then seek for His strength to overcome the assaults of sin; for let us remember, the assaults of original sin will ever return; and we must not be surprised, when one conflict is over, that another arises. This contest is unavoidable, for the enemy is within us. It makes us more careful and humble to know this, than if we believe that we had only to encounter with sin from without and not from within. And if we desire to feel less evil in us than God suffers us to have, we may be assured, this desire proceeds either from pride, seeking to glory in our own righteousness, or from an impatient wish to get rid of the trouble of striving always against sin; whereas it should be enough for us that God suffers it, lays it not to our charge, and carries us through all dangers.

> Let the redeemed of the Lord
> The wonders of His grace record.
> Israel the nation which He chose,
> And rescued from their mighty foes.
> He feeds and clothes us all the way;
> He guides our footsteps lest we stray
> He guards us with a powerful hand,
> And brings us to the heavenly land.

APRIL 14.

Verily thou art a God that hidest thyself, O God of Israel, the Saviour.—Isa. xlv. 15. *All the paths of the Lord are mercy and truth.*—Ps. xxv. 10. *The Lord of Hosts is wonderful in counsel, and excellent in working.*—Isa. xxviii. 29. *O Lord, how great are thy works! and thy thoughts are very deep.*—Ps. xcii. 5.

GOD is wonderful in all His doings! His ways are past finding out! At the end we can see best the wise and gracious steps He took with us; therefore, when things take such a wonderful turn that we are quite at our wit's end, and do not know which way to go, we may believe the hand of the Lord is in it, and some good will come of it at last. As we experience the name of Christ to be wonderful at such times, we may well expect that He will shew Himself to be our Counsellor and mighty God also. At first, everything may seem to be against us and go quite contrary; but, at last, we see plainly that it was highly needful it should go contrary to our corrupt nature, and that thus it went well; for though the ways of God are marvelous, yet they are glorious.

> God moves in a mysterious way
>   His wonders to perform;
> He plants His footsteps in the sea,
>   And rides upon the storm.
>
> Deep in unfathomable mines
>   Of never-failing skill,
> He treasures up His bright designs,
>   And works His sovereign will.
>
> Judge not the Lord by feeble sense,
>   But trust Him for His grace;
> Behind a frowning providence
>   He hides a smiling face.
>
> His purposes will ripen fast,
>   Unfolding every hour;
> The bud may have a bitter taste,
>   But sweet will be the flower.

APRIL 15.

Remember the Sabbath day, to keep it holy.—Ex. xx. 8. *I was in the Spirit on the Lord's day.*—Rev. i. 10.

READER, may God bless this meditation to thy soul! Perhaps thou art a careless sinner, who has trifled with Sabbaths. Oh! do not profane the Lord's day any more; but if thou valuest thy soul, attend upon His worship, and desire to be "in the Spirit on His day;" then wilt thou see and feel thy malady; look to Jesus for pardon, and Sabbath days will become precious to thy soul. Perhaps thou art a self-righteous Pharisee, punctual in outward services; so far is praiseworthy; but awful is thy mistake, if thou makest any outward service the ground of thy acceptance, especially as the language of the day is, "In the Lord have I righteousness and strength;" and so wilt thou say, if "in the Spirit." Or thou mayest have been a splendid professor, but now a grievous backslider. Oh! may thou be "in the Spirit on the Lord's day!" then thou wilt look to God for pardon, to Jesus for fresh sprinklings of His blood, and to the Spirit for His quickening influences. If thou art a believer under sharp trials, mayest thou be "in the Spirit;" then, when tribulations abound, consolations may abound also. If thou art a believer walking close with God, rich in knowledge and experience, thou wilt wish to be "in the Spirit," that grace may be magnified, Jesus more loved, and His name more honored. Reader, whatever thou art, if thou wishest to be "in the Spirit," and wouldst have thy temporal and spiritual concerns prosper, make conscience of keeping the Sabbath day holy.

> The Sabbath is designed, I know,
> To train my soul for heav'n;
> Then let me keep and think it too
> The best of all the seven.

April 16.

Nehemiah's Prayer :—*Remember me, O my God, for good.*—Neh. xiii. 31.

Divine Answer :—*Is Ephraim my dear son? is he a pleasant child? For since I spake against him, I do earnestly remember him still; therefore my bowels are troubled for him: I will surely have mercy upon him.*—Jer. xxxi. 20.

"O MY God, have mercy upon me!" is the prayer of every true penitent; and as soon as that prayer ascends to God, scented with the odor of faith, God hears it, and He keeps a bottle for the tears which produced it. Grant, Lord, that I may be enabled daily to offer this prayer; and grant me to bear steadily in mind, that as soon as I appear with my prayers before the Lord, He writes all my petitions in His book of remembrance. Should I not pray much? Yes, O Lord! and though I have many things already in thy book, yet will I give thee occasion to write down more and more every hour. Thus, nothing can be forgotten; all will be granted by Him. Delays we must expect; but all shall be made up with so much the larger gifts in due time, though the best will be reserved for a blissful eternity.

> Now let the Lord my Saviour smile,
>   And shew my name upon His heart;
> I would forget my pains awhile,
>   And in the pleasure lose the smart.
>
> Dear Lord, imprint upon my breast,
>   And in the book of life my name;
> I'd rather have it *there* impress'd
>   Than in the bright records of fame.
>
> When the vast fire burns all things here,
>   Those letters shall securely stand,
> And in the Lamb's fair book appear,
>   Writ by the eternal Father's hand.

APRIL 17.

And in this mountain shall the Lord of Hosts make unto all people a feast of fat things, a feast of wines on the lees; of fat things full of marrow, of wines on the lees well refined.—Isa. xxv. 6. See also Ps. xxiii. Matt. viii. 11.

A FEAST bespeaks plenty, harmony and joy. Many feasts were appointed under the law, in commemoration of various deliverances and mercies. The Gospel appoints one great perpetual festival, in consequence of the one grand blessing, which comprehends all other mercies—"Redemption by the blood of Christ." The table is always spread, the company are always welcome, the season is always pleasant, and the joy is always new. Lord, I once was feeding upon husks, upon ashes, upon the wind, and drinking down iniquity like water; but, oh! wonderful love! thou didst invite and bring me to thine own feast! Thou feedest me with the bread of life, and causest me to drink of the wine of thy consolation. May I never more have an appetite for the vanities of the world; but may I always have the Lord for my Shepherd, leading me by green pastures, and by the still waters; and may I, from sitting at His table in this wilderness, rise and go to sit at that table which is forever spread in heaven, at which Abraham, Isaac and Jacob are guests; and where Jesus, my Redeemer, is forever present.

> Why was I made to hear thy voice,
>   And enter while there's room,
> When thousands make a wretched choice,
>   And rather starve than come?

> 'Twas the same love that made the feast,
>   That sweetly forced us in;
> Else we had still refused to taste,
>   And perished in our sin.

April 18.

He believed in the Lord; and He counted it to him for righteousness.—Gen. xv. 6. Rom. iv. 5.

It is no uncommon thing in Scripture to put the act for the object, especially with regard to faith and hope. Thus hope signifies the object of hope (Jer. xiv. 9; 1 Tim. i. 1; Heb. vi. 18). And faith is often put for the object or doctrine of faith, or that which is believed in; as when it is said, Paul preached the faith which once he destroyed; and Felix heard him concerning the faith of Christ; and when the Scripture speaks of keeping and contending for the faith. Thus, when Abraham is said to believe in the Lord, the meaning is, he believed in the promise of God, that he should have a seed, and a very numerous one; he believed that the Messiah would spring from his seed; he believed in Him as his Saviour and Redeemer; he believed in Him for righteousness; and he believed in His righteousness as justifying him before God. It was not the act of his faith, but the object of it; not the promise he believed, but what was promised, and his faith received even Christ and His righteousness. See this explained fully in Rom. iv. 3, 10, 22-24. Reader, mark well how Abraham was justified before God—not by faith as a work, but as apprehending Christ; and follow this example of the father of the faithful. It is by faith in Jesus Christ alone that we can be justified before God; by faith all the Old Testament saints were justified, as well as the New. This distinguishes the Christian religion from all systems of morality: and to err in this, is to err in the fundamentals of Christianity.

> Give me the faith which can remove
>   And sink the mountains to a plain;
> Give me the child-like praying love
>   Which longs to build thy house again.

April 19.

This do in remembrance of me.—Luke xxii. 19.

Come, my soul, obey thy dying Lord's command! Let it be thy delight, as it is thy privilege, to attend thy Master at table, to take a near review of His bleeding love, and, by a renewed act of faith, obtain a fresh taste and renewed pledge of the precious benefits contained therein. Stagger not through unbelief. It is a blessed truth, Jesus died for sinners—this is the foundation of a sinner's hope. Let this encourage thee, O my soul!—thou art a sinner, guilty and defiled; Jesus' blood cleanses from all sin; He is the fountain opened for thy uncleanness;—thou art by nature a child of wrath, condemned by the Law, exposed to the curse; but Jesus was made a curse for thee;—thou art unrighteous, unholy; but Jesus is made of God unto thee righteousness and sanctification; thou art weak, beset with enemies; His strength shall be perfected in thy weakness, and thou, by faith, shall be more than conqueror through Him that loved thee. Thou art afraid of perishing at the last! look to Jesus; He purchased thee with His blood; He will not give thee up; none can pluck thee out of His hand. Rise, then, O my soul, and come to the banquet of love, and partake of the blessings of the everlasting covenant; beseech the Lord to manifest His love, and seal thy pardon, renew thy strength, and enable thee to travel the remaining part of the pilgrimage, till thou come to Mount Zion, and be admitted a welcome guest at the marriage supper in heaven.

> I thank thee, O my dying Lord,
>   For thine appointed feast;
> Vouchsafe to meet me at thy board,
>   And smile upon thy guest.

April 20.

I write unto you, little children, because your sins are forgiven you for His name's sake; to you, fathers, because ye have known Him that is from the beginning; to you, young men, because you have overcome the wicked one.—1 John ii. 12, 13.

GOD has more communion with some of His saints than others. Out of the multitude He chose twelve, out of the twelve He chose three, and out of the three He chose John to be His peculiar darling and bosom favorite, of whom it is said five times in St. John's gospel, that "he was the disciple whom Jesus loved." So now at this day, God hath His babes, who live upon milk, and nothing else. He "has children also," who know their Father, and are assured of His love; moreover, He "has His young men, who go out to war, and fight the Lord's battles victoriously;" and He has "fathers in Israel," who abound in gray-headed experience and wisdom; for they knew Him from the beginning, and they remembered His words. It is a great mercy to be one of God's "little ones," yea, the least of all; to be a star, though not of the first magnitude; to be a disciple, though not one of the three, nor one of the twelve, nor one of the seventy; but to be a John, a darling, and to lean on His breast, to lie in His bosom, oh! how great a mercy! It is a mercy to be new-born, to be taken into the family of God and household of faith; but to grow up to a perfect stature, to be a man in Christ Jesus, oh! how great a mercy! Lord, thou knowest my desire, perfect that which concerns thy servant.

It doth not yet appear how great we must be made;
But when we see our Saviour there, we shall be like our Head.
We would no longer lie like slaves beneath the throne;
My faith shall Abba, Father, cry, and thou thy kindred own.

APRIL 21.

Take thy son, thine only son Isaac, whom thou lovest, and get thee into the land of Moriah; and offer him there for a burnt-offering.—Gen. xxii. 2.

Abraham desired earnestly to see into the mystery of redemption; and God let Abraham feel, by experience, something of the depth of that mystery. "Take now thy son, thine only son Isaac, the staff of thine age, the hope of thy family, and offer him up for a burnt-offering; and in this transaction see my love to sinners, in giving up my only Son Jesus a sacrifice for them." Abraham obeyed; he virtually sacrificed his son; a ram was substituted in his place, and blessings were poured upon the faithful patriarch. In the whole story we have a lively type of greater things. We have seen the day when God spared not His own Son; when He was bound with cords; when He bore His cross, and on this mountain, probably on this very spot, was offered up an offering for sin; when He, triumphant over the grave, rose again to live for evermore, and saw His seed, even His redeemed people, whom no man can number, and whose possessions are the glories of eternity. My soul, think on these things. Art thou a son of Abraham? Is there in thine heart a darling sin? Draw forth the knife and smite it away. Hath God not spared His Son for me, and shall I spare what He commands me to sacrifice? No! gracious Saviour, no! Help me to keep back nothing from thee. Search my heart, and when thou hast tried me, crown the faith thou hast bestowed, and the obedience thou hast wrought, with that unfading glory thou hast promised to the faithful.

> I thank, thee, Father, for the gift
>   Of thy beloved Son;
> Now bid me give myself to thee,
>   And live to thee alone.

April 22.

God who is rich in mercy, for His great love wherewith He loved us, even when we were dead in sins, hath quickened us together with Christ, (by grace ye are saved;) and hath raised us up together, and made us sit together in heavenly places in Christ Jesus.—Eph. ii. 4-6.

CHRIST being the head of the body, His Church, all who are His real members, are, together with Him, dead, buried, raised up, and seated in heavenly places; for He is the new Adam, and has done all these things as our representative, in our stead, and for our good. Therefore a true believer may rejoice and say, "I have suffered in thee, O my glorious head, for all my sins already. I am discharged. I have no punishment to fear any more respecting the guilt and curse of sin. Thou hast fully answered the charge against me, satisfied the infinite justice of God for me, and it is impossible, with its equity and love, to require a double payment of my debts: consequently, I die no more; nay, I live already, and have my place with thee eternally in heaven, since the head cannot, nor will ever part even with the weakest of His members, but influence and draw them after Him wherever He goes."

> O Lord, we praise thee for thy Son,
> Who joined our nature to His own;
> Adam, the Second, from the dust
> Raises the ruins of the first.
>
> By the rebellion of one man,
> Through all the seed the mischief ran;
> And by one man's obedience now,
> Are all his seed made righteous too.
>
> Where sin did reign and death abound,
> There have the sons of Adam found
> Abounding life; their glorious grace
> Reigns through the Lord our Righteousness.

April 23.

God has made Him to be sin for us, who knew no sin; that we might be made the righteousness of God in Him.—2 Cor. v. 21. *To him that worketh not, but believeth on Him that justifieth the ungodly, his faith is counted for righteousness.*—Rom. iv. 5. See also Gen. xv. 6.

These are very sweet and precious words to those who look upon their own best virtues and performances by nature as sinful, and upon their best condition by grace as extremely weak and imperfect. How comfortable a thing is the justification of the penitent by faith, when the soul is first stripped quite naked before God, and thoroughly convinced of its wickedness and weakness! A mere moral man does not meddle with this. He pretends to make amends for his former sins, by altering his course, and doing better works; but this is not making amends at all, since we are but unprofitable servants, and want continually forgiveness of sin, even when we have done all. There is but one way to be justified, and to obtain and preserve the blessing of a good conscience, which is by humbling and confessing ourselves guilty, and looking only for forgiveness and righteousness in Christ. Thus we are made by Him the righteousness of **God** itself. May the Lord put us all in this way!

> No more, my God, I boast no more
>   Of all the duties I have done;
> I quit the hopes I held before,
>   To trust the merits of thy Son.
>
> Oh! yes, I must and will esteem
>   All things but loss for Jesus' sake;
> Oh! may my soul be found in Him,
>   And of His righteousness partake!
>
> The best obedience of my hands
>   Dares not appear before thy throne
> But faith can answer thy demands,
>   By pleading what my Lord has done.

APRIL 24.

God has exalted Christ Jesus with His right hand, to be a Prince and a Saviour, for to give repentance to Israel, and forgiveness of sins.—Acts v. 31. *Unto you first, God, having raised up His Son Jesus, sent Him to help you, in turning away every one of you from his iniquities.*—Acts iii. 26.

SAY not, What reason have I to repent? I am no murderer or robber; for thou art both. By thy sins thou hast murdered the Son of God, and by thy pride robbed God of His due service; therefore, if thy old heart be not changed into a new one, and yet thou feelest some uneasiness about thy salvation, do not look on this concern as a fit of the vapors, or as a temptation of the devil; but believe it is the work of Christ, who now awakes thee from the sleep of sin, and offers thee repentance; and who will change thy heart, and make thee a new man, if thou canst yield up thyself unto Him: "He stands at the door and knocks, and says, If any man hear my voice and open the door, I will come in to him and sup with him" (Rev. iii. 20).

> Now Christ will ev'ry want supply,
> And fill our hearts with peace;
> He gives, by cov'nant and by oath,
> The riches of His grace.
>
> Our hearts, that flinty, stubborn thing
> That terrors cannot move,
> That fears no threat'nings of His wrath,
> Shall be dissolv'd by love.
>
> There shall His sacred Spirit dwell,
> And deep engrave His law,
> And ev'ry motion of our souls
> To swift obedience draw.
>
> Thus will He pour salvation down,
> And we shall render praise;
> He'll bless the people of His love,
> And we'll adore His grace.

APRIL 25.

God is not a God of confusion.—1 Cor. xiv. 33.
*He has made everything beautiful in its season.
Also, no man can find out the work that God
maketh from the beginning to the end.*—Eccles.
iii. 11.

O LORD, I am like a little child, knowing neither the beginning nor end of my ways. I daily go in a strange path, the sides whereof are vanity, and the end destruction. I see not my way in it, yet my wicked heart tells me not to leave it. One pleasure after another bids me stay, yet the sweets thereof I never taste. I am weary of it; it is a perplexing path. But thou, who art the Wonderful Counsellor, make it my only wisdom to be advised and ruled by thee. Oh! shew me, then, always thy way in all things, even in the least, that I may never miss to do thy work in due season and due order. Make me such a faithful steward, as not to go one inch from thy will, but on all occasions to act and suffer according to thy pleasure.

> Whither, oh! whither shall I fly,
>   But to my loving Saviour's breast,
> Secure within thy arms to lie,
>   And safe beneath thy wings to rest.
>
> I have no might t' oppose the foe;
>   But everlasting strength is thine.
> Shew me the way that I should go;
>   Shew me the path I should decline.
>
> Which shall I leave, and which pursue?
>   Thou only my Adviser be;
> My God, I know not what to do!
>   But, oh! mine eyes are fixed on thee.
>
> Foolish, and impotent, and blind,
>   Lead me a way I have not known;
> Bring me where I my heaven may find
>   The heaven of loving thee alone!

APRIL 26.

Now He who stablisheth us with you in Christ, and hath anointed us, is God; who hath also sealed us, and given the earnest of the Spirit in our hearts.—2 Cor. i. 21, 22. *But ye have an unction from the Holy one, and ye know all things.*—1 John ii. 20.

A SENSIBLE joy of faith, and great delight in prayer, are not the only evidences of this earnest and sealing of the Spirit; these sometimes are wanting when we know we are sealed by these marks—namely, when we receive Christ in all His offices, and have a sincere desire to do the will of God in all things; when we love the ordinances of Christ, and regard the children of God with a brotherly affection, and seek to do them good; when we hate sin, and watch and pray against it; and, lastly, when we are poor in spirit, vile in our own eyes, and are led into further acquaintance with Christ himself, and with His Gospel, by the Spirit. These are constant marks even for the weakest.

> Why should the children of a King
>   Go mourning all their days?
> Great Comforter, descend, and bring
>   Some tokens of thy grace.
>
> Dost thou not dwell in all thy saints,
>   And seal the heirs of heaven?
> When wilt thou banish my complaints,
>   And shew my sins forgiven?
>
> Assure my conscience of her part
>   In the Redeemer's blood;
> And bear thy witness with my heart,
>   That I am born of God.
>
> Thou art the earnest of His love,
>   The pledge of joys to come;
> And thy soft wings, celestial Dove,
>   Will safe convey me home.

APRIL 27.

Christian's Prayer:—*God be merciful to me a sinner.*—Luke xviii. 13. *Look upon mine affliction and my pain, and forgive all my sins.*—Ps. xxv. 18.
Divine Answer:—*The Lord is gracious, and full of compassion, and of great mercy; the Lord is good to all, and His tender mercies are over all His works.*—Ps. cxlv. 8, 9. *My son, be of good cheer; thy sins are forgiven thee.*—Matt. ix. 2.

JUSTIFICATION, or remission of sins before the tribunal of God, and the comfortable assurance of it in the heart, do not always go together. The pardon is passed in heaven at once, and in the most perfect manner; yet the sense of it may be wanting; for the assurance of that pardon is mostly given by degrees, as believers are able to receive it. Feeble glimpses appear now and then; and many love-tokens usually pass between Christ and a believing soul, before the Spirit gives a full and clear witness to his conscience. Therefore a penitent soul must converse much with the Gospel, and pray continually for more light, and a greater degree of faith and peace. It must narrowly scrutinize its own feelings and desires, and bring these, at all times, to the test of the Bible; and in this work the glimmerings of the dawn of assured hope will begin to dispel its darkness.

> O God of mercy! hear my call;
>   My load of guilt remove;
> Break down this separating wall,
>   That bars me from my love.
>
> Give me the presence of thy grace;
>   Then my rejoicing tongue
> Shall speak aloud thy righteousness
>   And make thy praise my song.
>
> A soul oppressed with sin's desert,
>   My God will ne'er despise;
> An humble groan, a broken heart,
>   Is our best sacrifice!

April 28.

Delight thyself in the Lord, and He shall give thee the desires of thine heart.—Ps. xxxvii. 4. *Cast thy burden upon the Lord, and He shall sustain thee.*—Ps. lv. 22. *Commit thy works unto the Lord, and thy thoughts shall be established.*—Prov. xvi. 3.

If thou desirest to delight thyself only in the Lord, and art more solicitous for the increase of faith, love and holiness, than temporal happiness—and wouldst even part with some earthly good, provided it would enlarge thy spiritual welfare—this comes not from nature, but is an infallible mark of grace and regeneration; and the Lord shall give thee also the desires of thine heart, and even more than thou desirest. Nothing can be more foolish than to harbor one or more secret lusts in our hearts, after we have been once awakened. We must certainly suffer for it; our conscience will check us; we cannot enjoy it with half the pleasure as before; our course is hindered and our peace disturbed. How much more prudent and profitable, then, would it be to forsake all and follow Christ straight, who only can satisfy the desires of our heart! Consider this, O my soul! act the wiser part; let thine eye be single, and cleave to Him alone; while others, seeking to serve two masters, God and Mammon, are woefully disappointed at last; avoid thou this folly, and be wholly for Christ. Thus thou wilt be able to taste the kisses of His mouth, and the crystal streams of His comfortable and heavenly love.

> Dear Saviour, let thy beauties be
>   My soul's eternal food;
> And grace command my heart away,
>   From all created good.

APRIL 29.

Jeremiah's Prayer:—*Heal me, O Lord, and I shall be healed.*—Jer. xvii. 14.

Divine Answer:—*I am the Lord that healeth thee.*—Exod. xv. 26. *They that be whole need not a physician, but they that are sick.*—Matt. ix. 12. *I have seen his ways, and will heal him.*—Isa. lvii. 18; lxi. 1; lxiii. 7.

CHRIST'S healing all bodily sickness, was a token of His power and grace to heal all spiritual diseases of our souls, though ever so dangerous. Therefore, give thyself only up to His care; He understands thy distemper also, and will certainly restore thee. He has healed a great many already: nay, all those who ever desired it, of all their infirmities. Thou canst never be too miserable and bad for Him; He is ever willing and able to help. The worse thy case is, the more He will pity thee and have patience. Before we can be made whole, His way is to make us thoroughly sensible of our sickness, and lay our wounds more and more open. But, as the Physician then is most wanted, we must be the more earnest to implore His help, and He will surely bind us up again and heal us; not at once, but by degrees; often slowly and wonderfully, yet thoroughly at last; for He heals all, even the most incurable diseases (Ps. ciii. 3).

> Bind up, O Lord, and cheer my soul
>   With thy forgiving love;
> Oh! make my broken spirit whole,
>   And bid my pains remove.
>
> Let not thy spirit quite depart,
>   Nor drive me from thy face;
> Create anew my vicious heart,
>   And fill it with thy grace!
>
> Then let my heart with grateful love,
>   And grace abounding be;
> And let thy name all names above,
>   Be ever praised by me.

April 30.

Confess your faults one to another.—James v. 16.

It is related of St. John, the Evangelist, that he was once set upon by a company of thieves, amongst whom was a young man, their captain. To him St. John applied himself, by way of wholesome counsel and advice, which took so good effect, that he was converted, and went to all his fellow-thieves, and besought them, in the name of Jesus Christ, to walk no longer in their wicked ways. He told them that he was troubled in conscience for his former wicked life, and earnestly entreated them, as they tendered the welfare of their own souls, to leave off their old courses. The counsel was good, and well taken, so that many of them became converts. Thus one sinner's confession of his faults to another, may happily prove the conversion of one by the other. Hence that precept, "Confess your faults one to another," is thus interpreted by some:—That those who have been partners together in sin, should go and seriously confess their sins each to the other. He that hath been a drunkard, or any otherwise a wicked liver, let him go to his companions in iniquity, and tell them that he is troubled in mind because of his former excess, and he may be a mean of converting them. Reader, art thou converted?—follow this method;—go to thy old companions, warn them of their danger, and thou wilt either be a mean of converting them, or hereby get rid of their troublesome company. Again, he who has injured another, should confess his fault to that other, as well as to God, and beg forgiveness from both.

> If I have wronged my neighbor aught,
>   Or led a soul astray,
> Lord, give me grace to own my fault,
>   And to amend my way.

He that covereth his sins shall not prosper: but whoso confesseth and forsaketh them shall have mercy.—Prov. xxviii. 13.

———:o:———

I acknowledged my sin unto thee, and mine iniquity have I not hid.

I said, I will confess my transgressions unto the Lord; and thou forgavest the iniquity of my sin.—Ps. xxxii. 5.

May 1.

David's Prayer:—*Lord, enter not into judgment with thy servant.*—Ps. cxliii. 2.

Divine Answer:—*Verily, verily, I say unto you, he that heareth my word, and believeth on Him that sent me, hath everlasting life, and shall not come into condemnation; but is passed from death unto life.*—John v. 24. See also chap. viii. 51; Isa. xxv. 8.

SINCE the Judge Himself is our Brother, our Bridegroom, the Lord of death and life, yea, even our life, believers cannot die eternally; because "they are passed from death unto life." He that owns the justice of God's judgment, confesses himself guilty in all things, and appeals from the judgment-seat to the mercy-seat, him the Lord will own and justify through the righteousness of His Son; for "if we would judge ourselves, we should not be judged. Nay, we shall even sit in judgment together with Christ" (1 Cor. vi. 2). And surely in that day we shall not pass a sentence of condemnation on ourselves, much less will Christ; for He loves us more than we do ourselves. Oh! let us then humble ourselves before God, and come as condemned criminals to His seat of mercy, for pardon and for grace to help in the time of need.

> Who shall the Lord's elect condemn?
>   'Tis God that justifies their souls;
> And mercy, like a mighty stream,
>   O'er all their sins Divinely rolls.
>
> Who shall adjudge the saints to hell?
>   'Tis Christ that suffer'd in their stead!
> And their salvation to fulfill,
>   Behold Him rising from the dead.
>
> Then never shall my soul despair
>   Her pardon to procure;
> Who knows God's only Son has died
>   To make her pardon sure.

May 2.

Jeremiah's Prayer:—*Give heed to me, O Lord, and hearken to the voice of them that contend with me.*—Jer. xviii. 19.

Divine Answer:—*Behold, He that keepeth Israel shall neither slumber nor sleep.*—Ps. cxxi. 4. *Casting all your care upon God; for He careth for you.*—1 Pet. v. 7. *Cast thy burden upon the Lord, and He will sustain thee.*—Ps. lv. 22.

WHATEVER cares and anxieties perplex the people of God, whether they be temporal or spiritual, whether they be great or small, they also concern God. He knows their afflictions; He knows their anxieties. The care of our Lord, which He takes for His little ones, infinitely exceeds the care of the most tender mother over her weak and helpless child. Then, whilst I feel and own myself weak, foolish, and wretched, the Lord being the guardian of such babes, He will have patience with me; for they are the vessels of His grace. Knowing myself, therefore, to be always a weak and ignorant child, I will labor to keep close to Jesus in waiting and prayer. And since He is the Minister of the Sanctuary, He will never let me want anything that is good for me; but will defend me, and feed me, and train me up in the best and most suitable manner.

> Be thou my counsellor,
>   My pattern, and my guide.
> And through this desert land,
>   Still keep me near thy side.
> Oh! let my feet ne'er run astray,
> Nor rove, nor seek the crooked way!
>
> Should all the hosts of death,
>   And powers of hell unknown,
> Put their most dreadful forms
>   Of rage and mischief on,
> I shall be safe, for Christ displays
> Superior power and guardian grace.

May 3.

They said unto the woman, Now we believe, not because of thy saying, etc.—John iv. 42. *If so be ye have tasted that the Lord is gracious.*—1 Pet. ii. 3.

It is an important thing to know assuredly that the Scripture has such a witness as experience and that there is a real correspondence between the saints and the Word, between the believer and Christ. This matter lieth out of the common road of the world. Sinners not awakened can have no experience of this kind; and therefore it is often ridiculed by them. But, oh! what an empty thing would religion be without experience, and a heart-felt knowledge of its truth! Experience is the sure and secret mark whereby the Christian knoweth the Scripture is of God, and feeleth his own interest in Christ; he has been often helped out of a dark plunge by the sealing of the word on his heart. Oh! what an excellent interpreter is experience!—taste and see, for thus the serious Christian getteth a view of the Scripture and spiritual things, which the most subtle and piercing eye of unsanctified schoolmen cannot reach. (Ps. xxxiv. 8, and cxvi. 10; 2 Tim. i. 12; Gal. ii. 16; Heb. iv. 3.) This cannot be found in books; it confoundeth the wise and disputer of this world, while the meanest and simplest Christian understands it well. Reader, press after experience; live not by hearsay—upon the comforts of others; but seek to the Lord, that He would give thee this inward testimony; it will help thee in future trials, remove many of thy fears make thy passage through life easy and comfortable, and be as a pledge of thy future glory.

> 'Tis well to hear and read the Word,
>   Its truth to see and own;
> But there must be experience too,
>   Or yet thou art undone.

MAY 4.

Whosoever will come after me, let him deny himself, and take up his cross daily, and follow me; for whosoever will save his life, shall lose it; but whosoever shall lose his life for my sake, the same shall save it.—Mark viii. 34, 35; Luke ix. 23.
Whosoever he be of you that forsaketh not all that he hath, he cannot be my disciple.—Luke xiv. 33.

This doctrine is discarded by all who call Christ "Lord, Lord, but do not the things which He saith." The language of their heart is, "Speak unto us smooth things, prophesy deceits" (Isa. xxx. 10). How different was that of the Apostle! "So fight I, not as one that beateth the air; but I keep under my body, and bring it into subjection; lest that, by any means, when I have preached to others, I myself should be a castaway" (1 Cor. ix. 26, 27). No cross, no crown: let us not then be afraid of the cross; for when we bear it, it bears us; and when we refuse to take it up, we refuse the staff of every Christian pilgrim, and the weapon of every Christian soldier; we renounce the tree of life for that of knowledge, and practically "deny Jesus Christ and Him crucified."

> Give me, O Lord, a sober mind,
>   A steady, self-renouncing will,
> That tramples down, and casts behind
>   The deadly baits of pleasing ill.
>
> Oh! for a heart to praise my God,
>   A heart from sin set free,
> A heart that always feels thy blood
>   So freely shed for me.
>
> An humble, lowly, contrite heart,
>   Believing, true and clean,
> Which neither life nor death can part
>   From Him that dwells within.

May 5.

What things soever ye desire, when ye pray, believe that ye receive them, and ye shall have them.—Mark xi. 24. *Verily, verily, I say unto you, Whatsoever ye shall ask the Father in my name, He will give it you. Hitherto ye have asked nothing in my name; ask, and ye shall receive, that your joy may be full.*—John xvi. 23, 24. *But ask in faith, nothing wavering; for he that wavereth is like a wave of the sea; let not that man think that he shall receive anything of the Lord.*—James i. 6, 7.

HEROD promised with an oath to give the daughter of Herodias whatever she would ask, even to the half of his kingdom. How advantageous was his promise! but how much more so that of the Lord! "By myself have I sworn," says He, "that in blessing I will bless thee" (Gen. xxii. 16, 17). When He bids us ask, He does not lay us under a restriction of not asking above half a kingdom. No; we may ask a whole kingdom, even the kingdom of heaven, consisting both of grace and glory. Both are purchased for us by the blood of the Lamb; both promised to believers in the word of the Gospel; and both actually bestowed: grace upon praying souls in the church militant; glory upon praising souls in the church triumphant. If now we do not enjoy the kingdom of grace, righteousness, peace, and joy in the Holy Ghost, it is merely because we have not asked, or have asked amiss; this is, without faith, without patience, or in our own name, and not in the all-prevailing name of Jesus.

> Faith, mighty Faith, the promise sees,
>   And looks to Christ alone;
> Laughs at impossibilities,
>   And cries, IT SHALL BE DONE.

May 6.

David's Prayer :—*O Lord, pardon mine iniquity; for it is great.*—Ps. xxv. 11.
Divine Answer :—*Where sin abounded, grace did much more abound.*—Rom. v. 20. *For God will abundantly pardon.*—Isa. lv. 7.

It is all one with God to forgive a repenting sinner his trespasses, whether great or small, many or few; for they are all paid with one ransom. No sin properly speaking, is little in itself ; and none greater than the grace of God, and the infinite price laid down for it. Whatever sins, therefore a man feels, yet he may throw himself upon the abounding grace of God : but this grace must always be our comfort, to depend upon it alone, even when it is best with us ; for then only it is best with us when we depend alone on grace, and live in it as in our element. The grace of the Gospel not only redeems the soul from death, and quickens it to newness of life, but it brings it into a very near relationship with God, and fits it for a full participation of the eternal glory and blessedness which God has in store for those who fear Him.

> Why does your face, ye humble souls,
>   Those mournful colors wear?
> What doubts are these that waste your faith,
>   And nourish your despair?
>
> What though your num'rous sins exceed
>   The stars that fill the skies;
> And aiming at th' eternal throne,
>   Like pointed mountains rise !
>
> See here an endless ocean flows
>   Of never-failing grace ;
> Behold a dying Saviour's veins
>   The sacred flood increase !
>
> It rises high and drowns the hills,
>   Has neither shore nor bound !
> Now, if we search to find our sins,
>   Our sins can ne'er be found.

MAY 7.

David's Prayer :—*Have mercy upon me, O Lord, for I am weak.*—Ps. vi. 2. *And strengthen me with strength in my soul.*—Ps. cxxxviii. 3.

Divine Answer :—*My grace is sufficient for thee; for my strength is made perfect in weakness.*—2 Cor. xii. 9. *The Lord delights not in the strength of a horse; he takes not pleasure in the legs of a man. The Lord taketh pleasure in them that fear Him, in those that hope in His mercy.*— Ps. cxlvii. 10, 11. *The Lord* our Strength, mighty God, and Immanuel, *will give strength unto His people.*—Ps. xxix. 11.

IN whatever part we are weak and most beset by corrupted nature, we may yet be strong enough, through grace, to come off conquerors; therefore, hope against hope, and despair not of overcoming by the power of God, be thy corruptions within, and thy enemies without, ever so strong and obstinate. I am weak, indeed, but Christ is strong; I am poor, He is rich; I am sick, He is the Physician of the sick; I am a sinner, He is the Saviour of sinners; consequently He suits me, and I suit Him extremely well. But let me look to Him daily, seek His face earnestly, and grace to help in every time of need:

> Let me but hear my Saviour say,
> "Strength shall be equal to thy day;"
> Then I rejoice in deep distress,
> Leaning on All-sufficient grace.
>
> I glory in infirmity,
> That Christ's own power may rest on me;
> When I am weak, then I am strong,
> Grace is my shield, and Christ my song.
>
> I can do all things, or can bear
> All sufferings, if my Lord be there;
> Sweet pleasures mingle with the pains,
> While His kind hand my head sustains.

May 8.

Wherewithal shall a young man cleanse his way? By taking heed thereto according to thy word. Open thou mine eyes, that I may behold wondrous things out of thy law. Remove from me the way of lying, and grant me thy law graciously. I have chosen the way of truth; thy judgments have I laid before me. Teach me, O Lord, the way of thy statutes, and I shall keep it unto the end.—Ps. cxix. 9, 18, 29, 30, 33.

NEITHER the old nor the young can walk uprightly without taking heed to the Word of God; if they depart from that, they soon fall into error and vicious courses; but if they would make the Word their rule, they must read it carefully, and pray diligently for the enlightening of the Holy Spirit. If David considered his eyes as shut, how much more should we consider ours so, and pray, "Open thou mine eyes," etc. He who doth not fervently pray thus, is still blind, and hath not an eye; even though he should think himself a profound divine, and be so esteemed by others. Lord, give me to see the wonders both of thy Law and Gospel, and turn my feet from every crooked path. Let thy commandments be always before me as my guide, and enable me to choose the narrow path of truth, and steadfastly walk in it to the end; for this was David's request throughout this long psalm.

> How shall the young secure their hearts,
>   And guard their lives from sin?
> Thy Word the choicest rules imparts
>   To keep the conscience clean.
>
> Then teach me, Lord, the perfect way
>   Of thy precepts Divine,
> And to observe it to the end,
>   I shall my heart incline.

May 9.

David's Prayer :—*Teach me thy way, O Lord, and lead me in a plain path, because of mine enemies.*—Ps. xxvii. 11. *Teach me thy way, O Lord; I will walk in thy truth: unite my heart to fear thy name.*—Ps. lxxxvi. 11.

Divine Answer :—*Good and upright is the Lord; therefore will He teach sinners in the way. What man is he that fears the Lord? Him shall he teach in the way that he shall choose.*—Ps. xxv. 8, 12.

O Lord, be pleased to fulfill this gracious promise in me also. Thou hast inclined my heart to do thy will, and yet I am often in darkness about thy will. Here it is written, "Good and upright is the Lord; therefore will He teach sinners in the way." It is thy own word; I may depend upon it, and would plead it with thee. Many times thou hast fulfilled this promise already; thou art willing and able to do it evermore for thy own name's sake. Thou art ever mindful of thy word, and I would keep close unto it. Then let thy Spirit well explain thy Word, and write it on my heart, enabling me to understand, to love, and practice it.

> I lift my soul to God,
>   My trust is in His name;
> Let not my foes that seek my blood
>   Still triumph in my shame.
>
> Sin and the powers of hell
>   Persuade me to despair;
> Lord, let me know thy cov'nant well,
>   That I may 'scape the snare.
>
> The Lord is just and kind;
>   The meek shall learn His ways;
> And every humble sinner find
>   The methods of His grace.
>
> For His own goodness' sake
>   He saves my soul from shame;
> He pardons (though my guilt be great)
>   Through my Redeemer's name.

MAY 10.

David's Prayer :—*Turn again our captivity, O Lord.*—Ps. cxxvi. 4.

Divine Answer :—*The Lord has appointed me to preach good tidings unto the meek, to proclaim liberty to the captives, and the opening of the prison to them that are bound.*—Isa. lxi. 1. *For thus saith the Lord, etc., I will give thee for a covenant of the people, etc., that thou mayest say to the prisoners, Go forth; to them that are in darkness, Shew yourselves: they shall feed in the ways, and their pastures shall be in all high places: they shall not hunger nor thirst.*—Isa. xlix. 8-10. See also chap. xxxv. 10.

O LORD, I am hungering after the righteousness and freedom, not only of faith, but of holiness also; not that I may make holiness the foundation of hope, but the evidence of faith; and that I may be able to rejoice and take comfort of thy righteousness alone, without deceiving my soul. Grant, therefore, that I may be truly filled, and may be strong, easy, and free, so as to be kept no longer in any of the most subtle bonds, either of the Law, unbelief, and a bad conscience, or of a worldly mind!

> Buried in shadows of the night,
> We lie till Christ restores the light;
> Wisdom descends to heal the blind,
> And chase the darkness from the mind.
>
> Jesus beholds where Satan reigns,
> Binding his slaves in heavy chains;
> He sets the prisoners free, and breaks
> The iron bondage from our necks.
>
> Poor helpless worms in thee possess
> Grace, wisdom, power, and righteousness;
> Thou art our mighty ALL, and we
> Give our whole selves, O Lord, to thee.

May 11.

David's Prayer:—*How long wilt thou hide thy face from me, O Lord?*—Ps. xiii. 1.

Divine Answer:—*For a small moment have I forsaken thee; but with great mercies will I gather thee, etc.*—Isa. liv. 7-9.

When the Lord is pleased to quicken us in our prayers with a lively impression of one or more promises, we are apt to think that the hour of His help is come. But afterward, it may be, He not only hides Himself for a great while again, but things take even such a strange and contrary course, as if all had been nothing, or as if nothing was more uncertain than the word of God; nay, even than God Himself. They who deny such temptations, are strangers both to themselves and to the devices of Satan. But Christians must then be prudently upon their guard, thinking that God is going to do some glorious things for them; for if they be first more convinced of their utter unworthiness, if they act with faith and patience, and be more earnest in prayers, they are fit to receive so much more grace afterward. Though yet, after all, God, as a Sovereign, will give such measures of grace at such seasons, and to such persons, as He pleases.

> Dear Lord, behold our sore distress;
>   Our sins attempt to reign;
> Stretch out thine arm of conq'ring grace,
>   And let thy foes be slain.
>
> If thou despise a mortal groan,
>   Yet hear a Saviour's blood;
> An advocate so near the throne
>   Pleads and prevails with God.
>
> How boundless is our Father's grace,
>   In height, in depth, and length!
> He made His Son our righteousness;
>   His Spirit is our strength!

MAY 12.

David's Prayer :—*How long wilt thou forget me, O Lord?*—Ps. xiii. 1.

Divine Answer :—*Can a woman forget her sucking child, that she should not have compassion on the son of her womb? Yea, they may forget, yet will I not forget thee. Behold, I have graven thee upon the palms of my hands; thy walls are continually before me.*—Isa. xlix. 15, 16.

THE wickedness and the evil of our hearts, and the great heap of our actual transgressions which we daily transgress against the Lord, are no easy matters to get rid of. We need to wrestle and strive like Jacob, and hold the Lord till He bless us with His pardoning and His purifying grace. Were all our sins and afflictions easily to be prayed away with a few words, whence these sad and repeated complaints of David?—Why should God advise us to wait for Him, and persevere in hope? —And how could faith and patience be exercised? In our closets we may be lifted up with high speculations, seem to be strong, and able to leap over all the walls; but in great distress we see how dejected and distrusting our hearts often are (Ps. xxx. 7, 8), but the Lord preserves us.

> God's is an unchanging love,
> Higher than the heights above,
> Deeper than the depths beneath,
> Free and faithful, strong as death.
>
> Thou shalt see my glory soon,
> When the work of grace is done;
> Partner of my throne shalt be
> Say, poor sinner, lov'st thou me?
>
> Lord, it is my chief complaint,
> That my love is weak and faint;
> Yet, I love thee, and adore;
> Oh! for grace to love thee more.

MAY 13.

David's Prayer : — *Shew me thy ways, O Lord, and teach me thy paths.*—Ps. xxv. 4.
Moses' Prayer :—*Shew me now thy way, that I may know thee.*—Exod. xxxiii. 13.
Divine Answers :—*I will instruct thee, and teach thee in the way which thou shalt go: I will guide thee with mine eye.*—Ps. xxxii. 8. *My presence shall go with thee, and I will give thee rest.*—Exod. xxxiii. 14.

O LORD, suffer me not to step aside one inch from thy way, much less to fall away from thee, the true Vine, and Fortress of my soul, by the plausible insinuations of my own brain and imagination. May I never run, before thou hast called me, to the hurt of my soul; but constantly and confidently abide in thee, always drawing first the necessary light and strength from thee, by never-ceasing supplications. Grant that, my eye being fixed continually upon thee, I may be guided into all truth, my doings being attended with thy blessing, and my whole life be a constant progress toward heaven.

CHRIST'S ANSWER :—I will keep thee as the apple of mine eye, that no evil shall come near thee. As a careful mother watches over her child, so have I undertaken to teach thee my path, and guide thee with my own eyes. Whatever faintings and failings may befall thee, yet will I be ever faithful, raising thee up again, and leading thee on evermore in thy ways. Nay, as a good Shepherd, I will carry thee in my own arms whenever thy increasing weakness shall require.

> My honor is engaged to save
>   The meanest of my sheep;
> All that my heavenly Father gave,
>   My hands securely keep.

May 14.

By these, (books,) *my son, be admonished.*—Eccles. xii. 12. *But, as new-born babes, desire the sincere milk of the word, that ye may grow thereby.*—1 Pet. ii. 2.

NEW-BORN babes must not self-conceitedly be desirous of high things and strong meat. Such have more need experimentally to understand the first oracles of Christ, and taste the milk and saving power of the Gospel. This would best make them grow in grace, and wean them from the world, since a sucking child esteems nothing else in comparison of its mother's breast; and those that delight in more lofty, vain imaginations than the Bible, do not follow the right spirit, and at last must come to their catechism again; for the more a Christian is approaching to his end, and desires to be duly prepared for heaven, the more he walks in deep humility and godly simplicity, placing himself on the lowest bench of weak and little children. And thus they are the fittest vessels of grace; they will certainly be enlightened, and have the mystery of Christ revealed in their hearts (Matt. xi. 25).

> There was an hour when Christ rejoiced,
>   And spoke His joy in words of praise,—
> Father, I thank thee, mighty God,
>   Lord of the earth, and heaven, and seas.
>
> I thank thy sov'reign power and love,
>   That crowns my doctrine with success;
> And makes the babes in knowledge learn
>   The height, the breadth, the length of grace.
>
> But all His glory lies concealed
>   From men of prudence and of wit;
> The prince of darkness blinds their eyes,
>   And their own pride resists the light.
>
> Father, 'tis thus, because thy will
>   Chose and ordained it should be so;
> 'Tis thy delight t' abuse the proud,
>   And lay the haughty scorner low.

May 15.

I bow my knees unto the Father of our Lord Jesus Christ, etc., that He would grant you, according to the riches of His glory, to be strengthened, etc. —Eph. iii. 14-16. Read on to verse 21.

This is a prayer, and a form fit to be used by all Christians. It may be used as a daily prayer; we should offer it up in faith, without apprehending that the favor we ask is too great. God will do exceedingly more for us than we can either ask or understand. Whatever we ask, He will grant us still more; for though we are sinners, yet Jesus hath received gifts even for sinners; and to every one of us (v. 7) is given grace according to the measure of the gift of Christ, that we may enjoy all things richly,—Christ being rich toward all them that call upon Him. O God, thou art our Father, reconciled to us in Christ; grant us therefore power, great power, according to the riches of thy glory, not according to the narrowness of our hearts. We stand in need of great power, for we have great enemies. Strengthen us by thy Spirit, Lord Jesus; do thou dwell in our hearts, and grant us to be rooted in thy love, that we may know it more and more, and that it may be shed abroad in our hearts, and that we may be filled with all the fullness of God.

> To thee, my God, I daily sigh,
> But not for golden stores;
> Nor covet I the brightest gem
> On the rich eastern shores.
>
> No pleasure's soft enticing charms,
> My fond desires allure;
> Far greater things than earth can yield,
> My wishes would secure.
>
> Those blissful, those transporting smiles,
> That brighten heaven above;
> The boundless riches of thy grace,
> And treasures of thy love.

May 16.

Thy word have I hid in my heart, that I might not sin against thee. Stablish thy word unto thy servant, who is devoted to thy fear. Then shall I not be ashamed, when I have respect unto all thy commandments. Therefore, remember the word unto thy servant, upon which thou hast caused me to hope. I will run the way of thy commandments, when thou shalt enlarge my heart.—Ps. cxix. 11, 38, 6, 49, 32.

"THAT the word may become effectual to salvation, we must attend thereunto with diligence, preparation, and prayer, receive it with faith and love, lay it up in our hearts, and practice it in our lives." —*Shorter Catechism.* Gospel-comforts sweetly and powerfully urge us to obedience ; and law-terrors check us from resting on that obedience. Both are needful to guard us from security and legality. Whosoever despises or neglects obedience entertains a false notion of the Gospel, and is running headlong into licentiousness and ruin ; and he who relies on his obedience to justify him, defeats the design of the Gospel, and frustrates the grace of God, making it of no effect. May the Lord lead and keep us in the right way!

> Laden with guilt, and full of fears,
>   I fly to thee, my Lord ;
> And not a glimpse of hope appears
>   But in thy written word.
>
> This is the judge that ends the strife,
>   Where wit and reason fail ;
> My guide to everlasting life,
>   Through all this gloomy vale.
>
> Oh ! may thy counsels, mighty God,
>   My roving feet command ;
> Nor I forsake the happy road
>   That leads to thy right hand !

May 17.

Through the law I am dead to the law, that I might live unto God. I am crucified with Christ; nevertheless I live; yet not I, but Christ liveth in me; and the life which I now live in the flesh, I live by the faith of the Son of God, who loved me, and gave Himself for me.—Gal. ii. 19, 20.

CHRIST being our Head, in whom all fullness dwells, He will certainly fill all His members with life and strength, according to His promise, (John xiv. 19). "I live, and ye shall live also;" and (chap. xvii. 3). "This is eternal life, that they may know thee the only true God, and Jesus Christ, whom thou hast sent." To know Christ, and God in Christ, as love, is true light and life; he that has this has enough. Oh! the excellency of the knowledge of Christ! O Lord, teach me to know thee as the Bridegroom of my soul, that the Law may not rush into my conscience, now thy bridechamber, and condemn me any more! I desire to be devoted to thee alone. (Rom. vii. 4.) Grant therefore, that my whole heart and life, all my words and actions, may be governed only by a living faith on thee, who hast loved and given thyself for me.

    Come, dearest Lord, descend and dwell,
      By faith and love in every breast;
    Then shall we know, and taste, and feel
      The joys that cannot be exprest.

    Come fill our hearts with inward strength,
      Make our enlarged souls possess,
    And learn the height, and breadth, and length
      Of thine unmeasurable grace.

    Now to the God whose power can do
      More than our thoughts or wishes know,
    Be everlasting honors done,
      By all the Church, through Christ His Son!

MAY 18.

David's Confession :—*I am poor and needy, and my heart is wounded within me.*—Ps. cix. 22.
Divine Answer :—*I know thy poverty, but thou art rich.*—Rev. ii. 9. *For, blessed are the poor in spirit, for theirs is the kingdom of heaven.*—Matt. v. 3. *The meek shall eat and be satisfied; they shall praise the Lord that seek Him: your hearts shall live for ever.*—Ps. xxii. 26. *The Lord healeth the broken in heart; the Lord lifteth up the meek.*—Ps. cxlvii. 3, 6. *A bruised reed shall He not break, and smoking flax shall He not quench, till He send forth judgment unto victory.*—Matt. xii. 20.

SUCH are the tender mercies of Christ toward the weakest of His people, that He supplies them from time to time with all proportionable strength, till at last they are able to gain a complete victory. As soon, therefore, as we are sensible of our poverty or miserable condition, and are desirous of grace and strength to overcome sin, and evidence that desire to be sincere by constant prayer, we have actually some grace and spiritual life, and are delivered already from the jaws of hell; for there is no such feeling in dead souls; and in hell there is only a desire to be delivered from the punishment of sin, but not from sin itself.

> Blessed are the humble souls that see
> Their emptiness and poverty;
> Treasures of grace to them are given,
> And crowns of joy laid up in heaven.
>
> Blessed are the men with broken heart,
> Who mourn for sin with inward smart:
> The blood of Christ divinely flows,
> A healing balm for all their woes.

May 19.

I am the light of the world; he that followeth me shall not walk in darkness, but shall have the light of life.—John viii. 12. Therefore, *walk while ye have the light, lest darkness come upon you; for he that walketh in darkness knoweth not whither he goeth.*—Chap. xii. 35.

He that is faithful, keeping ever close to Christ and His light, strictly watching and obeying the motions of His Spirit, will be evermore tender in conscience, and receive so much more light: consequently, he will be, from time to time, more deeply rooted in repentance, faith, and assurance, so as either to be preserved from many combats and disorders, or at least be carried sooner through the same. He may meet with dark valleys in his pilgrimage, for nature is covered with darkness, and grace sometimes only glimmers like a spark; yet by degrees it will blaze, and at last break through and enlighten all our darkness. The glory of the Lord is often seen beaming in the cloud.

> Is He a star?—He breaks the night,
> Piercing the shades with dawning light;
> I know His glories from afar,
> I know the bright, the morning star.
>
> Is He a sun?—His beams are grace;
> His course is joy and righteousness;
> Nations rejoice when He appears,
> To chase their clouds and dry their tears.
>
> Nor earth, nor seas, nor sun, nor stars,
> Nor heaven His full resemblance bears;
> His beauties we can never trace,
> Till we behold Him face to face.
>
> Oh! let me climb these higher skies,
> Where storms and darkness never rise;
> There He displays His powers abroad,
> And shines and reigns th' incarnate God.

May 20.

I am the Lord God, which teacheth thee to profit, which leadeth thee by the way that thou shouldst go. Oh! that thou hadst hearkened to my commandments! then had thy peace been as a river, and thy righteousness as the waves of the sea.—Isa. xlviii. 17, 18. *Behold, I stand at the door, and knock; if any man hear my voice, and open the door, I will come in to him, and will sup with him, and he with me.*—Rev. iii. 20.

How often and how variously does the Lord knock at the door of our hearts, by the voice of His word, the voice of His Spirit, or the voice of conscience! But how seldom are we inclined to give Him the hearing! We are often so distracted with business or pleasure, that we can hardly observe His voice through the hurry and noise of worldly things; and we are not at home when He knocks, and seeks to take up His abode with us. Well, even now He is knocking by this paper. Hearken to His voice and open the door for Him directly, since He desires nothing from us that might be grievous; but intends to make our heart a glorious residence and banqueting-room of love, to fill it with heavenly treasure, and give us everything along with Himself.

> I'll bring Him to my mother's home;
> Nor does my Lord refuse to come
> To Zion's sacred chambers, where
> My soul first drew the vital air.
>
> He gives me there His bleeding heart,
> Pierced for my sake with deadly smart;
> I give my soul to Him, and there
> Our loves their mutual tokens share.
>
> I charge you all, ye earthly toys,
> Approach not to disturb my joys;
> Nor sin, nor hell, come near my heart,
> Nor cause my Saviour to depart!

May 21.

I am the true Vine, and my Father is the Husbandman; every branch in me that beareth fruit, He purgeth it, that it may bring forth more fruit. Abide in me, and I in you. He that abideth in me, and I in him, the same bringeth forth much fruit.—John xv. 1-5.

O Lord I trust that this word will have its accomplishment in me also, though as yet I have great reason to be humbled on account of my barrenness. Grant, therefore, that I always may abide in thee faithfully and quietly: since there is everything in thy power, and nothing can be done by our own strength; but as it is thy will, and it tends both to the glory of thy Father and thine own, I depend upon being replenished in due season with fruits of righteousness. Oh! suffer nothing in me which may dishonor thy name, and which would prove hurtful to myself and offensive to others. But whatever thou thinkest as yet fit for me to suffer, let it work for my real good.

How can I sufficiently adore the patience of the Lord, my gracious Husbandman, who still bears with me, the weakest of all His branches. He has not cut me off yet, but still dresses me to bring forth more fruit; though, like a degenerate plant, I have yielded little else but wild grapes. Why then shouldst thou grumble, O my heart, at the application of His pruning-knife? It is really for thy good. He is angry only with the degenerate, unfruitful branches. The more these are purged, the more fruit thou shalt bring forth.

> Is Christ a Vine?—His heavenly root
> Supplies the boughs with life and fruit;
> Oh! let a lasting union join
> My soul to Him, the Living Vine.

MAY 22.

I am glorified in them; I have declared unto them thy name, and will declare it, that the love wherewith thou hast loved me may be in them, and I in them; I in them, and thou in me, that they may be made perfect in one.—John xvii. 10, 26, 23.

CHRIST is the Head of His Church, and He is glorified in it, in having it to present to the Father a glorious Church, the members of which are washed clean in His own Blood, and are as stones fitly set. Christ loves His Church. He loves the individual members of it, and they derive all their nourishment from Him. Oh! glorious promise! how could He love us more! What blessed and intimate union is this! Oh! for such a faith that could always truly believe it! Christ is the Vine, believers are branches; He the Bridegroom, they the bride; He the Head, they the members of His body, of His very flesh, and very bones, and consequently, one body with Him. And whoever hated his own flesh? So in loving and cherishing believers, He loves Himself (Eph. v. 28, 29). Whenever He shall cease to love Himself, then, and no sooner, shall He cease to love and cherish them also. It is His own delight to do them good, more than the mother that suckles her child.

> Lord, what a heaven of saving grace
> Shines through the beauties of thy face,
> And lights our passions to a flame!
> Lord, how we love thy charming name!
>
> When I can say my God is mine,
> When I can feel thy glories shine,
> I tread the world beneath my feet,
> And all that earth calls good and great.
>
> Send comforts down from thy right hand,
> While we pass through this barren land;
> And in thy temple let us see
> A glimpse of love, a glimpse of Thee!

May 23.

David's Prayer :—*I am weary with groaning.*—Ps. vi. 6.

Divine Answer :—*He gives power to the faint, and to them that have no might He increases strength.*—Isa. xl. 29. *I have satiated the weary soul, and I have replenished every sorrowful soul.*—Jer. xxxi. 25. See also Matt. xi. 28-30.

HERE Christ is commending His own meekness, both as a pattern for imitation, and as an encouragement for heavy-laden sinners to draw near to Him with confidence. And His rest is promised, not for the merit of our labor and humility, but merely for our coming to Him and believing in Him. He says, "Take my yoke upon you." "But how shall I take it?" says the sinner. "Why," says Christ, "learn of me. Let me be your Teacher; and though you are blind and foolish, fretful and forgetful, yea, wholly polluted with sin, I can yet bear with you; because I am meek and lowly in heart,—not rough and haughty to offenders, as Pharisees usually are, but full of compassion toward them, willing to receive them, aud ready to forgive and comfort them," etc. Come, therefore, to Him, O sinner, with all thy load of sin and misery, and He will in no wise cast thee out, but receive thee gladly!

> Come hither, all ye weary souls,
>   Ye heavy-laden sinners, come!
> I'll give you rest from all your toils,
>   And raise you to my heavenly home!
>
> Bless'd is the man whose shoulders take
>   My yoke, and bear it with delight;
> My yoke is easy to his neck,
>   My grace shall make the burden light!
>
> Jesus we come at thy command,
>   With faith, and hope, and humble zeal,
> Resign our spirits to thy hand,
>   To mould and guide us at thy will!

MAY 24.

David's Prayer :—*I have gone astray like a lost sheep; seek thy servant.*—Ps. cxix. 176.
Divine Answer :—*Behold, I, even I, will both search my sheep, and seek them out. I will seek that which was lost, and bring again that which was driven away, and will bind up that which was broken, and will strengthen that which was sick.*—Ezek. xxxiv. 11, 16. *He shall feed His flock like a shepherd; He shall gather the lambs with His arm, and carry them in His bosom.*—Isa. xl. 15.

HE that is wise in his own conceit, as philosophers usually are, does not pray like David to be sought after and healed by Jesus Christ; and therefore he continues, amidst all his boasted wisdom, deeply ignorant of his fallen nature and his ruined state. But as thou hast given me, O thou good Shepherd, to understand my lost and helpless condition; and that, like a wandering sheep, I can neither find myself when lost, nor advise myself how to return, I beseech thee to seek, heal, lead, feed, carry and strengthen me also as my various needs require; that I may be able to say with David, "The Lord is my Shepherd, I shall not want."

> My Shepherd will supply my need,
>   Jehovah is His name;
> In pastures fresh He makes me feed,
>   Beside the living stream.
>
> He brings my wand'ring spirit back
>   When I forsake His ways;
> And leads me, for His mercy's sake,
>   In paths of truth and grace.
>
> The sure provisions of my God
>   Attend me all my days;
> Oh! may thy house be mine abode,
>   And all my work be praise.

MAY 25.

I am not worthy of the least of all the mercies, and of all the truth, which thou hast shewed unto thy servant.—Gen. xxxii. 10. *Who am I, O Lord God? and what is my house, that thou hast brought me hitherto?*—2 Sam. vii. 18. *When I consider thy heavens, the work of thy fingers, the moon and the stars, which thou hast ordained; what is man, that thou art mindful of him? and the son of man, that thou visitest him?*—Ps. viii. 3, 4.

A SOUL truly humbled highly esteems every favor, and judges itself utterly unworthy of the least; looking upon everything as a free gift, and bestowed only for Jesus Christ's sake. Now, O my dear Father! it is true, in myself, I deserve none, no not the least, of thy mercies; but as thou hast graciously looked upon me, and given me, thine only Son, who hath purchased all blessings at a high price for sinners, I do believe that goodness and mercy will follow me all the days of my life. Amen. Be it so, holy Father, to thy glory and my everlasting joy!

> Now to the power of God supreme
>   Be everlasting honors given;
> He saves from hell (we bless His name),
>   He calls our wand'ring feet to heaven.
>
> Not for our duties or deserts,
>   But of His own abounding grace,
> He works salvation in our hearts,
>   And forms a people for His praise.
>
> 'Twas His own purpose that began
>   To rescue rebels doomed to die;
> He gave us grace in Christ His Son,
>   Before He spread the starry sky.
>
> Jesus, the Lord, appears at last,
>   And makes His Father's counsels known;
> Declares the great transactions past,
>   And brings immortal blessings down.

MAY 26.

I beseech you, that ye present your bodies a living sacrifice, holy, acceptable unto God, which is your reasonable service. And be not conformed, etc.—Rom. xii. 1, 2. See also 1 Cor. vi. 19.

THE presenting our bodies a living sacrifice unto God, when attended with serious prayer and reading the Scriptures, is the best means of knowing the will of God. To neglect this, and use other means, is tempting God, and exposing ourselves to the temptations and siftings of the wicked one. We may think ourselves to be divinely convinced by faith of the will of God, though we follow our own imaginations, and spoil the best of our actions. Self-will generally takes quick resolutions, and has a great deal of assurance; whereas God very often leads His people blindly, and takes methods quite different from ours. "Who therefore believes shall not make haste" (Isa. xxviii. 16). Let every one be careful that he does not mistake self-will and plausible representation for Divine convictions and assurance of faith; always strictly examine himself first, whether his body, soul, will, affections, are entirely offered up to the good-will and pleasure of God; for God requires the service of the whole man even a sacrificing our whole selves to Him, not only at church, but in all other places, that we do not conform to the world, but be daily transformed by the renewing of our minds.

> Though lifted eyes salute the skies,
>   And bended knees the ground,
> Yet God abhors the sacrifice
>   Where truth cannot be found.
>
> Lord, search my thoughts, and try my ways,
>   And make my soul sincere;
> Then shall I stand before thy face,
>   And find acceptance there.

MAY 27.

I will greatly rejoice in the Lord, my soul shall be joyful in my God; for He hath clothed me with the garments of salvation, He hath covered me with the robe of righteousness.—Isa. lxi. 10.

CHRIST has a garment of the finest work for every saint. It is this garment they must wear, no other one will do in the sight of God. Then, O my soul, put on this garment. It is one of unspotted whiteness; thou canst wear it by faith. In vain dost thou dress up and adorn thyself before thou approachest Christ. To Him thou must come, filthy, naked, and miserable as thou art; He will clothe and adorn thee Himself; and in this ornament alone thou shalt rejoice. For the very best of our robes and performances are not without spots, but still want to be washed in the blood of Christ, and covered with this ornament. "These are they who come out of great tribulation, and have washed their robes, and made them white in the blood of the Lamb" (Rev. vii. 14). This, and this alone, is the way to enjoy and maintain true peace. This will enable us to rejoice that our names are written in heaven.

> Awake, my heart,—arise, my tongue,
>   Prepare a tuneful voice;
> In God, the life of all my joys,
>   Aloud will I rejoice.
>
> 'Tis He adorned my naked soul,
>   And made salvation mine;
> Upon a poor, polluted worm
>   He makes His grace to shine.
>
> The Spirit wrought by faith and love,
>   And hope, and every grace;
> But Jesus spent His life to work
>   The robe of righteousness.
>
> Strangely, my soul, art thou arrayed
>   By the great sacred Three;
> In sweetest harmony of praise
>   Let all thy powers agree.

MAY 28.

David's Confession:—*I have sinned against the Lord.*—2 Sam. xii. 13.

Divine Answer:—*The Lord also hath put away thy sin; thou shalt not die.*—2 Sam. xii. 13. *For if we would judge ourselves, we should not be judged.*—1 Cor. xi. 31.

He that with unfeigned repentance accuses and judges himself, accounting his own righteousness and best doings as filthy rags, and seeks for mercy through Jesus, may expect to receive forgiveness of all his sins at once, though chastisement may follow; for pardons are not bestowed in parcels or various measures, as spiritual gifts are. God, through Christ, receives the whole person of a penitent sinner into His favor, forgiving both original and actual sins in one instant; so that either none or all are forgiven; but though repentance be needful to humble a sinner, and to bring him to Christ, yet no sins are forgiven on account of this repentance, but through faith alone in the blood of Christ. This fountain washes away the guilt of all sins, though ever so numerous and heinous; for it is written, "The blood of Christ cleanseth from all sin" (1 John i. 7). Come, then, my soul, believe and be washed in this fountain.

> Shew pity, Lord, O Lord forgive!
> Let a repenting rebel live.
> Are not thy mercies large and free?
> May not a sinner trust in thee?
>
> My lips with shame my sins confess,
> Against thy law, against thy grace;
> Lord, should thy judgment grow severe,
> I am condemned, but thou art clear.
>
> My crimes are great, but don't surpass
> The power and glory of thy grace;
> Great God, thy nature has no bound;
> So let thy pardoning love be found!

MAY 29.

Having the understanding darkened, being alienated from the life of God through the ignorance that is in them, because of the blindness of their heart, etc.—Eph. iv. 18, 19.

IF a man be naturally dead, bring a candle into the room, he sees it not; let the sun shine in his face, he perceives not the beauty, nor feels the warmth thereof; offer him rich presents, he receives them not; he hath no eye to see them, no heart to desire them, no hand to reach out unto them. Thus it is with one that is spiritually dead. Let the sunshine of the Gospel blaze out ever so clear, he sees it not, because he is in darkness; though he lived under plentiful means and dispensations, yet he is blind and sottish; offer unto him the rich pearls of the Gospel, those rich treasures of grace in Christ Jesus, yet he hath no heart to them, no hand of faith to lay hold upon them; so blind, so sottish, so stupid and senseless is he, that though these rich treasures, these graces, these pearls of the Gospel be conveyed unto him in earthen vessels, in a plain and familiar manner, yet he doth not, he cannot apprehend them; judgments do not affright him, and mercies cannot allure or persuade him; yet this creature is all life in the element of sin; he loves it, he pleads for it, he commits it with greediness. This is St. Paul's account of the unconverted Gentiles; and how many such have we under a Christian name! O Lord, exert thy great power, quicken all that are thus dead in trespasses and sins; "turn them from darkness to light, and from the power of Satan to thine own self." Amen.

> A carnal soul is blind within,
>   And has no want of Jesus' grace;
> He feels and fears no harm in sin,
>   And turns from God his haughty face.

May 30.

David's Declaration :—*I wait for the Lord, my soul doth wait.*—Ps. cxxx. 5.

Divine Answer :—*They that wait upon the Lord shall renew their strength, etc.*—Isa. xl. 31. *For the Lord is good unto them that wait for Him, to the soul that seeks Him.*—Lam. iii. 25.

It is not enough to utter words which form a prayer, but these words must express the desires and wishes of our heart. Nor is this enough; prayer without expectation is no prayer at all. Unless we desire and eagerly look for the coming of what we have prayed for, how can it be called prayer? it will only be a solemn mocking of God. Therefore, when we have prayed, we must remember to wait also, and to look anxiously for the answer; for this is well pleasing to the Lord, and expressly commanded by Him. The more we wait and keep instant in prayer, so much more will He give; nay He always hears and grants our petitions directly, and lays them up for His children; but that we may not abuse them, He gives the enjoyment only when it is most needful; therefore we may confidently say, Such and such gifts I shall have, since I have prayed for them: they are actually laid up for me; and the use and benefit thereof I shall reap in due season, especially in death and in eternity.

> My spirit looks to God alone,
> My rock and refuge is His throne;
> In all my fears, in all my straits,
> My soul on His salvation waits.
>
> Trust Him, ye saints, in all your ways,
> Pour out your hearts before His face.
> When helpers fail and foes invade,
> God is our all-sufficient aid.
>
> For sov'reign power reigns not alone,
> Grace is a partner of His throne;
> Thy grace and justice, mighty Lord,
> Shall well divide our last reward.

May 31.

In the multitude of my thoughts within me thy comforts delight my soul.—Ps. xciv. 19. *Blessed be God, even the Father of our Lord Jesus Christ, the Father of mercies, and the God of all comfort; who comforteth us in all our tribulation, that we may be able to comfort them which are in any trouble, by the comfort wherewith we ourselves are comforted of God.*—2 Cor. i. 3, 4.

A CONTENTED man, with afflictions, is ready to place his trust and seek his comforts in temporal things. Earthly desires crowd upon him, filling his soul with vanity; and he cannot well taste the sweet comforts of God's Word, but under the burden of the cross. Here we often enjoy more solid rest than if we were without the cross, and then that word is fulfilled which Christ says (Matt. xi. 30), "My yoke is easy, and my burden is light." Thus our hearts are set against the world, reconciled to heavenly things, and easily separated from many idols which we could not resist nor forsake before. Well then may we bear these salutary burdens, which, when sanctified, will produce present comfort, and soon issue in eternal rest and glory. And since the Lord has promised to give strength sufficient for the day, that we may not be tempted above measure, there is abundant reason again to say that His burden is light indeed, and His yoke is truly easy.

'Tis good for me to wear the yoke,
  For pride is apt to rise and swell;
'Tis good to bear my Father's stroke,
  That I may learn His statutes well.

Father, I bless thy gentle hand;
  How kind is thy chastising rod,
That forced my conscience to a stand,
  And brought my wand'ring soul to God!

June 1.

I determined not to know anything among you, save Jesus Christ, and Him crucified.—1 Cor. ii. 2. *The fear of the Lord is the beginning of wisdom; a good understanding have all they that do His commandments; His praise endureth for ever.*—Ps. cxi. 10. *The wisdom that is from above is first pure, then peaceable, gentle, and easy to be entreated, full of mercy and good fruits, without partiality, and without hypocrisy.*—James iii. 17. *Knowledge puffeth up, but charity edifieth.*—1 Cor. viii. 1.

CHRIST crucified, and He alone, is the power and wisdom of God; Him all Christians, and especially divines, should make their particular practice to study well. Were our faith built on human wisdom then surely carnal philosophers would be the greatest believers; whereas they are sometimes the worst infidels, or, at best, the most silly and faithless people in times of distress. And besides, their being puffed up is another evidence that they have not the true wisdom; for the wisdom from above is only with the lowly and babes, who pray for it earnestly (Prov. xi. 2; Matt. xi. 25). What would all knowledge avail us, then, without the knowledge of Christ! One spark of pure love yields more power than all the stores of empty human learning. May the Lord Jesus shed His love abroad in my heart! as, whatever others may do, Him have I determined only to know, and Him have I determined only to serve: His love to the cross I account for my greatest wisdom and glory.

> They that would grow divinely wise,
>   Must with His fear begin;
> Our fairest proof of knowledge lies
>   In hating every sin.

June 2.

Christian's Prayer :—*I will not let thee go, except thou bless me.*—Gen. xxxii. 26. *Forsake me not, O Lord, O my God.*—Ps. xxxviii. 21.

Divine Answers :—*Behold, I am with thee, and I will keep thee in all places whither thou goest; for I will not leave thee, until I have done that which I have spoken to thee of.*—Gen. xxviii. 15. *I know thee by name, and thou hast also found grace in my sight.*—Ex. xxxiii. 12. *I will never leave thee, nor forsake thee.*—Heb. xiii. 5.

GOD will have me to be faithful; and should not He be so Himself? Am I to trust in His word? Then surely He will not forsake me, but be as good as His word. Heaven and earth must pass away, but His word will not; He is ever faithful. If I do not believe this, I think blasphemously of God, and can have no help or comfort from His word; but if I truly believe Him to be faithful, I believe enough. This is what He only desires, and if I really do, my faith will not be moved even in the hottest trials; the word will hold me up, though I receive it even in weakness. But my faith must be attended with continual prayer.

> Begin, my tongue, some heavenly theme,
>   And speak some boundless thing;
> The mighty works, or mightier name,
>   Of our eternal King.
>
> Tell of His wondrous faithfulness,
>   And sound His power abroad;
> Sing the sweet promise of His grace,
>   And the performing God.
>
> Proclaim salvation from the Lord
>   For wretched, dying men;
> His hand has writ the sacred Word
>   With an immortal pen.
>
> Engraved, as in eternal brass,
>   The mighty promise shines,
> Nor can the powers of darkness raze
>   Those everlasting lines.

June 3.

I say unto you, that every idle word that men shall speak, they shall give account thereof in the day of judgment.—Matt. xii. 36. *Let no corrupt communication proceed out of your mouth, but that which is good, to the use of edifying, etc.*—Eph. iv. 29. See also chap. v. 4.

Here all corrupt communication, jesting, foolish talking, or whatever is not convenient and good to the use of edifying, is plainly forbidden. But who truly believes the report and the truth of these awful words? Surely the world does not believe them at all. This is quite plain, from that very common and shocking practice of judging, lying, swearing, jesting, and talking all manner of filthiness; yea, even religious people very often do not believe and consider them enough. How many heedless, slanderous, idle, and unprofitable words are sometimes spoken by these! Be therefore careful, O my reader, to weigh every word, and to make light of none; for such will increase thine account. Whenever we are going to speak, let the question be first, Is it needful to speak?—does it tend to the glory of God?—will it profit me or others? O Lord, grant that never an idle word may drop from my lips. Whenever I am to converse with others, give me grace first to converse with thee by secret prayer. In all companies let thy presence be before mine eyes, always looking upon thee as the chief person in the place, and receiving direction when and what I am to speak. May thy good Spirit always teach me, and sanctify all my thoughts and words!

> And must I give a strict account
>   Of every idle word?
> Then set a watch upon my lips,
>   And guard my tongue, O Lord.

June 4.

Let every man abide in the same calling wherein he was called.—1 Cor. vii. 20.

MOST of the employments of life are in their own nature lawful; and all those that are so may be made a substantial part of our duty to God, if we engage in them only so far, and for such ends as are suitable for beings who are to live above the world. This is the only measure of our application to any worldly business; it must have no more of our hands, our hearts, or our time, than is consistent with a hearty, daily, careful preparation of ourselves for another life. For since all true Christians have renounced this world to prepare themselves, by daily devotion and universal holiness, for an eternal state of quite another nature, they must look upon worldly employments as upon worldly wants and bodily infirmities,—things not to be desired, only to be endured and suffered, till death and the resurrection have carried us to an eternal state of real happiness. A person's being called into the kingdom of grace, is not designed to make void the duties that arise from his peculiar calling or situation in life, but to enforce the practice of them in such a way as may be most to the glory of God. He, therefore, that does not consider the things of this life as of little moment, or even nothing, in comparison of the things that are eternal, cannot be said either to feel or believe the greatest truths of Christianity.

> Lord, save me from my calling's snare,
>   From fraud, and from the love of gain;
> My hand be filled with worldly care,
>   But all my heart with thee remain.
>
> In honor of thy glorious name,
>   Let all my worldly deeds be done;
> And may the thoughts be to the same,
>   Of all who dwell beneath the sun.

June 5.

And the loftiness of man shall be bowed down; and the haughtiness of man shall be made low; and the Lord alone shall be exalted in that day.—Isa. ii. 17. *I will cause the arrogancy of the proud to cease, and I will lay low the haughtiness of the terrible.*—Isa. xiii. 11. *The Lord God omnipotent reigneth.*—Rev. xix. 6.

"PRIDE was not made for man," says the son of Sirac; "and the proud in heart are an abomination to the Lord;" and yet what is more common than pride and self-righteousness among the fallen children of Adam? So deeply are they ingrafted in our corrupt natures, that nothing short of Almighty grace can root them up. It is the great design and effect of the blessed Gospel, wherever it is applied to the heart by the Spirit of God, to mortify this cursed tempter. In that day, the haughtiness of man—his self-will which he set up in opposition to the will of God—shall be brought down; and his self-righteousness, by which he thought to recommend himself to the favor of God, shall be made low; and Christ and His righteousness alone shall be exalted.

Hath this precious promise ever been fulfilled in thy experience, O my soul? Is the will of God thy rule? Is the righteousness of Christ thy hope? and is the language of thy heart and life, "Let God in all things be exalted in me, and by me, through Christ Jesus?" Without this, O my soul, thy profession is vain, thy faith is also vain, and thou art yet in thy sins. Grant, O Lord, that I may be humble in heart and soul.

> Lord, lay my legal spirit low,
>   And every lofty look subdue;
> Bid all my heart to Jesus bow,
>   Exalt, and love, and trust Him too.

June 6.

I know also, my God, that thou triest the heart, and hast pleasure in uprightness.—1 Chron. xxix. 17. *The Lord looketh on the heart.*—1 Sam. xvi. 7.

As God searches the heart and tries the reins, He cannot be deceived by outward form. We ought not therefore to deceive ourselves in this particular. It is no certain proof of a real conversion to God, if we only reform the grosser sins of our former lives, much less if we only abstain from such things as by nature we are not so much inclined to indulge; but if our hearts are so renewed, by the grace of the Holy Spirit, as to be firmly and habitually opposed to our most beloved lusts, we have good evidence of a real conversion; for these inward capital enemies the Lord and all His upright followers attack most before all the rest. If we would give over that which is dearest to us, we must first know and believe that Christ is able and willing to help us, and has engaged His Word that none shall seek His face in vain. Let us keep this thought ever in our minds. It will both stir up faith, and encourage diligence in seeking after salvation.

> Mistaken souls that dream of heaven,
> And make their empty boast
> Of inward joys and sins forgiven,
> While they are slaves to lust.
>
> Vain are our fancies, airy flights,
> If faith be cold and dead;
> None but a living power unites
> To Christ the living Head.
>
> 'Tis faith that changes all the heart;
> 'Tis faith that works by love;
> That bids our sinful joys depart,
> And lifts the thoughts above.
>
> Faith must obey her Father's will,
> As well as trust His grace.
> A pard'ning God is jealous still
> For His own holiness.

June 7.

I will hedge up her way with thorns, and make a wall that she shall not find her paths; and she shall follow after her lovers, but she shall not overtake them; then shall she say, I will go and return unto my first husband, for then was it better with me than now.—Hosea ii. 6, 7.

As it is only with thee, O my dear Saviour, that I can be happy, I would never leave thee any more; and that I may not slip from thee unawares, even under good pretences, I desire to have my way well hedged up, and be encompassed everywhere with thorns. Let me quickly discover and crucify everything which would give the least disturbance to the enjoyment of thy love, that I may always closely walk with thee alone, and never take a step out of thy way, for fear of running myself into the thorns, and bringing unnecessary sufferings upon me; though I do not mean to avoid the cross of Christ in other respects, but would willingly submit to any sufferings, which are never without good fruit. Glory be to thee, O my blessed Saviour, that thou hast not given me up yet, and suffered me to run into destruction in my own ways! Oh! be pleased to restrain me evermore; and whenever I am in danger of sliding into the broad way, let me find no rest till I am brought back, though it be through the briers of affliction.

> I know thy judgments, Lord, are right,
>   Though they may seem severe;
> The sharpest sufferings I endure
>   Flow from thy faithful care.
>
> Before I knew thy chastening rod,
>   My feet were apt to stray;
> But now I learn to keep thy Word,
>   Nor wander from the way.

June 8.

And he said, Art thou my very son Esau? And he said, I am.—Gen. xxvii. 24.

THERE are certainly some circumstances in this affair which may help a little to excuse Jacob and his mother, but cannot justify them. The case may be thus stated:—It cannot be denied, on the one hand, but that both Jacob and his mother were justly to be praised for having a due esteem of the father's solemn blessing, and for their endeavoring to attain it; since this could proceed from no other motive than a full persuasion of the truth of God's promises and covenant with Abraham. And thus, from the consideration of the goodness of the end, and from Jacob's title to the blessing as accompanying the birthright, as also from the fore-appointment of God, together with Isaac's approbation of the thing when done, may be drawn some arguments to lessen their crime. But, on the other hand, it must be confessed, that the means used to attain their ends were highly criminal. Rebecca was wrong in her advice to her son, and he was wrong in following it; for though God, before he was born, designed him to inherit the blessing, yet he ought to have waited until the Divine Wisdom opened the way, and not have anticipated God, and procured the blessing by an irregular act of his own. Besides, both of them, by this act, presumed to limit the power of God, by thinking that fraud was needful to accomplish God's purpose.

> Let not your hearts with anxious thoughts
>   Be troubled or dismayed;
> But trust in Providence Divine,
>   And trust my gracious aid.

June 9.

Lest any of you be hardened through the deceitfulness of sin.—Heb. iii. 13. *Every man is tempted, when he is drawn away of his own lust, and enticed.*—James i. 14.

DOTH sin present itself? – turn away from it with loathing and prayer. Give it not a look, lest it ensnare thee. If thou committest sin, and diest without repentance, thy soul is lost, and thy redemption ceaseth for ever ; or if thou committest sin and dost repent, yet expect hidings of God's face and breaking of bones, as David felt to his cost. Oh! what bitter pangs—what painful throes —what shadows of death—what terrors of hell may seize upon thee, before thou canst make thy peace, or settle thine assurance! Wilt thou give way to sin because it is delightful, or because it is pardonable? Who loves poison because it is sweet? or who drinks poison because he may have an antidote? seeing it will work to his trouble, if it work not out his life! I have a precious soul, shall I lose it for a lust? I have a gracious God, shall I venture Him for a sin? No, Lord, give me grace to resist sin, give me victory over it. Let me always reject that, for the indulgence of which I am sure to lose my peace, and endanger the loss of my immortal soul.

> A tender conscience give me, Lord,
>   And put thy fear within,
> That I may tremble at thy Word,
>   And 'scape the snares of sin.
>
> All mine iniquities blot out,
>   Thy face hide from my sin ;
> Create a clean heart, Lord, renew
>   A right spirit me within.
>
> Cast me not from thy sight, nor take
>   Thy Holy Spirit away ;
> Restore me thy salvation's joy ;
>   With thy free Spirit me stay.

June 10.

This is He that came by water and blood, even Jesus Christ; not by water only, but by water and blood: and it is the Spirit that beareth witness, because the Spirit is truth. He that believeth on the Son of God hath the witness in himself. And this is the record, that God hath given to us eternal life; and this life is in His Son. He that hath the Son hath life.—1 John v. 6, 10-12.

Jesus came with water and blood; not with water alone to sanctify us, but also with His blood to make atonement for our sins. We should, therefore, first of all, penitently seek and obtain remission of sins in His blood, then may we hope to obtain the water of life, the Holy Ghost, for our inward purification and sanctification. And His Holy Spirit will bear witness within us, that the Gospel is truth, and that God will fulfill His word by giving us everlasting life, as He hath promised. We have three witnesses of it in heaven, and three on earth. And if we believe in Christ, we have this true testimony in ourselves, and may therefore assuredly know, "that having the Son of God, we have life, eternal life; for He is (according to verse 20) life eternal;" and, consequently, being in Him, we are already entered into everlasting life.

> Let all! our tongues be one
>   To praise our God on high;
> Who from His bosom sent His Son,
>   To fetch us strangers nigh.
>
> My Saviour's pierced side
>   Poured out a double flood;
> By water we are purified,
>   And pardoned by the blood.
>
> It cost Him cries and tears
>   To bring us near to God;
> Great was our debt, and He appears
>   To make our payment good.

June 11.

No man hath ascended up to heaven, but He that came down from heaven, etc.—John iii. 13; Eph. iv. 9; Deut. xxx. 11-14; Matt. xi. 27.

No mere man whatsoever has entered, or can enter into the secrets of God's heart in heaven, relating to the great mysteries of salvation, so as immediately and perfectly to understand them and make them known to others; but this privilege is peculiar to the Messiah, who is spoken of under the character of "the Son of Man" (Ps. lxxx. 17, and Dan. vii. 13), and always had an existence in heaven as the Son of God, and who came from thence into an incarnate state, that He might reveal God's counsels to men. As many are perplexed about the Divinity of Christ, the following note may help them to conceive of that matter more properly: As the Divine and human natures were united in the person of Christ, some things are attributed to one nature which properly belong to the other. Thus, when it is said (1 Cor. ii. 8) "The Lord of glory was crucified;" and (Acts xx. 28) He is called "God who purchased the Church with His own blood;"—the meaning is not, that He, as the Lord of Glory Divine, was crucified, or, as God, shed His blood—as if that nature could be crucified and bleed—but that the person who was the Lord of Glory in one nature, was crucified in the other, etc. So when it is said, "The Son of Man is in heaven," the meaning is not, that He, as the Son of Man, was there whilst He was on the earth; but that He, who was here in His human nature, was there in His Divine.

> My Saviour, whilst He dwelt on earth,
> As God in heaven had His abode;
> So let me, by an heavenly birth,
> Live in the world, yet dwell with God.

June 12.

I will perform my good word toward you: for I know the thoughts that I think toward you, saith the Lord; thoughts of peace, and not of evil, to give you an expected end. Then shall ye pray unto me, and I will hearken unto you; and ye shall seek me, and find me.—Jer. xxix. 10-13.
See also Ps. xxiii. 4, 9.

There is a valley where neither sun, moon, nor stars are seen, and in which the Christian has often to travel; yet in the darkest place of it God is very nigh. This is the valley of extremity. It is into this valley that every soul must go before it can get a hold of Christ. It is here the sinner struggles with Jesus, and says, "I will not let thee go except thou bless me." It is hard work traveling in this valley. Were it a light matter to rely on the faithfulness of God in times of distress, what need to give us so many and various promises? If our faith be right, we must also endure and wait His time with patience, which certainly is not an easy task; since the promise of our Lord not only tarries very often, but sometimes His providence goes contrary to His Word, and makes His Word seem to fall to the ground; yet then we must remember, that these are the very ways and methods of God, which have ever been in the deep, and acted contrary to our expectation. This the corruption of our natures requires; and the wisdom of God ever chooses first to help us inwardly, by exercising faith and patience, and so prepares us for a right use of His outward favors. Thus we receive a double blessing at once from His hands.

> Who shall pretend to teach Him skill,
> Or guide the counsels of His will?
> His wisdom, like a sea divine,
> Flows deep and high beyond our line.

June 13.

Behold, I will allure her, and bring her into the wilderness, and speak comfortably unto her.—Hos. ii. 14. *Come, my beloved, let us go forth into the field; let us lodge in the villages.*—Song of Sol. vii. 11.

The Lord forsaketh not His saints;—though the great waves of affliction come upon them, and nigh overwhelm them, because they have forgotten their first love; and though the heavy tide of temptation be running strong against them, and they with their little bark of faith be unable to stem it; though they have given their hearts to that in which the Lord delighteth not; though they have backslidden often and far,—yet the Lord "will allure them, and bring them into the wilderness and speak comfortably unto them." O Lord, this world is nothing to me but a wilderness, a place of tribulation, where, being tossed to and fro, I enjoy no rest; but when I lift up my heart and look for peace in thee, I am supported and comforted. Grant that I may thus be strengthened for the time to come, whenever I am at a loss what course to take. Let me always firmly believe thee to be a present help in trouble, who art willing and able to bear me up under all outward distresses, till I shall safely arrive at the rest of the people of God.

Lord! what a wretched land is this, that yields us no supply,
No cheering fruits, no wholesome trees, nor streams of living joy!
But prickling thorns, through all the ground, and mortal poisons grow,
And all the rivers that are found, with dang'rous waters flow.

Yet the dear path to thine abode lies through this horrid land;
Lord! we would keep the heavenly road, and run at thy command.
Our souls would tread the desert through, with undiverted feet;
And faith and flaming zeal subdue the terrors that we meet.

JUNE 14.

When we pray, say, Our Father, etc.—Luke xi. 2.
Ye ask and receive not, for ye ask amiss.—Jas. iv. 3.

MANY say the Lord's Prayer who do not pray it. They do not care that God should say Amen, though they themselves will say so. They say, "Our Father;" but if He be their Father, where is His honor? They say, "Which art in heaven;" but did they believe it, how durst they sin as they do upon earth? They say, "Hallowed be thy name;" yet take God's name in vain. They say, "Thy kingdom come;" yet oppose the coming of His kingdom. They say, "Thy will be done on earth as it is in heaven;" yet will not stand to their word: for this is the will of God, their sanctification; but they want none of that. They say, "Give us this day our daily bread;" yet mind not the feeding of their souls with "the bread (Christ Jesus) which came down from heaven." They say, "Forgive us as we forgive others;" but, alas! if God should take them at their word, how undone were they, whose hearts burn with malice and revenge! They say, "Lead us not into temptation;" yet run into it. They say, "Deliver us from evil;" and yet deliver themselves *to* evil, and give up themselves "to fulfill the lusts of the flesh," etc. Yea, those generally sin most against this prayer who stickle most for the saying of it. Reader, how often hast thou been guilty of such vain petitions and repetitions? Wonder not, if thou prayest in such a manner as this, that thou receivest nothing. Labor to get a deep sense of God's majesty and mercy, that thy prayers may be fervent and earnest, and God will bless thee.

> Assist and teach me how to pray;
> Incline my nature to obey;
> What thou abhorrest let me flee,
> And only love what pleases thee.

June 15.

Jesus Christ, the same yesterday, to-day, and for ever.—Heb. xiii. 8. *Who of God is made unto us wisdom, and righteousness, and sanctification; that, as it is written, he that glorieth, let him glory in the Lord.*—1 Cor. i. 30, 31. *He has finished the transgression, He has made reconciliation for iniquity, He has brought in everlasting righteousness.*—Dan. ix. 24; Isa. xlv. 24.

WHEREIN have we that we should glory before the Lord? Have we obeyed the law? Have we satisfied, or can we satisfy, the Divine justice? Where is the righteousness which we have of ourselves to give to God? Let us look back upon our past lives—is it there? Let us look into our own hearts—is it there? Alas! in ourselves we find nothing but misery; but in Christ we find all that is good; nay, He is Himself our All. He works and gives what is necessary to salvation, therefore we cannot, and need not, bring anything to Him of our own; but since He is made unto us wisdom, righteousness, sanctification, and our All, we may, and must, rely only on His name, and draw everything from Him by the continual prayer of faith. And when by living faith in Christ He becomes our All, the law, sin, Satan, and even our own judgments, have lost their power and right of condemnation over us.

> Jehovah speaks, let Israel hear;
> Let all the earth rejoice and fear,
> While God's eternal Son proclaims
> His sov'reign honors and his names.
>
> I am the Last, and I the First,
> The Saviour-God, and God the just,
> There's none besides pretends to shew
> Such justice and salvation too.
>
> In me alone, shall men confess,
> Lies all their strength and righteousness;
> But such as dare despise my name,
> I'll clothe them with eternal shame.

June 16.

Beloved, if God so loved us, we ought also to love one another.—1 John iv. 2. *I say unto you, Love your enemies; bless them that curse you; do good to them that hate you; and pray for them that despitefully use you.*—Matt. v. 44.

Hypocrites may counterfeit the children of God in many things, but they cannot love their enemies from their hearts; and yet by this we must try and know ourselves, whether we are really children of God or not. The world very easily, but very falsely, suppose themselves to be God's children; but sincere Christians find it often very hard to believe it without a Divine sense and assurance of it; it costs them many a sore conflict; for if Satan disputeth the Sonship of Christ, much less will he spare any of us. But since a true love to the children of God, and to our enemies, is a sure evidence of our state of grace, we have our title clear to it, though we shall walk in darkness, and be destitute of all pleasant sensations. Give us, then, O thou Father of our spirits, the heart filled with love, that is able not only to love those that are of the same mind with ourselves, but also to love those that are opposed to us, and even to love those sincerely that do us wrong. Give the meek, the lowly, and the loving heart which Jesus had.

> Now by the bowels of my God,
>   His sharp distress, His sore complaints;
> By His last groans, His dying blood,
>   I charge my soul to love the saints.
>
> Clamor, and wrath, and war begone;
>   Envy and spite for ever cease;
> Let bitter words no more be known
>   Amongst the saints, the sons of peace.
>
> Tender and kind be all our thoughts,
>   Through all our lives let mercy run;
> So God forgives our numerous faults,
>   For the dear sake of Christ His Son.

JUNE 17.

And he said to his servant, Go up now, look toward the sea. And he went up, and looked, and said, There is nothing. And he said, Go again seven times.—1 King xviii. 43; Jas. v. 17, 18. *Seven times a-day do I praise thee because of thy righteous judgments.*—Ps. cxix. 164. *Daniel kneeled upon his knees three times a-day, and prayed, and gave thanks before his God.*—Dan. vi. 10.

Six times Elijah's servant looked toward the sea before he could see anything; the seventh time he saw a cloud, but no bigger than his hand; yet that cloud, within a few hours, covered the heavens with darkness, and the earth with rain. Just so may be the case with many a one when he is praying to his God, as Caleb's daughter did unto her father (Judges i. 15). Thou hast hitherto made me the owner of a dry, a barren heart; but give me now some springs of water, some feeling, at least, some sorrow for my sins. Well, though at six times bending of thy knees God doth not grant it, and though at the seventh there appears but one small drop swimming in thine eyes, yet be not discomforted; that drop may prove a shower—the beginning of that may at last dissolve thy whole heart to water; and as there is a full joy for the thorough conversion of a sinner, there may be a suitable measure of joy for one tear, nay, for one desire of a tear, of any one sinner that repenteth. Grant, O Lord, that I may be able to come unto thee at all times in holy confidence of prayer, and that my prayers may not only be unceasing, but that I may with expectation wait upon an answer.

> If six or sixty prayers are past,
> Pray on and never faint;
> A blessing surely comes at last,
> To cheer a drooping saint.

June 18.

Ye shall drive out all the inhabitants of the land. But if you will not drive out the inhabitants of the land from before you, then it shall come to pass, that those which ye let remain of them shall be pricks in your eyes, and thorns in your sides, etc.—Numb. xxxiii. 52, 55. See this fulfilled, Judges i. 27; chap. ii. 14,—*Manasseh did not drive out the inhabitants of Bethshean, etc., and the Canaanites would dwell in that land; so that they* (the Israelites) *could not any longer stand before their enemies.*

THE very same is to be observed in the holy and spiritual battles of the Lord. He that fights only against outward sins, is but very little, if at all, acquainted with the dangerous enemies in his heart, or the deep corruption of original sin, and so the tempter may easily gain an advantage over him. Experienced Christians guard more against the inward assaults of wickedness; they are at peace with no sin, but keep up a constant war with all their most subtle and darling lusts. However, though the Canaanites, our inbred foes, must be conquered, they will dwell in the land, and cannot be wholly thrust out of the bosom, which makes the Christian warfare continue till death; yet give me grace, O Lord, never to spare my sinful lusts or tempers, but to look unto thee to destroy them without delay, as soon as they begin to move or stir, that I may not be destroyed by them.

> O Prince of Peace, forgive my guilt,
>   Though more than I can tell;
> And from the power of sin release,
>   And from the host of hell.
>
> Furnish me, Lord, with heavenly arms,
>   From Grace's magazine,
> And I'll proclaim eternal war
>   With every darling sin.

June 19.

In the beginning God created the heaven and the earth. And the earth was without form, and void; and darkness was upon the face of the deep; and the Spirit of God moved upon the face of the waters.—Gen. i. 1, 2. *We are His workmanship, created in Christ Jesus* (Note) *unto good works, which God has before ordained that we should walk in them.*—Eph. ii. 10.

THEREFORE, before we can really grow in holiness, we must be born again. How is it possible for a man to grow in sanctification, without a real change being first wrought in his heart? It is the Spirit's way first to strip us of our own righteousness and strength, to shew us our nakedness and nothingness, to fill us with godly sorrow for sin, and then lead us to Jesus for pardon, sanctification and justification. Christ being the Vine, we must first be planted in Him, and draw nourishment and strength from Him by faith. When it is fulfilled, "they shall feed and lie down" on His pasture, "and none shall make them afraid" (Zeph. iii. 13); then we shall be able to bring forth good fruits, and obtain victories; for it is God Himself that thus makes us perfect in every good work, and prepares a table for us in the presence of our enemies.

> I ask not honor, pomp or praise,
>   By worldly men esteemed;
> I wish from sin's deceitful ways
>   To feel my soul redeemed.
>
> I wish, as faithful Christians do,
>   Dear Lord, to live to thee,
> And by my words and walk to shew
>   That thou hast died for me.
>
> Oh! grant me, through thy precious blood,
>   Thy Gospel thus to grace;
> Renew my heart, O Lamb of God,
>   Thus shall my works thee praise.

JUNE 20.

In the Lord have I righteousness and strength.—
Isa. xlv. 24; 2 Cor. ii. 14, and v. 19.

JUSTIFICATION through faith in Christ, at first, is a very dark doctrine, hard to be understood, but afterward we find, by experience, that it would be impossible to be saved in any other way, and that nothing can be surer than this, though all mankind should turn away from it. And when we are made to see that our best performances are unclean in the sight of God, and could not be accepted without the covering of Christ's righteousness, then we are brought to submit entirely to Christ, and at last to look upon ourselves wholly justified through Him, which alone produceth rest, strength, and a gentle spirit, the true image of Christ.

In vain do we hope to procure this rest by any reasonings or strong resolutions of our own; for if we are sometimes able to master our affections by our own strength, this is yet a building of our own, and keeps us from earnest wrestling in prayer. We have now a form of godliness without its power, and are still deceiving our own souls; for nothing can be pleasing in the sight of God, and profit us in the last day, but what He works Himself. Away, therefore, with all these doings of our own. Let us acknowledge the weakness and nothingness of our strength, and apply, in our poor, blind, naked, lost and miserable condition, to the blood and righteousness of Christ; then we shall also find power and dominion over sin (Isa. xxxiii. 24).

> Sinners shall hear the sound;
> Their thankful tongues shall own,
> Our righteousness and strength is found
> In thee, the Lord alone.

JUNE 21.

David's Declaration:—*In the day of my trouble I will call upon thee; for thou wilt answer me.*—Ps. lxxxvi. 7.

Divine Answer:—*Then shalt thou call, and the Lord shall answer; thou shalt cry, and He shall say, Here I am.*—Isa. lviii. 9. *The Lord is rich unto all who call upon Him; and it shall come to pass, that whosoever shall call upon the name of the Lord shall be saved*—(this, to the comfort of the weak, is several times repeated in Scripture) Joel ii. 32; Acts ii. 21; Rom. x. 12, 13, 20. *Therefore when the righteous cry, the Lord heareth them, and delivereth them out of all their troubles.*—Ps. xxxiv. 17, and cxlv. 18; James v. 16.

OH! glorious promise! how can God deny me anything now that I pray for? He has passed His word for it; His Son has purchased it; the Holy Spirit inspires the prayer; the Word holds it forth; and the prayer of faith lays hold of it, and actually receives it. Prayer is the mouth of faith. If thou wilt have much, "open thy mouth wide, and it shall be filled." Who, then, should not be stirred up to pray much! Oh! what foolishness is this, that we have nothing, but may obtain all from God, and yet are so loath to pray much and pray right! Oh! thou Hearer and Answerer of prayer, pour out upon my soul the spirit of prayer. Give me assured trust in thee, that thou wilt hear my prayer; and, oh! let not my hope of an answer rest on anything but the all-prevailing merits of my Redeemer.

> God knows the pains His servants feel,
>   He hears His children cry;
> And, their best wishes to fulfill,
>   His grace is ever nigh.

June 22.

Swear not at all; neither by heaven; for it is God's throne: nor by the earth; for it is His footstool: neither by Jerusalem; for it is the city of the great King. Neither shalt thou swear by thy head, because thou canst not make one hair white or black. But let your communication be, Yea, yea; Nay, nay: for whatsoever is more than these cometh of evil.—Matt. v. 34-37. See also James v. 12.

SWEAR not by the creatures; that, in effect, is swearing by their Maker. Neither swear by thy Maker, unless called to it by authority for the putting an end to strife: swear not falsely, that is calling the God of truth to witness a lie: swear not needlessly or rashly, as Saul did (1 Sam. xiv. 39). Such oaths or vows are ensnaring; better broke than kept, but best not made at all. Swear not idle, common oaths, such as, O Christ!—O God! —Faith and troth!—By my soul!—As I live!—God bless me! If we must give account for every idle word, much more for every idle oath, and most of all for horrible cursing and blasphemy, that profanes God's name, and is the very language of hell. He that is guilty of perjury, not only is destroying his own soul, but is seeking to ruin his neighbor, by perverting justice, and robbing the innocent of his right. Yea, sometimes God takes a false-swearer and self-curser at his word, and strikes him dead on the spot. Lord, help the guilty to repent of their sin, and help all to watch and pray against it.

> From false, and rash, and idle oaths,
>   Defend my tongue, O Lord;
> Let salt of grace hang on my lips,
>   To season every word.

June 23.

Dearly beloved, avenge not yourselves, but rather give place unto wrath; for it is written, Vengeance is mine; I will repay, saith the Lord.—Rom. xii. 19. *Say not, I will do so to him as he hath done to me; I will render to the man according to his work.*—Prov. xxiv. 29. See also Lev. xix. 18. *Recompense to no man evil for evil.*—Rom. xii. 17.

JUDGE ye then, my brethren, would it be wise to snatch the rod out of the all-powerful hand of God, to take it into our own, even was it in our power to do it? We are taught by the holy prophet not to avenge ourselves, it being daring presumption to usurp God's province, and to step into His throne. He that chastiseth the nations, shall He not correct? Might may overcome right for a time, to try God's children; but whether that is done with a close hand, so as not to be discovered, or with a high hand, so as not to be controlled, God will, in His due time, shew Himself, and assert His right of vengeance against all that would take it from Him. It is therefore our wisdom to call to mind our blessed Lord's silence when He suffered, "who, when He was reviled, reviled not again; when He suffered He threatened not," and to copy after it, committing ourselves to Him that judgeth righteously.

> Grace dwells with justice on the throne,
>   And men that love thy word
> Have in thy sanctuary known
>   The counsels of the Lord.
>
> When God, in His own sov'reign ways,
>   Comes down to save the opprest,
> The wrath of man shall work His praise,
>   And he'll restrain the rest.

June 24.

If any man be in Christ, he is a new creature.—
2 Cor. v. 17.

Let no man be discouraged from coming to Christ because he finds not in himself that godly sorrow for sin, that ability to repent, that disposition of heart which he desires to have : we must first be in Christ before we are new creatures. This is a common fault among us ; we would fain have something before we come. We think God's pardons are not free, but we must bring something in our hand ; whereas the proclamation runs thus: "Buy without money,"—that is, come without any excellency at all : because we are commanded to "come and take the water of life freely." Therefore do not say, I have a fretful disposition, and a hard heart, and cannot mourn for sin as I should, therefore I will stay till that be done. It is all one as if you should say, I must go to the physician, but I will have my wounds well, and my disease healed first. The end of going to Christ is, that this very hardness of thy heart may be taken away ; that this very deadness of thy spirit may be removed ; that thou mayest be enlightened, quickened, healed ; that thou mayest hate sin, for He is thy Physician. Look not for sanctification, nor for genuine fruits of righteousness, till thy soul is united unto Christ by a living faith ; for it is faith that purifies the heart, and works (*i. e.*, produces good works) by love. Thou must first be in Christ, grafted into Christ by faith, before thou canst be a new creature.

> Lord, graft me in thyself, the vine,
>   And feed me from thy root,
> So shall I in thine image shine,
>   And bear much heavenly fruit.

June 25.

All things are lawful unto me, but all things are not expedient; all things are lawful for me, but I will not be brought under the power of any.— 1 Cor. vi. 12. See chapters x. 23, and viii. 8.

MANY that are well affected to religion, and receive instructions of piety with pleasure and satisfaction, often wonder how it comes to pass that they make no greater progress in that religion which they so much admire. Now, the reason of it is, because religion lives only in their head, while something else has possession of their heart, and therefore they continue, from year to year, mere admirers and praisers of piety, without ever coming up to the reality and perfection of its precepts. If it be asked why religion does not get possession of their hearts?—the reason is, not because they live in gross sins or debaucheries,— for their regard to religion preserves them from such disorders,—but because their hearts are constantly employed, perverted, and kept in a bad state by the wrong use of such things as are lawful to be used; for our souls may receive very great hurt, merely by the abuse of innocent and lawful things. What is more innocent than rest and retirement? and yet what more dangerous than sloth and idleness? What is more lawful than eating and drinking? and yet what more destructive of virtue than sensuality and indulgence? How lawful and praiseworthy is the care of a family? and yet what so prejudicial as an anxious worldly temper? Reader, follow the apostle, and beware of lawful things; keep thy heart free from the power of them.

> O Lord, direct me in the use
> Of things that lawful are;
> For lawful things may have abuse,
> And prove a fatal snare.

June 26.

There are diversities of operations; but it is the same God which worketh all in all.—1 Cor. xii. 6.

SOME believers are remarkable for the strength of their faith in trials, even unto death; others for liveliness and activity in duty; others for wisdom, conduct and prudence, in temporals and spirituals; others for their zeal in defence of the truth; others for knowledge in the mysteries of truth; others for meekness and patience; others for outward usefulness; and some for an inward and spiritual life of communion with God; but all these are the various gifts and graces of the Holy Spirit, dividing severally to every man as He will, and are given to profit withal. My fellow-Christians, let us hence learn a lesson of forbearance to our brethren. It is not right to judge of another by thine own pattern. Art thou a warm and active Christian? Condemn not him whose endowments may be more placid and contemplative than thine. He who now creeps as a snail in humble silence, may, by one lift of Divine power, be raised higher than thou art. The same may be said of other differences among the followers of Jesus. Let us then no longer envy one another, or indulge a rash and censorious spirit; but rather covet earnestly the best gifts, and faithfully improve the talent committed to our trust, that each of us may receive that heart-reviving word, "Well done, good and faithful servant, enter thou into the joy of thy Lord."

> There is a voice of sovereign grace
>   Sounds from the sacred Word;
> O ye despairing sinners, come
>   And trust upon the Lord.
>
> My soul obeys th' Almighty call,
>   And runs to this relief;
> I would believe thy promise, Lord;
>   Oh! help my unbelief!

JUNE 27.

Every good gift, and every perfect gift, is from above.—James i. 17. See also Job i. 21.

READER, it is a point of the greatest importance for thee to know, that every evil thing is of thyself, and every good thing of God. Without faith we cannot be saved; but, saith St. Paul (Eph. ii. 8) "By grace are ye saved, through faith, and that not of yourselves, it is the gift of God." We are called upon to repent; but (in Acts v. 31) we read that Christ is exalted at the Father's right hand, to be a "Prince and a Saviour, for to give repentance to Israel." We must be born again, but regeneration is wholly of God's will: "Which were born, not of blood, nor of the will of the flesh, nor of the will of man, but of God" (John i. 13). Saving knowledge is likewise the gift of God: "To you it is given to know the mysteries of the kingdom of heaven" (Matt. xiii. 11). Effectual calling is also of God's grace (2 Tim. i. 9). Justification is of God's grace; we are justified freely. Adoption also is an act of grace; He vouchsafes that high privilege, not in common to all, but only to so many as He pleaseth. Perseverance in duty is also God's gift; for "we are preserved by the power of God to salvation." Eternal life is also a gift; for "the gift of God is eternal life, through Jesus Christ." A right knowledge of these things, reader, will keep thee humble and dependent upon God; and not only dispose thee to give Him the glory of His grace, but to seek to Him diligently for it.

> Whate'er I have, or may possess,
>   It flows from God above;
> Comes from His bounty and His grace,
>   And undeserved love.

June 28.

We would see Jesus. Search the Scriptures; for in them ye think ye have eternal life, and they are they which testify of me.—John xii. 21, and v. 39. *Seek ye out of the book of the Lord, and read.*—Isa. xxxiv. 16. See also chap. viii. 20.

It is remarkable that the wise men traveling to find Christ followed only the star; and as long as they had that in view, were assured that they were in the right way, and we may believe had great pleasure in their journey; but when they entered Jerusalem,—whereas the star led them not thither, but to Bethlehem,—and there would be instructed where Christ was born, they were not only ignorant of the place where, but had also lost the sight of the star which should guide them thither. Whereby we are taught this useful lesson, that when we are going to learn Christ, and seek Christ, who is above, to beware we lose not the star of God's Word, which only is the mark that shews us where Christ is, and which way we may come to Him. To which may be added, that if, with David, we make the Word of God "a lamp to our feet, and a light to our paths," we shall not be led aside by every false fire that presents itself to us; but by keeping close to the Word of God, we shall be brought to the knowledge of Christ here, and to the full enjoyment of Him hereafter. Reader, this little book is only designed to lead thee to "search the Scriptures," which are able to make thee wise unto salvation, through faith in Jesus Christ.

> Eternal life God's Word imparts,
> Whereon each fainting spirit lives;
> Here sweeter comforts cheer our hearts,
> Than all the round of nature gives.

June 29.

Let no corrupt communication proceed out of your mouth, but that which is good to the use of edifying, that it may minister grace unto the hearers; and grieve not the Holy Spirit of God. Let not filthiness be once named among you, nor foolish talking, nor jesting, which are not convenient.—Eph. iv. 29, 30, and v. 4. *But now ye also put off all these; anger, wrath, malice, blasphemy, filthy communication out of your mouth. Lie not one to another.*—Col. iii. 8. 9.

IDLE words are hurtful words; they grieve the Holy Spirit, destroy what power has been obtained by prayer, and cause nothing but levity and distraction of mind. Let this be a caution against talking too much; for if it does not tend to the glory of God, it is nothing but corrupt communication, the end of which is destruction and misery. May all Christians take heed to refrain their tongues, and never speak unadvisedly; but always consider first, whether their words can be profitable to others, and acceptable to God in heaven. O Lord, teach me, by thy wisdom, "to keep my mouth as it were with a bridle," and to weigh all my words like gold! Let my heart and lips be moved and governed by thy Spirit, that both my silence and talking may be according to thy will and direction! Grant that I may always chiefly converse with thee in prayer and thanksgiving for the good of my own soul and others; and whenever I am to open my lips in due time, let my words be so seasoned and blessed as to administer grace to the hearers.

> So let our lips and lives express
> The holy Gospel we profess;
> So let our words and virtues shine,
> To prove the doctrine all Divine.

JUNE 30.

And he dreamed, and behold a ladder set up on the earth, and the top of it reached to heaven; and behold the angels of God ascending and descending on it.—Gen. xxviii. 12.

THIS ladder the Lord Jesus Christ applies to Himself (John i. 51), and it may be considered as representing the Divine Providence, which governs all things. The several steps of the ladder are the motions and actions of Providence; the angels going up and down, shew that they are the great ministers of Providence, never idle, but always employed in the preservation of the just; their ascending, means their going up to receive the Divine orders and commands; and their descending, their coming down upon earth to put them in execution. So that, in this representation, God signified to Jacob, now full of care and uneasy apprehensions, that the man who was under the custody and protection of Divine Providence wanted not company in a wilderness, wanted not security in the midst of dangers, wanted not direction in the most difficult undertakings; since there were so many ministering spirits holding correspondence between earth and heaven, and daily and hourly "sent forth from God's presence to minister unto them who shall be heirs of salvation." Seeing, then, that these ministering spirits of God are still active in their work, shall I not enjoy the care and the direction of such holy beings? Shall I not give up my poor soul into their hands? Alas! how it clings to its own foolish ways! May the God of grace deliver it from these; for they are indeed folly!

> Thou, Jesus, my safe ladder art,
>   To lift me to the skies;
> And on it when I find I'm got,
>   My heart begins to rise.

July 1.

Alleluia: for the Lord God omnipotent reigneth.
—Rev. xix. 6.

God is the Lord of Hosts; He is the great commander of heaven and earth; He it is that directs all conflicts in war; no field is pitched, no battle fought, but by His special order and commission; and all for the accomplishment of His glory. But it befalleth us as it doth them who stand in the same level wherein two great armies are ready to engage: they conceive them to be a disordered multitude; whom, notwithstanding, if they beheld from a high hill, they would discern that they were artificially ranged, and every man serving under his own colors. Even so men, who behold the state of the world with the eyes of flesh and blood, dim by reason of the corruption of their judgments and weakness of their affections, think all things out of order, they "see servants riding on horses, and princes going on foot; that the worse men are, the better they fare; and they fare the worse the better they are:" but if they would go into God's sanctuary, and judge of occurrences by heavenly principles, then they would confess that no army on earth can be better marshaled than the great army of all the creatures of heaven and earth, yea, and of hell too; and that, notwithstanding all appearances to the contrary, all is well, and will end well, especially to God's people; and that the God of order will bring light out of darkness, and order out of the greatest confusion, could they but have patience, and let Him alone with His own work.

> The Lord God omnipotent reigns,
>   Commanding whatever He will;
> And rebels that fear not His word
>   Are under His government still.

JULY 2.

Thou hast thrust sore at me, that I might fall; but the Lord helped me.—Ps. cxviii. 13. *Preserved in Jesus Christ, and called.*—Jude 1.

JESUS was in the council, undertook our cause, struck hands in the covenant as our surety, wrought out a righteousness for us, suffered our curse on the tree to redeem us, ever lives, and ever loves, and ever pleads our cause, while He represents our persons before the everlastingly gracious and infinitely just and righteous Jehovah, His Father and our Father, now well pleased with us, because accepted and preserved in the Beloved. Are these things so? And has the Lord, the Spirit, the glorifier of Jesus, enlightened our understandings to see these things, enabled us to believe, and assured our hearts of our own happy share and interest in them! O my soul, stop, reflect, dwell on such wonderful power, marvelous favor, distinguishing love, and appropriated mercy! Now let all mine enemies exert their utmost power, I will not be afraid. Afflictions, pains, temptations, may await me, waves and storms may go over my head, Satan may sift me as wheat, the waters of death may prove bitter to my taste, yet I will not be discouraged; He that died for me will take care of me; He that pardoned my aggravated offences will heal my infirmities; He that knew the power of temptation will support and deliver me out of all. This I believe; Lord, help my unbelief! The wisdom, the power, the love, the promise, the covenant, and the oath of Jehovah, stand all engaged for the preservation of a poor, unworthy believer in Jesus. Alleluia.

> Why should I fear, though mighty foes
> Thrust at me every day?
> The Lord, who offers me His help,
> Is stronger much than they.

JULY 3.

Learn of me, for I am meek and lowly in heart; and ye shall find rest unto your souls.—Matt. xi. 29. *Be clothed with humility; for God resisteth the proud, and giveth grace to the humble. Humble yourselves therefore under the mighty hand of God, that He may exalt you in due time.*—1 Pet. v. 5, 6.

Such as are haughty and self-conceited, rush against the mighty hand of God, and destroy themselves; but those that are humbled under it, will be protected by the same. Whatever knowledge or skill we may obtain in the schools of human learning, the Scriptures do not yet allow us to be truly wise, but calls us blind and mere worldly students, till we learn to be poor in spirit, lowly in heart, and dead to the world (Prov. xi. 2; 1 Cor. i. and ii). Therefore, "the more a man dies to this world, the more is he enlightened;" and the more humiliating views he obtains of his worthlessness in the sight of Jehovah, the greater will be his capacity of grace, and the more abundant supplies of grace will be administered to his soul. What is more precious in the sight of God than the soul that is broken from its own conceits and vanities, and has enlisted itself under the banner of Jesus,—a meek and lowly soldier of the Cross? As nothing, then, O my soul, bend thyself in the presence of the Lord! Lay that aside which is of this world, and putting on the garment of heavenly meekness, walk humbly with thy God.

Lord, if thou thy grace impart, poor in spirit, meek in heart,
I shall as my Master be, rooted in humility.
Simple, teachable, and mild, changed into a little child:
Pleased with all the Lord provides, weaned from all the world besides,
Father, fix my soul on thee; every evil let me flee;
Nothing want, beneath, above; happy in thy precious love.

July 4.

And Jacob went on his way, and the angels of God met him.—Gen. xxxii. 1.

As Jacob was favored with a heavenly vision when he first departed from his father's house, so the Divine Being thought proper again to favor him with the same token of His protection on his return thither, in order to encourage him to meet with confidence those dangers he had to encounter. Hence we may observe, that when God designs His people for extraordinary trials, He prepares them by extraordinary comforts. We should think it had been more seasonable for these angels to have appeared to him just in the heat of his engagement, either with Laban before, or Esau after, than in this calm and quiet interval, when he saw not himself in any imminent peril. But God will have us when we are in peace to provide for trouble, and when trouble comes, draw comfort and encouragement from former experiences; knowing assuredly, that He who has delivered in six troubles will also deliver in seven, and in due time out of all. This may be a representation of God's people at death, who, after a life of sore trial and heavy conflict with the triple-armed enemy of their souls, are triumphantly returning to Canaan, to their heavenly Father's house; and then the angels of God shall meet them, to congratulate the happy finishing of their labors, and carry them to their everlasting rest; there to dwell with God and the Lamb, and in company with the whole multitude of redeemed saints, to sing the songs of praise in the New Jerusalem.

> May Jesus guide me on my way,
>   And guard from threatening woes;
> His presence turns my night to day,
>   And disconcerts my foes.

JULY 5.

For by thy words thou shalt be justified, and by thy words thou shalt be condemned.—Matt. xii. 37.
If any man among you seem to be religious, and bridleth not his tongue, but deceiveth his own heart, this man's religion is vain.—James i. 26.
I will take heed, that I sin not with my tongue; I will keep my mouth with a bridle, while the wicked is before me.—Ps. xxxix. 1.

THE general turn of a man's discourse will clearly discover the bent of his mind; for "out of the abundance of the heart the mouth speaketh." Other outward marks may be imitated; but not to offend in tongue, to be free from detraction and boasting, to speak the truth in love, to "let no corrupt communication (nothing contrary to peace or holiness) proceed out of the mouth," this is the finger of God. Here the hypocrite and formalist always fail. Let us earnestly pray for grace to bridle the tongue. "O Lord, set a watch before my mouth, keep the door of my lips," that I may never bring a reproach upon my profession, by speaking proud, false, foolish, or censorious words. But, on the contrary, may I speak the words of wisdom, and, out of a meek and a pure heart, adorn the doctrine which I profess, by a holy and quiet conversation. Especially defend me in the presence of them who fear not thy name, that I bring not a reproach thereon, by any foolish word that I may let slip out of my mouth.

> The tongue, that most unruly power,
> Requires a strong restraint;
> We must be watchful every hour,
> And pray, but never faint.
>
> Lord, can a feeble, helpless worm,
> Perform a task so hard?
> Thy grace must all the work perform,
> And give the free reward.

July 6.

Loose them and bring them unto me. And if any man say ought unto you, ye shall say, The Lord hath need of them, and straightway he will send them.—Matt. xxi. 2, 3. *The Spirit of the Lord came mightily upon him, and the cords that were upon his arms became as flax that was burnt with fire, and his bands loosed from off his hands.*—Judges xv. 14.

THUS the Spirit of the Lord makes us free from all spiritual bonds; for "where the Spirit of the Lord is, there is liberty" (2 Cor. iii. 17). Though I was torn from Christ by the enemy, yet, as a robber, he gets no right to me. Christ does not give up for this reason His right which He has to me on so many accounts; and as soon as I am willing by His grace to give up myself to Him, and desire to be delivered from the power of Satan, He vindicates and saves me as His property; I am His, Satan looses his hold, and nothing in the world can withhold me from Him. All the fetters must fall off. "The Spirit of the Lord came mightily upon him, and the cords that were upon his arms became as flax that was burnt with fire, and his bands loosed from off his hands." Help me to resign myself wholly into thy hands, and may the Spirit of the Lord loose my bonds, the bonds of sin.

> What though the hosts of death and hell
>   All armed against me stood,
> Terrors no more shall shake my soul;
>   My refuge is my God!
>
> Arise, O Lord, fulfill thy grace,
>   While I thy glory sing;
> My God hath broke the serpent's teeth,
>   And death has lost his sting.
>
> Salvation to the Lord belongs,
>   His arm alone can save;
> Blessings attend thy people here,
>   And reach beyond the grave.

July 7.

Make you a new heart and a new spirit; for why will ye die, O house of Israel?—Ezek. xviii. 31. See also 2 Cor. v. 17-21.

Many are converted, but not entirely to Christ and from their own righteousness, so as to be truly sensible of their abominable wickedness, and earnestly to flee to Christ for a reconciliation and righteousness; and therefore they never seek to Jesus to make the new heart and new spirit, but continue on in their mere outward moral state year after year. But to be truly a member of the spiritual body of Christ Jesus, there must not only be an outward morality, there must also be the inward spirituality, the sanctification of the heart, the renewing of the whole inner man in that heavenly knowledge, righteousness and holiness, which adorned the soul before the fall. O Lord, let me daily receive a word from thee, to nourish and strengthen my soul, so as to be renewed daily by it more and more.

> Oh! for a heart to love my God;
>   A heart from sin set free;
> A heart that always feels the blood
>   So freely shed for me.
>
> A heart resigned, submissive, meek,
>   My dear Redeemer's throne;
> Where only Christ is heard to speak,
>   Where Jesus reigns alone.
>
> A lowly and believing heart,
>   Abhorring self and sin;
> A constant heart, which nought can part
>   From Christ, who dwells within.
>
> A child-like heart, that cries for food,
>   And pines for love Divine;
> An upright heart, by grace renewed,
>   A copy, Lord, of thine.

July 8.

Martha, Martha, thou art careful and troubled about many things.—Luke x. 41. *Keep thy heart with all diligence; for out of it are the issues of life.*—Prov. iv. 23. *This people draweth nigh unto me with their mouth, and honoreth me with their lips; but their heart is far from me.*—Matt. xv. 8.

As the virtue of a strong spirituous liquor evaporates by degrees in a vial which is not closely stopped, in like manner the life and power of the Spirit insensibly vanishes away, if the heart is not kept with all diligence. Of the former, remains only water; of the latter, nothing but the form of religion, or perhaps some false principles and errors crept in. Therefore many must be tried and sifted, that they may know, like Hezekiah, what is in their hearts (2 Chron. xxxii. 31): consequently, what more needful than to take heed to our own spirits, and to keep close to the written Word? for as the latter times draw nearer, the more plausible will errors and seducements appear, both on your right hand and on your left. Beware of being drawn off from the truth, either by the worldly prudence of half-hearted professors, or by pretences to merit in the self-righteous Pharisee.

> O Lord, permit me not to be
> A stranger to myself and thee;
> Amidst a thousand thoughts I rove,
> Forgetful of my highest love.
>
> Call me away from flesh and sense,
> One sovereign word can draw me thence;
> I would obey the voice Divine,
> And all inferior things resign.
>
> Be earth, with all her scenes, withdrawn;
> Let noise and vanity be gone:
> In secret silence of the mind
> My heaven, and there my God, I find.

July 9.

My soul thirsteth after thee as a thirsty land.—Ps. cxliii. 6. *Let him that is athirst come; and whosoever will, let him take the water of life freely.*—Rev. xxii. 17. *If any man thirst, let him come unto me and drink. He that believeth on me, as the Scripture hath said, out of his belly shall flow rivers of living water.*—John vii. 37, 38.

When thou art dry and barren, examine thyself closely what may be the cause; ask pardon for all known offences, and take care to amend them. And though thou shouldst not find anything particular, yet humble thyself deeply before the Lord; but, at the same time, remember that thou art accepted, beloved, justified and blessed in Christ; and in this disposition quietly wait the returns of some new drops of living water and grace; but be also sure afterward to cherish and make a right use of them. Thus thou shalt be under the immediate care of the mighty God of Jacob. "And the Lord shall guide thee continually, and satisfy thy soul in drought, and make fat thy bones; and thou shalt be like a watered garden, and like a spring of water, whose waters fail not" (Isa. lviii. 11).

> For thee I thirst, O Lord, I mourn!
> When will thy smiling face return?
> Shall all my joy on earth remove,
> And God for ever hide His love?
>
> ANSWER.
>
> No! ye that pant for living streams,
> And pine away and die,
> Here you may quench your raging thirst
> With springs that never dry.
>
> Rivers of love and mercy here
> In a rich ocean join;
> Salvation in abundance flows,
> Like floods of milk and wine.

July 10.

My soul waiteth upon God; from Him cometh my salvation. He only is my defence; I shall not be greatly moved. Therefore, trust in Him at all times; ye people, pour out your heart before Him: God is a refuge for us.—Ps. lxii. 1, 2, 8.

The more patient, believing and single-eyed we are, the sooner we shall see the salvation and victory of the Lord. Double-minded souls have the greatest struggle; and the slothful must tarry the longer. Sometimes, it is true, though we are faithful, yet we must cry out, "O Lord, how long?" (Ps. vi. 3.) But nevertheless, He always hears and delivers us, though we do not see and feel it directly, but seem to suffer continually. In heaven we shall certainly see it, and reap the blessed fruits of all our afflictions and prayers. While we are upon this earth, the face of the Lord may often be obscured and hid from us, yet at length we shall "see the glory of the Lord in the cloud," and deliverance shall come out of the troubles that seemed to overwhelm us. Thus it is that the Lord works with His people, to keep them always in remembrance of Himself. Shall we not wait then for Him, even though He tarry long? Yes, my soul, wait thou upon the Lord; He is a refuge for thee.

> Almighty God of truth and love,
>   In me thy power exert;
> The mountain from my soul remove,
>   The hardness of my heart.
>
> From thee, that I no more depart,
>   No more thy goodness grieve;
> The filial awe, the fleshy heart,
>   The tender conscience give.
>
> Quick as the apple of an eye,
>   O God, my conscience make!
> Awake, my soul, when sin is nigh,
>   And keep it still awake.

July 11.

I have been young, and now am old; yet have I not seen the righteous forsaken; nor his seed begging bread.—Ps. xxxvii. 25.

SWEET declaration! encouraging experience! The Lord indeed careth for the righteous,—for those who, having seen the want of mercy, rely for it upon the promise of God, that there is forgiveness with Him through the meritorious life and death of Jesus Christ. He hath promised that He will never leave nor forsake them; that He will withhold from them no manner of thing that is good. He careth also for their seed; so that they shall not beg their bread. He frequently provides for them, when their parents are no more, in such unexpected ways, that many who see it are constrained to acknowledge, "This is the Lord's doing." And sometimes, while they are living, He brings bread to their mouths, and also furnishes them with opportunities to hear of and seek for the bread which came down from heaven, and which endureth unto everlasting life; thus snatching them from the jaws of ignorance and destruction. O Lord, if mine ears have heard—if mine eyes have seen—and, more especially, if I partake of such blessings, thankfully may I own that thou art a God keeping covenant and mercy; and make this proof of thy faithfulness a ground of reliance upon thee for all needful promised blessings! Help me to cast all my cares on thee, and endeavor, by prayer, instruction, and example, that thy goodness may be sanctified to my seed.

> The Lord, for His own mercy's sake,
>   Will bless believers and their seed;
> The parents He will not forsake,
>   Nor let the children beg their bread.

July 12.

Strengthened with all might, according to His glorious power, unto all patience and long-suffering with joyfulness.—Col. i. 11. *And they departed from the presence of the council, rejoicing that they were counted worthy to suffer shame for His name.*—Acts v. 41. *That He would grant you, according to the riches of His glory, to be strengthened with might by His Spirit in the inner man.*—Eph. iii. 16. *But the fruit of the Spirit is love, joy, peace, long-suffering, gentleness, goodness, faith, meekness, temperance.*—Gal. v. 22.

OH! my soul, what encouraging words are these! How full of meaning! The Lord our righteousness is the Lord our strength. He is near at hand, believer, to strengthen thee according to thy need; not in one or two respects, but with all might, with a supply suited to every various occasion, and that to the utmost, answerable to what may be expected from the exertion of "His own glorious power." Happy state of the believer in Jesus! though feeble in himself, surrounded with enemies, and exercised with a continual warfare, he shall not be overpowered; for the promise and the arm of God is on his side. The Lord, who can do what He pleaseth, is in alliance, yea, in covenant with a believer; and therefore he shall be made more than a conqueror through Christ who has loved him.

> Let me but hear my Saviour say,
> "Strength shall be equal to thy day;"
> Then I rejoice in deep distress,
> Leaning on All-sufficient grace.
>
> I glory in infirmity,
> That Christ's own power may rest on me;
> When I am weak, then am I strong,
> Grace is my shield, and Christ my song.

JULY 13.

Christian's Declaration:—*My beloved is mine, and I am his.*—Song of Solomon ii. 16.

Divine Answer:—*I will betroth thee unto me for ever; yea, I will betroth thee unto me in righteousness, and in judgment, and in loving-kindness; and thou shalt know the Lord.*—Hos. ii. 19, 20.

By faith in the blood of Christ we are accepted, and closely united to Him as our bridegroom. By faith we daily eat His flesh, drink His blood, and are sprinkled all over; and need there is of a daily sprinkling, that our persons and services may be accepted, since the best of our works, our prayers and praises, our duties and graces, are all unclean till washed in the blood of Jesus. This appears from Heb. ix. 19-21, where it is said, that all the vessels of the ministry, and even the book, were sprinkled. By faith let us cling to this blood of sprinkling, which emanates from the cross, and let us abide in Jesus, without whom we can bring forth no fruit; for "as the branch cannot bear fruit of itself, except it abide in the vine; no more can ye, except ye abide in Him" (John xv. 4).

> Hark! the Redeemer from on high
> Sweetly invites His fav'rites nigh;
> From caves of darkness and of doubt,
> He gently speaks, and calls us out.
>
> "My sister and my spouse," He cries,
> "Bound to my heart by various ties;
> Thy powerful love my heart detains
> In strong delight, and pleasing chains."
>
> Dear Lord, our thankful heart receives
> The hope thy invitation gives;
> To thee our joyful lips shall raise
> The voice of prayer, the voice of praise.
>
> I am my Love's and He is mine;
> Our hearts, our hopes, our passions join;
> Nor let a motion, nor a word,
> Nor thought arise to grieve my Lord.

July 14.

David's Prayer:—*When thou saidst, Seek ye my face, my heart said unto thee, Thy face, Lord, will I seek.*—Ps. xxvii. 8. *I am thine, save me; for I have sought thy precepts.*—Ps. cxix. 94.

Divine Answer:—*They who seek me early shall find me.*—Prov. viii. 17. *The humble shall see this, and be glad; and your heart shall live that seek God.*—Ps. lxix. 32. *Seek, and ye shall find.*—Matt. vii. 7. *For whoso findeth me, findeth life.*—Prov. viii. 35. *For I am the life.*—John xiv. 6.

Such arguments and entreaties we may use with God, to strengthen us in faith; He does not want them, but we do; and He is well pleased when we take Him at His word. For if we would not draw near to God in prayer till our hearts are quickened, perhaps we might never come to it. Therefore we must not indulge ourselves in such a state of dullness, but rather put a force upon ourselves, and pray against our natural inclination. Being faithful and instant in this, we shall certainly have our affections warmed, and great power and blessings given from above, that our hearts may live. O Lord, I plead thy precious promises, and thou canst not deny thy word. Thou hast laid thyself under obligation to help a feeble praying soul. Then let thy Holy Spirit abide with me, to quicken my soul when fainting, and to rule my heart in all things, that no sin may have dominion over me.

> Lord, I address thy heavenly throne;
>   Call me a child of thine;
> Send down the Spirit of thy Son
>   To form my heart divine.
>
> There shed thy choicest love abroad,
>   And make my comforts strong,
> Then shall I say, My Father God,
>   With an unwav'ring tongue.

JULY 15.

David's Prayer :—*O my God, I trust in thee; let me not be ashamed.*—Ps. xxv. 2. *In thee, O Lord, do I hope; thou wilt hear, O Lord my God.*—Ps. xxxviii. 15. *Let none that wait on thee be ashamed.*—Ps. xxv. 3.

Divine Answer :—*Hope maketh not ashamed.*—Rom. v. 5. *They that trust in the Lord shall be as Mount Zion, which abideth for ever.*—Ps. cxxv. 1. *Pray for help; and though it tarry, wait for it; because it will surely come; it will not tarry.*—Hab. ii. 3. *Then thou shalt know, etc.*—Isa. xlix. 23.

DOES God delay His promises, and the enemy raise a suspicion against His faithfulness?—remember it is said, "Pray and wait." Wait for the coming of God's own good time. His time will come; and "though it tarry, wait for it, because it will surely come." Thou art still alive, and shalt yet be a witness to God's faithfulness. If He was not faithful and true, He could not be God. His faithfulness is eternal, and as sure and as great as Himself; above all our thoughts. Thou shalt at last the more gloriously experience it, and not be ashamed. Heaven and earth shall pass away, but His word shall not fail, because "He keeps truth for ever" (Ps. cxlvi. 6). Hath He promised, and shall He not perform? Hath He said, and will He not do? Yea, verily, His words are truth to the end of the world.

> Happy the man whose hopes rely
> On Israel's God : He made the sky,
> And earth, and seas, with all their train;
> And none shall find His promise vain.
>
> His truth for ever stands secure;
> He saves th' oppressed, He feeds the poor;
> He sends the laboring conscience peace,
> And grants the prisoner sweet release.

July 16.

And as Moses lifted up the serpent in the wilderness, even so must the Son of Man be lifted up.—John iii. 14. And I, if I be lifted up from the earth, will draw all men unto me.—John xii. 32.

This He spoke of His death. And it is the remembrance of His cruel death, of what He suffered, said, and finished, when He hung naked and wounded upon the cross, that relieves an afflicted conscience, and effectually captivates the sinner's heart to Himself. The sharpest convictions, if not relieved by this sight, will never teach the heart to love; the strongest resolutions, unless made with this bleeding object in view, will melt away like snow. But a crucified Saviour is a powerful loadstone indeed; multitudes have been drawn by it from sin to holiness, from Satan to God, from earth to heaven. Come then, my soul, contemplate thy Redeemer in all the stages of His humiliation work. Travel with Him from His birth to His cross, from His cross to His grave; and from the grave behold Him rising the first-fruits of them that sleep. Go, my soul, and spend an hour with Him in Gethsemane; see His bloody sweat, hear His groans, and think what all this was for. It was for thy sins; that He might redeem thee to God; that He might bring back to thy Father who is in heaven a pure and a redeemed spirit. Then love Him.

> Was it for crimes that I have done
> He groaned upon the tree?
> Amazing pity! grace unknown!
> And love beyond degree!
>
> But drops of grief can ne'er repay
> The debt of love I owe;
> Lord, I would give myself away;
> 'Tis all that I can do.

JULY 17.

Charity suffereth long, and is kind; charity envieth not; charity vaunteth not itself, is not puffed up, doth not behave itself unseemly, seeketh not her own, is not easily provoked, thinketh no evil; rejoiceth not in iniquity, but rejoiceth in the truth; beareth all things, believeth all things, hopeth all things, endureth all things. Charity never faileth.—1 Cor. xiii. 4-8.

O MY dear heavenly Father! I desire to love thee and my neighbor with a pure heart fervently, and beg thou wouldst let me know and enjoy thy love in Christ, as the only means of producing this love in me. For how can my heart be cold when resting at the cross of Christ, and feeling the virtue of His blood? Or how can it be hard, when lying in thy bosom, richly tasting of thy grace, and sweetly experiencing thine everlasting love to me, a vile miserable sinner? Oh! may a sense of thy love melt my hard heart into love, and change it thoroughly; and change my longing desires from those sinful things of time that gender strife.

> Had I the tongues of Greeks and Jews,
> And nobler speech than angels use,
> If love be absent, I am found,
> Like tinkling brass, an empty sound.
>
> Were I inspired to preach, and tell
> All that is done in heaven and hell;
> Or could my faith the world remove,
> Still I am nothing without love.
>
> Should I distribute all my store
> To feed the bowels of the poor;
> Or give my body to the flame,
> To gain a martyr's glorious name,—
>
> If love to God and love to men
> Be absent, all my hopes are vain;
> Nor tongues, nor gifts, nor fiery zeal,
> The work of love can e'er fulfill.

July 18.

David's Prayer :—*Unto thee, O Lord, do I lift up my soul.*—Ps. xxv. 1.
Divine Answer :—*Thou hast heard the desire of the humble, thou wilt prepare their heart, thou wilt cause thine ear to hear.*—Ps. x. 17.

FAITH only desires Christ, and does neither delight in the gain, nor grieve much at the loss of temporal things; but "faith, through an earnest desire for Christ and His Word, rises above all creatures, and overcomes all worldly pleasures and fears." And this, being the work of God, will certainly be accomplished; nay, is looked upon as really accomplished already in our desires and endeavors after it; in the same manner as evil desires are reckoned for deeds in the sight of God, though they never proceed to outward acts. Let the inward desires of my heart be, that God, even the God of Israel, may sanctify me by the Holy Spirit, and raise my faith to embrace Christ as far more precious than all this world possesses. May I, in my dear Saviour, see a Jordan in which I may wash and be clean; and may my heart not aim after the streams of earth, which have no healing power, but my health being in Christ, may He be all I seek after; as whatever I may do, may I always seek the Lord!

>I cannot bear thine absence, Lord;
> My life expires if thou depart;
>Be thou, my heart, still near my God,
> And thou, my God, be near my heart.
>
>I was not born for earth and sin,
> Nor can I live on things so vile;
>Yet I will stay my Father's time,
> And hope and wait for heaven awhile.
>
>Then, dearest Lord, in thine embrace,
> Let me resign my fleeting breath,
>And with a smile upon my face,
> Pass through the lonesome vale of death.

July 19.

Thou drewest near in the day that I called upon thee; thou saidst, Fear not. O Lord, thou hast pleaded the cause of my soul, and redeemed my life.—Lam. iii. 57, 58. *Fear not, for I am with thee.*—Isa. xliii. 5. *I am He that liveth and was dead: and, behold, I am alive for evermore; and have the keys of hell and of death.*—Rev. i. 18.

CHRIST has overcome death, led captivity captive, and "by one offering, perfected for ever them that are sanctified" (Heb. x. 14). Whoever leaves this world believing in Him, being perfected already, has nothing to fear after death. O my heavenly Father! dispose me to seek diligently after holiness; and though the work of sanctification will be imperfect in this life, which should humble me much, yet let it cause no fear of death, nor disturb my confidence in thee, since my salvation and my confidence do not depend on a perfect holiness here, but on my being in Christ and adopted through Him; which adoption the weakest child hath, as well as the strongest, though both are not equally sensible of it. For every true believer, whether weak or strong, hath eternal life, and shall not fall into condemnation. If, therefore, I am a child of God, though a weak one, I am still an heir, and shall find life and deliverance in death.

> I am Alpha, says the Saviour,
>   I Omega likewise am;
> I was dead and live for ever,
>   God Almighty and the Lamb.
>
> In the Lord is our perfection,
>   And in Him our boast we'll make;
> We shall share His resurrection,
>   If we of His death partake.

July 20.

What is the chaff to the wheat? saith the Lord. Is not my word like as a fire? and a hammer that breaketh the rock in pieces?—Jer. xxiii. 28, 29.

Is there not great condescension in the everlasting Father of all sending to the sinful sons of men a knowledge of Himself, the infinite God, in language so plain and simple, that our finite understandings can comprehend it? Was there ever humility mingled with love like this? Yes, I hear you say, the infinite God becoming man was greater. It was; but this plain, and simple, and pure word of God contains the knowledge and purport of this still more condescending event; and what were such an event without our knowledge of it? To value this precious gift of God's word aright, let us inquire of what use it is to us. Hear God's own declaration, "Is not my word like as a fire? saith the Lord, and like a hammer that breaketh the hard rock in pieces?" It is as a hammer to break down our hard and sinful hearts, and as a fire to melt and purify them. And what more convenient for our wants? Our hearts are hard, deceitful and filled with every wicked thing. They need to be broken, to be bended from their pride; they need to be melted to love and to godly sorrow; they need to be cleansed of their pollutions, and God's word is powerful to these. May the Spirit of the Lord help me to study and apply that sacred word, and may my soul by it be, every day, made wiser unto salvation.

> Thy word, almighty Lord,
>   Where'er it enters in,
> Is sharper than a two-edged sword
>   To slay the man of sin.

July 21.

Can two walk together except they be agreed?—
Amos iii. 3. *What agreement hath the temple of God with idols? Come out from among them, and be ye separate, saith the Lord, and touch not the unclean thing; and I will receive you.—*
2 Cor. vi. 16, 17.

READER, I suppose thee a religious person; one that has been converted by the power of grace; one that is desirous to glorify God in life and conversation; one that has an interest in Jesus, and wants to have it made more manifest to thine own self every day; one that considers this life as a passage to a better, and would be glad of a spiritual companion to go along with thee, for "two are better than one." Give not the right hand of fellowship to any before thou hast tried him, for two cannot walk comfortably together except they are agreed. Bring him to the law of God; the eternal, moral law of God, contained in the ten commandments, and ask him, Does he look upon that law of God as the rule of his life? If he denies it, avoid him. If he says he is not under the commanding power of it, turn away from him. But if he says that he sincerely takes it as God's revealed will to him, owning the authority thereof over his conscience and conversation, "Thus saith the Lord," breathing after universal obedience, repenting and mourning where he falls short, and fleeing by faith to Christ for all peace and pardon,—take such a one for a friend and companion. And may the Lord ever enable me to receive into my affections only those who are his dear children in Christ.

> Lord, draw my wand'ring heart to thee,
> And reconcile it to thy word;
> Then will it well with God agree,
> And find communion with its Lord.

July 22.

My soul fainteth for thy salvation. My soul is continually in my hand. Uphold me according to thy word, that I may live; and let me not be ashamed of my hope. Look thou upon me, and be merciful unto me, as thou usest to do unto those that love thy name.—Ps. cxix. 81, 109, 116, 132.

O Lord, I love thy name, it is dear unto my heart. And, since thou art called merciful, gracious, long-suffering, and even the Lord our righteousness, I therefore depend upon nothing of my own, but throw myself entirely upon thy free grace and righteousness, which alone keeps me in peace. Without thee I am ignorant and weak; and Satan being as wicked as he is cunning, what would become of me, if I was not kept and preserved by thee? Thy name is a strong tower, the righteous enter there and are safe; there let me abide also continually, so shall I be safe from every adversary. The power of Satan shall not prevail against me, neither shall the enticements of the body overwhelm the grace of the soul, but the Lord shall be my shield and my exceeding great reward. He is the Rock of Ages that stands unmoved, and on which all may find shelter.

> The arms of everlasting love,
>   Beneath my soul be placed;
> And on the Rock of Ages set
>   My slippery footsteps fast.
>
> The city of my blest abode
>   Is walled around with grace;
> Salvation for a bulwark stands,
>   To shield the sacred place.
>
> Satan may vent his sharpest spite,
>   And all his legions roar;
> Almighty mercy guards my life,
>   And bounds his raging power,

July 23.

Not unto us, O Lord, not unto us, but unto thy name be the glory.—Ps. cxv. 1. *For thine is the kingdom, and the power, and the glory, for ever. Amen.*—Matt. vi. 13.

How little reason have we to glory in anything of our own, since nothing but sin is ours, which even defiles that which is of God!

O Lord, grant that I may always give thee the praise of thy own, and may learn to delight and glory in thee, having no other aim but to walk before thee in godly simplicity and sincerity. For "he that walketh uprightly walketh surely" (Prov. x. 9). All disquiet of mind ariseth from our own lusts and unmortified tempers, which makes the bosom like a troubled sea; and no settled calm shall we find till we have a single eye to God's glory, and can count ourselves worthy of no good. Then we may draw comfort out of trouble, and learn to praise the Lord, both for what He giveth and for what He taketh away; being sure that all things are working for our good, and tending to God's glory, which He knows best how to promote; and that nothing but sin can make us unhappy and miserable.

> Great God! how infinite art thou!
>   What worthless worms are we!
> Let the whole race of creatures bow,
>   And pay their praise to thee.
>
> Our lives through various scenes are drawn,
>   And vexed with trifling cares,
> While thine eternal thought moves on
>   Thine undisturbed affairs.
>
> Oh teach our hearts to bless thy name,
>   For that almighty care,
> Which thou hast ever had for those
>   Thine own who truly are.

July 24.

Who shall lay anything to the charge of God's elect? It is God that justifieth; who is he that condemneth? It is Christ that died, yea rather, that is risen again; who is even at the right hand of God, who also maketh intercession for us.—Rom. viii. 33, 34.

There is a story, how the devil appeared to a dying man, and shewed him a parchment roll, which was very long, wherein was written, on every side, the sins of the poor sick man, which were many in number; and there were also written the idle words he had spoken in his life, together with the false words, the unchaste words, and angry words; afterward came his vain and ungodly words; and, lastly, his actions, digested according to the commandments. Whereupon Satan said, See here, behold thy virtues! see here what thy examination must be! Whereupon the poor sinner answered, It is true, but thou hast not set down all; for thou shouldst have added and set down here below, "The blood of Jesus Christ cleanseth us from all our sins;" and this also should not have been forgotten, that "Whosoever believeth in Him shall not perish, but have everlasting life." Whereupon the devil vanished. Thus, if the devil should muster up our sins, and set them in order before us, let but Christ be named in a faithful way, and he will give back, and fly away with all speed.

> My sins are great, I do confess,
>   And of a scarlet dye;
> But Jesu's blood can wash me clean,
>   As God does testify.
>
> Then let me to this cleansing flood
>   A daily visit make;
> And, washing white my sin-foul soul,
>   To holy life awake.

JULY 25.

But we all, with open face beholding as in a glass the glory of the Lord, are changed into the same image, from glory to glory.—2 Cor. iii. 18. *For He has left us an example, that we should follow His steps.*—1 Pet. ii. 21. See also Phil. ii. 5.

How pure and how holy is that life which the blessed Jesus led, when, a man of sorrows, He dwelt on our earth, enduring the same trials and temptations which we suffer! yet He overcame them all, leaving us an example, that we should follow His steps. If, before we say or do anything, we would always consider whether it was agreeable to the pattern of Christ, a multitude of sins would be avoided. O Lord, however guilty and miserable I am, yet, when I can humble myself before thee as the vilest of sinners, and look up unto thee by faith, depending only upon thy free grace, I enjoy peace. Grant, therefore, O my God, that this beholding of thee may be my constant exercise, and that, by this means, I may be strengthened cheerfully to follow thy pattern, and be daily more changed into the glorious image of thy love, patience, and humility, and thus be ripening for eternal life.

My dear Redeemer and my Lord!
I read my duty in thy word;
But in thy life the law appears,
Drawn out in living characters.

Such was thy truth, and such thy zeal,
Such deference to thy Father's will,
Such love, and meekness so divine,
I would transcribe and make them mine.

Be thou my pattern, make me bear
More of thy gracious image here;
Then God the Judge shall own my **name**
Among the followers of the Lamb.

July 26.

He maketh His sun to rise on the evil and good, and sendeth rain on the just and unjust.—Matt. v. 45.

MANY serious people give alms to the pious poor, but are afraid of relieving a common beggar; and it must be owned, that, as riches are a talent from God, they who have them must be discreet in the distribution of them. The religious poor have the best claim, but others ought not to be entirely overlooked; as is plain from the conduct of God Himself, for "He maketh the sun to rise on the evil and on the good." It may be said they will make an ill use of your bounty; but what then? Is not this the very effect of Divine goodness? Is not this the very goodness that is recommended to us in Scripture, by the imitating of which we may shew ourselves to be "the children of our Father which is in heaven, who sendeth rain on the just and on the unjust?" Do I beg of God to deal with me, not according to my merit, but according to His own great goodness; and shall I be so absurd as to withhold my charity from a poor fellow-creature, because he may perhaps not deserve it? Shall I use a measure toward him, which I pray God never to use toward me? Lazarus was a common beggar; and yet he was the care of angels, and carried into Abraham's bosom. "I was a stranger, and ye took me in," saith our blessed Saviour; but who can perform this duty, that will not relieve persons that are unknown to them? "As we have therefore opportunity, let us do good unto all men, especially unto them who are of the household of faith."

> Lord, give me faith which works by love,
>   And will good works command;
> Which makes a neighbor's grief my own,
>   And lends a helping hand.

JULY 27.

Though I walk through the valley of the shadow of death, I will fear no evil; for thou art with me; thy rod and thy staff they comfort me.—Ps. xxiii. 4. See also Exod. xiv. of the deliverance of the Israelites, and the destruction of the Egyptians in the Red Sea.

To rejoice in the light of God's countenance is certainly most pleasant, but not always so profitable to every one as sometimes to walk in the dark, nay, in the valley of the shadow of death. Some are more humble and cautious while walking in the dark than in the light; and glimpses of grace are then exceedingly precious; but such should consider for their humiliation, that darkness or deadness are commonly the effects of a wrong spirit and careless walk. O Lord, grant that when I am deprived of sensible comforts, I may yet be enabled to rely upon thy bare word, and in death may be refreshed by the light of thy countenance. Amen. Yes; thou hast declared, "that the righteous hath hope in his death" (Prov. xiv. 32).

> Death cannot make our souls afraid
>   If God be with us there;
> We may walk through our darkest shade,
>   And never yield to fear.
>
> May I but climb to Pisgah's top,
>   And view the promised land,
> My flesh itself shall long to drop,
>   And pray for the command.
>
> Clasp'd in my heavenly Father's arms,
>   I shall forget my breath,
> And lose my life among the charms
>   Of so divine a death.
>
> Oh! may Jehovah's powerful arms
>   Around me ever be;
> Then, though beset with death's alarms
>   My help shall be in thee.

THE GOLDEN TREASURY. 225

JULY 28.

Hear, ye children, the instruction of a father; and know understanding.—Prov. iv. 1. *We speak that we do know, and testify that we have seen.*—John iii. 11. *Beloved, believe not every spirit, but try the spirits whether they are of God.*—1 John iv. 1.

READER, let the following monitions, the result of long experience and observation, be acceptable unto thee. They are designed for thy spiritual good, will warn thee against errors, and, if complied with, will give thee a true relish of gospel peace and and redeeming love :—Let "the life thou now livest in the flesh be by faith in the Son of God." Labor after a constant soul-reviving fellowship with the Father and the Son, through the Holy Spirit. Watch over thy passions, conduct, and conversation so as that the Spirit of the Lord be not grieved, nor His comfortable influences withdrawn from thy soul. Be ready to every good work as thou hast ability and opportunity ; and take special care thy good be not evil spoken of through the manner of thy performing it. Let no external services whatever, either respecting thyself or others, make thee neglect a constant watchfulness over the inward motions of thine own heart. Let the written Word of God be thine invariable rule, both in principle and practice. Be very earnest after meekness, humility, patience, self-denial, inward holiness, and all other graces of the Spirit ; these carry their own evidence that they are wrought of God, and in their blessed effects will remain with thee for ever. " My son, if thine heart be wise, and experienced in these things, my heart shall rejoice, even mine."

> Lord, fill my heart with love and joy,
> And fill it with thy precious peace ;
> So will my tongue find sweet employ,
> And bless the Lord my righteousness.

July 29.

David's Prayer:—*Open thou mine eyes, that I may behold wondrous things out of thy law.*—Ps. cxix. 18. See also Ps. xiii. 3, and xxxii. 9.

Divine Answer:—*I am come a light into the world, that whosoever believeth on me should not abide in darkness.*—John xii. 46; Ps. cxlvi. 8.

MANY imagine their eyes are opened, and that they have clear notions of religion in their heads; but they see just like Eve after eating the forbidden fruit; their hearts being corrupted, are destitute of Christian simplicity and godly sincerity; for he that does not understand the word of God by the light of the Holy Spirit, through prayer and faith, but only by his natural reason, is certainly blind still (Rev. iii. 17); and one devilish and plausible temptation to error and sin, is enough to break the strongest chain of human reasoning; for it is only "faith that gets the victory" (1 John v. 4). O my soul! get faith; seek it earnestly from God; thou canst not buy it; thou canst not take it up of thyself; thou must get it. "By grace are ye saved, through faith, and that not of yourselves, it is the gift of God" (Eph. ii. 8). Nor canst thou get it until thou ask for it. Ask it then of God, and seek for it diligently.

> The souls enlightened from above,
>   With joy receives the word;
> They see what wisdom, power, and love,
>   Shines in their dying Lord.
>
> The vital savor of His name
>   Restores their fainting breath;
> But unbelief perverts the same
>   To guilt, despair, and death.
>
> Till God diffuse His graces down,
>   Like showers of heavenly rain,
> In vain Apollos sows the ground,
>   And Paul may plant in vain.

July 30.

Abide in me, and I in you. As the branch cannot bear fruit of itself, except it abide in the vine; no more can ye, except ye abide in me. I am the vine, ye are the branches; he that abideth in me, and I in him, the same bringeth forth much fruit; for without me ye can do nothing.—John xv. 4, 5. See also 1 John ii. 6.

I CAN no more do without thee, O my dear Saviour, than the branch can without the vine! Keep me therefore always in thee, else I shall have recourse to my own fancied stock of grace, though I have been a thousand times convinced of my insufficiency. May I never be left in the least thing to my own strength, but be directed, assisted and blessed by thee in all my doings; for as far as I trust to myself, I am distrustful of thee, and consequently weak; and, on the other hand, the more I distrust myself, the more I trust on thee, and shall be strengthened and blessed. Be thou my refuge and my never-failing friend.

> Son of God, thy blessing grant;
> Still supply my every want;
> Tree of Life, thine influence shed;
> With thy sap my spirit feed.
>
> Tend'rest branch, alas! am I;
> Wither without thee, and die;
> Weak as helpless infancy;
> Oh! confirm my soul in thee.
>
> Unsustain'd by thee, I fall;
> Send the strength for which I call;
> Weaker than a bruised reed,
> Help I every moment need.
>
> All my hopes on thee depend;
> Love me, save me to the end;
> Give me thy continuing grace,
> Take the everlasting praise.

July 31.

Offer unto God thanksgiving; and pay thy vows unto the Most High: and call upon me in the day of trouble; I will deliver thee, and thou shalt glorify me. Whoso offereth praise glorifies me; and to him that ordereth his conversation aright will I shew the salvation of God.—Ps. 1. 14, 15, 23. See also Isa. xxv. 9.

NOTHING moves God more to hear us than the glorifying Him by faith with thanksgiving, and the keeping up a child-like confidence in Him as our reconciled Father in Christ; and nothing quickeneth faith more than sure promises of answering our prayers. Thus God will certainly hear and deliver us, since all His ways are only designed to strengthen us in faith, and to save our souls. What need we then to be afraid in times of trouble? ought we not rather to draw near to God in prayer and thanksgiving, and glorify Him even beforehand,—confidently believing that we shall certainly meet with new deliverances and quickenings of faith? Yes, my soul, wait thou upon the Lord, He shall save thee, and thou shalt be glad and rejoice in His salvation; for in His favor is light, and with Him is power to order thy conversation aright.

> To what a stubborn frame
> Has sin reduced our minds!
> What strange ungrateful wretches we!
> And God as strangely kind!
>
> Turn, turn us, mighty God,
> And mould our souls afresh;
> Break, sov'reign grace, these hearts of stone,
> And give us hearts of flesh!
>
> Let old ingratitude
> Provoke our weeping eyes,
> And hourly as new mercies fall,
> Let hourly thanks arise!

Let us come before His presence with thanksgiving, and make a joyful noise unto Him with psalms.—Ps. xcv. 2.

Praise ye the Lord: for it is good to sing praises unto our God: for it is pleasant: and praise is comely.—Ps. cxlvii. 1.

—:o:—

Thou, Lord, wilt bless the righteous: with favor wilt thou compass him as with a shield.—Ps. v. 12.

The righteous Lord loveth righteousness: His countenance doth behold the upright.—Ps. xi. 7.

AUGUST I.

Say ye to the righteous, that it shall be well with them, for they shall eat the fruit of their doings. —Isa. iii. 10. Therefore, *mark the perfect man, and behold the upright; for the end of that man is peace.*—Ps. xxxvii. 37.

MANY are for having that first which is not to be expected till the end. They would be glad of the triumph, but will not fight; the waiting for the Lord seems to them too long;—but for the most glorious promises we must often wait the longest. Jacob was obliged to wait longer than Esau, though he had greater promises than he: and how long was it before the promise of Christ, the greatest of all, was accomplished? It ought, therefore, well to be observed, that it is said at last, "It shall be well with the righteous, and the end of the upright is peace." When his faith, love and patience are tried enough in the furnace of afflictions, then the acceptable year shall come,, and the blessed days of joy will appear. May I live the life and die the death of the righteous, and may my latter end be like His, full of peace, and joy, and rejoicing!

> As sparks break out of burning coals,
>   And still are upward borne,
> So grief is rooted in our souls,
>   And man grows up to mourn.
>
> Yet with my God I leave my cause,
>   And trust His promised grace;
> He rules me by His well-known laws
>   Of love and righteousness.
>
> Not all the pains that e'er I bore
>   Shall spoil my future peace,
> For death and hell can do no more
>   Than what my Father please.

AUGUST 2.

Examine me, O Lord, and prove me; try my reins and my heart.—Ps. xxvi. 2. *Search me, O God, and know my heart; and see if there be any wicked way in me, and lead me in the way everlasting.*—Ps. cxxxix. 23, 24.

WOULD David, the man after God's own heart, not trust himself, but present his heart to the Lord to be tried?—much less can or ought we to trust our hearts; "for he that trusts in his own heart," says the wise man, "is a fool" (Prov. xxviii. 26). We have more reason to be afraid of our own hearts than of all other enemies. It is not necessary for us to know when or by what means the Lord searches our hearts; but every one that is really in a state of grace, and walking in the fear of the Lord, will pray to Him to search the heart, and to deliver him from every wicked way. The Holy Spirit hath various ways of searching the hearts of His people, and makes use of different means with the same person. We are not to limit the mode nor the extent of His operations; but it is our duty to pray, that He will in everything guide us in the way that leadeth to everlasting life. Some may be worked upon very differently from what we have been; but the whole is under the direction of Infinite Wisdom, and tends to manifest the glory of Divine grace in our salvation. "All things work together for good to them that love God" (Rom. viii. 28).

> Lord, search my soul, try every thought;
> Though my own heart accuse me not
> Of walking in a false disguise,
> I beg the trial of thine eyes.
>
> Let not one wicked perverse way,
> Be found in all I do and say,
> But grant thy grace my soul to feed,
> And in the path of life me lead.

AUGUST 3.

Lord, all my desire is before thee. Teach me thy way; I will walk in thy truth; unite my heart to fear thy name.—Ps. xxxviii. 9, and lxxxvi. 11.

ENCOURAGED by thy blessed word of promise, O Lord, that before men call thou wilt answer, and whilst they are yet speaking, thou wilt hear (Isa. lxv. 24), I now draw nigh to thee, and present my supplication before thee. Teach me, by thy word and Spirit, the things of my everlasting peace. Let my soul be cast into the mould of the gospel, and let me be obedient to thy will in all things. Manifest thyself unto me, as thou dost not to the world; shew me my inward corruptions, and let me see into the depth of iniquity that is in my heart; grant me that "fear of the Lord which is the beginning of wisdom; incline my heart unto thy testimonies; lead me into all truth; help me to learn, that he that believeth will not make haste;" restrain the impetuosity of my natural temper, that I may do all things deliberately, as becometh one that feareth alway, that is ever looking unto thee for direction. Lord, preserve me calm in my spirit, gentle in my commands, and watchful, that I speak not unadvisedly with my lips; moderate in my purposes, yielding in my temper, where the honor of my God is not immediately concerned; and ever steadfast where needful. Lord, grant me thy protection; and may thy blessing be upon me, that I may not bring an evil report upon that good land I was permitted to spy out; but walk honorably through the wilderness, and pass triumphantly over Jordan into Canaan. Amen.

> Be with me, Lord, where'er I go;
> Teach me what thou wouldst have me do;
> Suggest whate'er I think or say;
> Direct me in the narrow way.

August 4.

Strive to enter in at the strait gate.—Luke xiii. 24. *Work out your own salvation with fear and trembling.*—Phil. ii. 12. *Forgetting those things that are behind, I reach forth unto those things which are before.*—Phil. iii. 13.

The road to heaven is called a narrow road, because the travelers on it are not permitted to turn either to the one side or the other; such turnings are sin. The gate to this road is called strait, because on entering, you deny yourselves to all the pleasures of the world. He that feeds only upon Christ, and yet with fear and trembling works out his own salvation, is in the narrow way; the former preventing discouragement, and the latter presumption. Grant, O God, that I may still continue to fight the good fight of faith, and never look back on the flesh-pots of Egypt; but "rather choose to suffer affliction with the people of God, than to enjoy the pleasures of sin for a season." May the painful death which thou sufferedst on the cross, have an abiding place in my heart, that thereby unbelief and slavish fear may be destroyed on the one hand, and security on the other; that I may walk at all times and in all places with holy and filial reverence, as in thy presence! Amen.

> As new-born babes desire the breast,
>   To feed, and grow, and thrive;
> So saints with joy the gospel taste,
>   And by the gospel live.
>
> Grace, like an uncorrupted seed,
>   Abides and reigns within;
> Immortal principles forbid
>   The sons of God to sin.
>
> Not by the terrors of a slave
>   Do they perform His will;
> But with the noblest powers they have,
>   His sweet commands fulfill.

AUGUST 5.

David's Prayer:—*Create in me a clean heart, O God; and renew a right spirit within me.*—Ps. li. 10.

Divine Answer:—*And I will give them one heart, and I will put a new spirit within you; and I will take the stony heart out of their flesh, and will give them an heart of flesh; that they may walk in my statutes, and keep mine ordinances, and do them; and they shall be my people, and I will be their God.*—Ezek. xi. 19, 20.

A GLORIOUS promise, which may be relied on, and will certainly be fulfilled if heartily pleaded in prayer. "And blessed are the pure in heart; for they shall see God" (Matt. v. 8). In regard to justification, we are perfectly clean by Christ's atonement; but in regard to sanctification, our hearts are not perfectly clean yet, but we have still need to pray, "Create in me a clean heart." Amen. O Lord! may thy blood and Spirit cleanse and sanctify me thoroughly from all my sins! Amen.

> Blessed with the joys of innocence
>   Adam our father stood,
> Till he debased his soul to sense,
>   And ate th' unlawful food.
>
> Now we are born a sensual race,
>   To sinful joys inclined;
> Reason has lost its native place,
>   And flesh enslaved the mind.
>
> Great God! renew our ruined frame,
>   Our broken powers restore;
> Inspire us with a heavenly flame,
>   And flesh shall reign no more!
>
> Eternal Spirit, write thy law
>   Upon our inward parts!
> And let the second Adam draw
>   His image on our hearts!

AUGUST 6.

And Enoch walked with God.—Gen. v. 24.

HAPPY they who, in their early days, are turned from sin, themselves, and the world, by repentance toward God, and faith in the promised seed, as Enoch was, who, from the time of his conversion, walked with God in a continued progress in his work and ways. To "walk with God," is to come out from a sinful generation and cleave to the Lord, as Noah and Caleb did; and God requires this of all believers (2 Cor. vi. 17). It is setting the Lord before our eyes continually, and fearing Him always, as Joseph and Nehemiah did; thereby avoiding everything that would offend Him. It is also making an open profession of faith in Him and zeal for His service, as our highest honor and best interest. And further, it is such a walk as obtains a holy intimacy and communion with God, which is kept up by constant meditation, prayer and praise; hearkening to the voice of His word and Spirit, and walking humbly before Him; hereby holiness is promoted and encouraged in the soul. Thus "Enoch walked with God;" thus he maintained a holy confidence in Him, committing all his ways to Him, always expecting help from Him, and rejoicing in the hopes of being with Him for ever.

For these happy ends the grace of God is sufficient for all that see their wants, and ask it. The Lord help us to seek it, that, like Enoch, we may walk with God here below, and live with Him for ever in glory. Amen.

> My heart is prone to rove, I see;
> Lord, plant it near thy bleeding side;
> Then will it kindly gaze on thee,
> And in thy love and fear abide.

AUGUST 7.

See that ye walk circumspectly; not as fools, but as wise. Be ye therefore not unwise, but understanding what the will of the Lord is.—Eph. v. 15, 17. *That ye may approve things that are excellent; that ye may be sincere, and without offence.*— Phil. i. 10. See also Luke xii. 36.

BELIEVERS have nothing more at heart than the will of God; being once convinced of that, they immediately set about it at all hazards; but sometimes they cannot come to a thorough knowledge of the same without great conflicts and patience. "For ye have need of patience, that after ye have done the will of God, ye might receive the promise" (Heb. x. 36). For the flesh is exceedingly crafty and froward; and though often forbid to go, it is as often calling out, "Howsoever, let me run" (2 Sam. xviii. 23). But the Lord will nevertheless carry them through. Yes, Lord, this thou hast done innumerable times. Oh! that I may trust thee also for the time to come, and not be so weak in faith any more. Oh! that my soul could feel at home with God, as in the presence of a kind father, and being glad in His presence, I might trust His offered grace, and walk not as the foolish, but as the wise, knowing and doing the will of the Lord.

> Beloved self must be denied,
>   The mind and will renewed;
> Passion suppressed, and patience tried,
>   And vain desires subdued.
>
> Flesh is a dangerous foe to grace,
>   Where it prevails and rules;
> Flesh must be humbled, pride abased,
>   Lest they destroy our souls.
>
> Lord, can a feeble, helpless worm,
>   Fulfill a task so hard?
> Thy grace must all my works perform,
>   And give the free reward.

August 8.

If ye be reproached for the name of Christ, happy are ye; for the Spirit of glory and of God resteth upon you.—1 Pet. iv. 14, 19. *Rejoice ye in that day, and leap for joy: for, behold, your reward is great in heaven.*—Luke vi. 23. *Whosoever shall confess me before men, him will I confess before my Father who is in heaven. But whosoever shall deny me before men, him will I also deny before my Father who is in heaven.*—Matt. x. 32, 33.

EVERY real Christian must expect persecution from the world; and though he should take heed of giving needless offence by self-will or rash conduct of any kind, yet should he not seek to shun the cross by what some men call prudence, or a sneaking compliance with the world, but be willing to suffer everything, rather than to hurt the cause of God in the least. We should openly confess Christ our Lord, and not mind being called fools by the wicked, as we know that at last they will call themselves by that name, therefore care not for the approbation and praise of the world; but count it a great honor to bear the reproach of Christ. Be willing rather to suffer persecution, and to be one of the despised in this world, than that the name of the Lord should suffer any dishonor by the countenance you may wish to give to some sin in order to avoid offence. O my soul, flee such temptation. It is not the will of the Lord that you yield.

> Blest are the suff'rers who partake
> Of pain and shame for Jesu's sake;
> Their souls shall triumph in the Lord;
> Glory and joy are their reward.
>
> The Lamb shall lead His heavenly flock
>   Where living fountains rise,
> And love Divine shall wipe away
>   The sorrows of their eyes.

AUGUST 9.

Take heed to your spirit.—Mal. ii. 15. *Those things which proceed out of the mouth come forth from the heart, and they defile the man.*—Matt. xv. 18. *The heart is deceitful above all things, and desperately wicked; who can know it?*—Jer. xvii. 9. *The imagination of the thoughts of man's heart is evil continually.*—Gen. vi. 5.

PRIVATE loop-holes, sinful lusts, can hide themselves at times so well as to seem quite dead; but if we grow careless, they spring up again on a favorable occasion, and sometimes appear in a spiritual shape, and take a fine spiritual name. Thus, though the flesh exceedingly likes sensual indulgences, yet to flatter its lust of pride, and the vanity of being thought a perfect man, it will sometimes endure great mortification. Therefore we ought always to be jealous of ourselves, and guard as much against self-righteousness as licentiousness; for the flesh is never more fleshly and dangerous than when it has the most spiritual appearance, and covers its lusts with the holiness and spirituality of angels.

> Sin has a thousand treach'rous arts
>   To practice on the mind;
> With flatt'ring looks she tempts our hearts,
>   But leaves a sting behind.
>
> With names of virtue she deceives
>   The aged and the young;
> And while the heedless wretch believes,
>   She makes his fetters strong.
>
> She pleads for all the joy she brings,
>   And gives a fair pretence;
> But cheats the soul of heavenly things,
>   And chains it down to sense.
>
> So on a tree divinely fair,
>   Grew the forbidden fruit;
> Our mother took the poison there,
>   And tainted all her blood.

AUGUST 10.

David's Prayer:—*O send out thy light and thy truth; let them lead me, let them bring me unto thy holy hill, and to thy tabernacles.*—Ps. xliii. 3.

Divine Answer:—*The path of the just is as the shining light, that shineth more and more unto the perfect day.*—Prov. iv. 18.

THE wiser we are in our own conceits, the more negligent are we in prayer, and the more destitute of true wisdom and faith; the more carnal are our feelings, the more trust and peace have we in our own righteousness: "for the Lord gives sight only to the blind, and to the babes," who pray for it. Therefore the deepest humblings go before the greatest blessings. O my blessed Saviour! since I am always blind and ignorant of myself, if I am not guided by thine eyes, I desire always to look up to thee, and do everything under thy direction. "O send out thy light and thy truth; let them lead me, let them bring me unto thy holy hill, and to thy tabernacles." "Let thy mercies come unto me, O Lord, even thy salvation, according to thy word" (Ps. cxix. 41).

> Prevent me, lest I harbor pride,
> Lest I in my own strength confide;
> Shew me my weakness; let me see
> I have my power, my all from thee.
>
> Enrich me always with thy love,
> My kind protector ever prove!
> The signet put upon my breast,
> And let thy Spirit on me rest.
>
> Assist and teach me how to pray;
> Incline my nature to obey;
> What thou abhorrest let me flee,
> And only love what pleases thee!
>
> O may I never do my will,
> But thine, and only thine fulfill!
> Let all my time and all my ways
> Be spent and ended to thy praise!

AUGUST 11.

By grace ye are saved. It is the gift of God.—Eph. ii. 5, 8. *Not by works of righteousness which we have done, but according to His mercy He saved us, by the washing of regeneration, and renewing of the Holy Ghost; which He shed on us abundantly through Jesus Christ our Saviour.*—Titus iii. 5, 6. See also John iii. 3, 5.

To rely on grace, and desire to be saved only by free grace, is a sweet exercise; but so far from being practiced enough, we have all need to learn the prayer of the Publican better still, since the Pharisee is ever busy to creep in again. But care must be taken that we do not build our faith only upon the sweet enjoyments of the grace of God, as it is procured by Christ, and promised to us through Christ; for which reason God sometimes denies us sensible enjoyments, that true faith may begin to act like itself, and depend upon nothing but His free grace in Christ. And this we have also boldness to do, should we ever seem to fall short of the due measure of faith, godly sorrow and repentance; for since there is no merit to be placed in these things, there is no certain measure and degree prescribed to all; but it is enough truly to hate sin, to desire grace, and sincerely to enter upon the Christian race.

> 'Tis not by works of righteousness
>   Which our own hands have done;
> But we are saved by sov'reign grace,
>   Abounding through His Son.
>
> 'Tis from the mercy of our God
>   That all our hopes begin;
> 'Tis by the water and the blood
>   Our souls are washed from sin.
>
> Raised from the dead, we live anew,
>   And justified by grace,
> We shall appear in glory too,
>   And see our Father's face.

AUGUST 12.

Whosoever committeth sin transgresseth also the law; for sin is the transgression of the law. And ye know that He was manifested to take away our sins.—1 John iii. 4, 5. *All unrighteousness is sin.*—Chap. v. 17. *When He had by Himself purged our sins, sat down on the right hand of the Majesty on high.*—Heb. i. 3.

THERE is a far greater power in the blood of Christ to save and cleanse, than in sin to defile and destroy (Rom. viii. 3). The law became weak to do good, but it hath power to condemn: "The strength of sin is the law:" the law gives strength to sin, because, by virtue of the curse of the law, sin reigns and defiles the souls of men, through that righteous curse, "The soul that sins shall die." But the blood of Jesus Christ hath greater power to save than sin, together with the law, hath to condemn; for the blood of Christ takes away and abolishes it utterly. Where this blood is applied and brought home, sin itself cannot ruin that soul. The soul is poisoned and corrupted by sin; but the blood of Christ takes away the guilt of sin, yet not the being of it; as we are sanctified but in part, we can only plead with God that we may be kept by Almighty power; and that Jesus may be for us, who is stronger than all that can come against us.

O dear incarnate Son of God,
Well wash me in thy precious blood!
Cast all my guilt into that sea,
And let no lust have power o'er me.
The shafts against my soul that sin and Satan wield,
Ward off, and be to me a refuge sure and shield.

In sore temptations be my guide,
My soul, in fiery trials, lead;
Me rescue from the power of hell,
Within thy house make me to dwell!
And, oh! at last, unspotted at thy Father's throne,
Present me through thy perfect righteousness alone.

August 13.

Be ye not as the horse, or as the mule, which have no understanding; whose mouth must be held in with bit and bridle, lest they come near unto thee. —Ps. xxxii. 9. Therefore, *if ye call on the Father, who without respect of persons judgeth according to every man's work, pass the time of your sojourning here in fear.*—1 Pet. i. 17.

READER, dost thou believe there is a God, and that He will shortly judge thee for every evil action thou hast done, and for all the secret iniquity of thy bosom?—how, then, canst thou meet thy Judge, unless thy heart be changed and thy sins are pardoned? There will be no room for dissembling, excusing, or escaping them. Begin therefore in time, O wretched man, to consider how thou must appear before that awful judgment seat! The door of mercy is yet open. Oh! call upon the Lord Jesus for repentance and pardon before the door be shut, and thou be lost for ever. The gulf of destruction is standing with an open mouth ready to receive thee; Jesus is also standing with His arms stretched widely out to receive and to welcome thee back to His Father and to thy Father's love. Whither dost thou choose to go! Oh! go to Jesus!

> O God, mine inmost soul convert;
> And deeply on my thoughtful heart
>   Eternal things impress;
> Give me to feel their solemn weight,
> And tremble on the brink of fate,
>   And wake to righteousness!
>
> Be this my one great business here,
> With serious industry and fear
>   My future bliss t' insure;
> Thine utmost counsel to fulfill,
> And suffer all thy righteous will,
>   And to the end endure!

August 14.

Be strong and of good courage. I will be with thee; I will not fail thee, nor forsake thee. Only be thou strong and very courageous. Oh! sweet commandment! *Be not afraid, neither be thou dismayed; for the Lord thy God is with thee whithersoever thou goest.* Oh! glorious promise! —Joshua i. 5, 6, 9. See also Isa. xiv. 4.

God calls upon us to be strong in faith; and strong faith will make men cheerful and courageous, and enable them to overcome strong difficulties. Therefore, if thy feet and heart are bound for Canaan, trust stoutly in the Lord to carry thee safely through all the trials and temptations that beset thy path, and to defend thee in all thy conflicts with the world and with Satan. Feeble as thou art, yet go on and fear nothing, for God is with thee. He that has but this one care, and fears not to displease Him, need not care for, or fear anything else; his safety is ensured in the promise of God, who will keep him harmless in all things. Oh! thou God of Israel, who didst lead thine ancient people to their desired rest, grant me to be strong and courageous in thee while traveling to *my* Canaan of peace; and may thy fear fill my heart!

> Awake, our souls, (away our fears,
>   Let every trembling thought be gone,)
> Awake and run the heavenly race,
>   And put a cheerful courage on.
>
> True, 'tis a strait and thorny road,
>   And mortal spirits tire and faint;
> But they forget the mighty God,
>   That feeds the strength of every saint.
>
> From Him, the overflowing spring,
>   Our souls shall drink a fresh supply;
> While such as trust their native strength
>   Shall melt away, and droop, and die.

August 15.

Behold the Lamb of God, who taketh away the sin of the world!—John i. 29. *These are they who came out of great tribulation, and have washed their robes, and made them white in the blood of the Lamb. Therefore are they before the throne of God, and serve Him day and night in His temple.*—Rev. vii. 14, 15.

These are they who have obtained pardon and purification through the blood of the Lamb; they are the Lamb's wife, arrayed in fine linen, clean and white; for the fine linen is the righteousness of saints (Rev. xix. 8). And it is because they are washed in the blood of the Lamb, that they are admitted to the immediate presence of God, and are before the throne. Nothing that is impure or unholy, or that defileth, can come there. He that washes himself continually in the blood of Christ, does not make light of sin, but detests it above all things; for what can be more abominable than sin, since it cannot be taken away but by the blood of the Son of God? This humbles true believers, and makes them watch against sin; and if it has not the same effect on thee, Reader, matters are not right with thy soul; for talking of the blood of the Lamb, and yet trifling with sin, cannot agree together, but shew a false or a deceived heart.

> Now will I hate those lusts of mine
>   That crucified my God;
> Those sins that pierced and nailed His flesh
>   Fast to the fatal wood.
>
> Yes, my Redeemer, they shall die,
>   My heart has so decreed;
> Nor will I spare the guilty things
>   That made my Saviour bleed.
>
> Whilst with a melting, broken heart,
>   My murdered Lord I view,
> I'll raise revenge against my sins,
>   And slay the murd'rers too.

August 16.

Verily I say unto you, They have their reward.—Matt. vi. 2. *Henceforth there is laid up for me a crown of righteousness, which the Lord, the righteous Judge, shall give me at that day; and not to me only, but unto all them also that love His appearing.*—2 Tim. iv. 8.

For this crown faith strives. And because this faith justifies, it makes the world say, Well, I also believe. But where is their conflict and conquest? It is answered, I rely on Christ and grace. But Canaan was also a free gift of grace, and yet it was not taken without conflicts. And moreover, as worldly people are unacquainted with the wickedness of their hearts, they do not trust alone upon grace, but on their duties and outward form of godliness,—self-love and pride still reigning in their hearts. When shalt thou, my soul, be driven from thy earthly stay? when shalt thou hope alone in Jesus, and be saved? How long shalt thou trust in an arm of flesh? Oh! turn now unto the Lord who begat thee, and in His strength fight, and thou shalt overcome all thine enemies; in Him have faith, and with thee all shall be well.

> No works nor duties of your own
> Can for the smallest sin atone;
> The robes that nature may provide
> Will not the least pollutions hide.
>
> Ye sons of pride, that kindle coals
> With your own hands to warm your souls,
> Walk in the light of your own fire,
> Enjoy the sparks that ye desire.
>
> This is your portion at my hands,
> Hell waits you with her iron bands;
> You shall lie down in sorrow there,
> In death, in darkness, and despair.

August 17.

Run with patience the race set before us.—Heb. xii. 1.

He that runs, and wants patience, will never get to the end of his race; for in the race of God's commandments men have foul play: one comes and rails on him for his zeal, for running so fast, when he thinks himself too slow; another gives him a blow and strikes him down, and up he gets and runs again. Every man will make room and give way to him that is in a race here; while he that runs the heavenly race may expect, and will find, many stand in his way, and stop him all they can, so that he will have great need of patience: without it everything will offend him. What is a wise man, a zealous man, without patience? He will bear nothing, suffer nothing, and can do no great good. David had many enemies that spake mischievous things against him, and laid snares for his life; but he was as a deaf man that "heard not; and as a dumb man that openeth not his mouth." Saul was twice in his power, yet he would not avenge himself of him; he wanted neither courage nor wisdom; he had a stirring spirit, a working head, was sensible of wrongs, knew himself innocent, his adversaries malicious; his thoughts must needs be troubled, and yet he was his own man under all; he committed his cause to God, his patience was in exercise, and he waited God's time of deliverance. Christ's active and passive obedience made him a complete Mediator: may thine, Reader, make thee a complete Christian!

> Awake, my soul, dismiss thy fears,
>   The sword of truth gird on,
> The Christian warfare boldly wage,
>   Nor think thou art alone;
> For Christ, thy King, by His all-strengthening power
> Shall safely guide thee till thy conflict's o'er.

August 18.

Whom God set forth to be a propitiation (mercy-seat) *through faith in His blood, etc.*—Rom. iii. 25.

God hath set forth the propitiation. From all eternity he proposed Christ to be the mercy-seat. The spring of all is from the Father, who is love. He proposed, revealed, and made Christ known to Adam, to Abraham, and to the prophets; He proposed the mercy-seat as an object of faith in all the sacrifices that were types of Christ;—this mercy-seat is clearly and fully set forth in the Gospel dispensation.

Whither shall I, a poor sinner, conscious of guilt and apprehensive of wrath, flee for refuge? Where shall I find it? Where but under the covert of atoning blood! While others have recourse to refuges of lies, and would establish a righteousness of their own, in the Lord, my righteousness, I find rest and safety. Having fled for refuge to lay hold on the hope set before me, in Christ, my hope, I shall have strong consolation. Does Jehovah from this mercy-seat offer pardon to me, a rebel sinner? Shall I not hear this voice of mercy, and live, and joy in God, through Christ? Will God commune with me from this mercy-seat, and bless me with the manifestation of His love? Oh! delightful interview, when most alone, retired from the world, but least alone when with my God! Oh! the inexpressible pleasure of secret devotion, of "a life hid with Christ in God!" If the contemplation of Divine love here below be so ravishing, oh! what shall I experience above? "My God, guide me here by thy counsel, and afterward receive me to glory."

> Lord, while I live, my light, my truth,
> My all-atoning Saviour be;
> While here, me by thy counsel guide;
> At death, take me to be with thee.

AUGUST 19.

No man can serve two masters; for either he will hate the one, and love the other; or else he will hold to the one, and despise the other. Ye cannot serve God and mammon.—Matt. vi. 24. *If I yet pleased men, I should not be the servant of Christ.*—Gal. i. 10. *Love not the world, neither the things that are in the world. If any man love the world, the love of the Father is not in him.*—1 John ii. 15.

DOTH Satan tempt thee, either by pleasures, dignities, or profits? O my soul, stand upon thy guard, gird on thy strength with such thoughts as these:—What can the world profit me if the cares of it choke me? How can pleasures comfort me if their sting poison me? or what advancement is this, to be triumphing in honor before the face of men here, and to be trembling with confusion before the throne of God hereafter? What are the delights of the world to the peace of my conscience, or the joy that is in the Holy Ghost? What are the applauses of men to the crown prepared by God? or what is the gain of the world to the loss of my soul? The vanity of the creature is far beneath the excellency of my soul; and the things of time not worthy to be mentioned with the things of eternity. Two masters, of such opposite principles as God and mammon, I cannot serve; therefore Satan, upon the most deliberate consideration, I must give thee and thy service up, for thou biddest me to my loss.

> Two masters are too much for me;
> Nor can the world with God agree;
> Then, tempting mammon, get thee gone,
> And let me serve my Christ alone.

August 20.

O taste and see that the Lord is good!—Ps. xxxiv. 8. *Jesus Christ the same yesterday, to-day, and for ever.*—Heb. xiii. 8.

There is an infinite fullness of all spiritual blessings treasured up in Christ Jesus for all His people; and out of His fullness they do receive, even grace for grace. But, alas! we are slow of heart to believe the truth; we please ourselves with small things, and come slowly forward to a daily growth out of that fullness. Young converts, enamored with what they have in hand, or living upon their feelings, are ready to flee from knowledge, as something dangerous and destructive of holiness; and mere professors are apt to deny and even deride those precious feelings, as though the affections had no share in the Christian religion, and that the whole consisted in having a crowded head. Come, then, O my soul, divest thyself from the pride of party and the strife of tongues! Be thou an humble supplicant at the feet of Jesus, for a live coal from off the altar, to purge away thine iniquity, and to warm thy affections; and likewise for the aid of the Holy Spirit, to lead thee into "the knowledge of the only true God, and Jesus Christ whom He hath sent." Then shalt thou not only taste but see, not only see but taste, both sweetly taste and clearly see, that "the Lord is good."

> Oh! the rich depths of love Divine;
> Of bliss a boundless store;
> Dear Saviour, let me call thee mine;
> I cannot wish for more.
>
> On thee alone my hope relies;
> Beneath thy cross I fall;
> Thou art my life, my sacrifice,
> My Saviour, and my All.

August 21.

We speak the wisdom of God in a mystery, even the hidden wisdom, which God ordained before the world to our glory.—1 Cor. ii. 7. *Even the mystery which hath been hid from ages and from generations, but now is made manifest to His saints.*—Col. i. 26.

There are some things declared in the Gospel, which are absolutely its own, that are proper and peculiar unto it; such as have no footsteps in the law, or in the light of nature, but are of pure revelation, peculiar to the Gospel. Of this nature are all things concerning the love and will of God in Jesus Christ; the mystery of His Incarnation, of His Offices and whole Mediation, of the Dispensation of the Spirit and our Participation thereof, and our Union with Christ thereby; our Adoption, Justification, and effectual Sanctification thence proceeding. In a word, everything that belongs unto the purchase and application of saving grace is of this sort. These tidings are properly evangelical, being peculiar to the Gospel alone. Hence the Apostle Paul, unto whom the dispensation of it was committed, puts that eminency upon them, that (in comparison) he resolved to insist on nothing else in his preaching (1 Cor. ii. 2). And to that purpose doth he describe his ministry (Eph. iii. 7–11).

Reader, observe these two things:—What God reveals in His Word, let thy reason submit unto;—what He proposes as objects or matter of faith, beg of Him to enable thee to believe.

> The hidden wisdom of God's grace
>   No reason can explore;
> Then help me, by the Spirit's light,
>   To see, believe, adore.

AUGUST 22.

Blessed be the God and Father of our Lord Jesus Christ, who hath blessed us with all spiritual blessings in heavenly places in Christ.—Eph. i. 3.

FROM natural constitution we earnestly expect present gratification. It is by no means sufficient, therefore, to explain to us our duty, or enforce it by future rewards and punishments. There must be pleasures at hand, to outweigh the enticements of sin, and outbid whatever that sorceress can offer. The religion of Jesus is constituted in this manner; it brings the possession of the best happiness here—a rich foretaste in this life of heavenly glory. Salvation cometh of the Lord to the sinner upon believing, just as a most ample estate bequeathed to a beggar in debt; at once it alters his whole condition, pays all he owes, supplies all he wants, gives him rank, figure and authority, to which before he was a perfect stranger. Such blessedness, in the pardon of all my sins, in access to God with confidence, in victory over my spiritual enemies, give me, O my God, to enjoy!

> Thou only Sov'reign of my heart,
>   My refuge, my almighty Friend;
> How can my soul from thee depart,
>   Or whom alone my hopes depend!
>
> Eternal life thy words impart,
>   On these my fainting spirit lives;
> Here sweeter comforts cheer my heart
>   Than all the round of nature gives.
>
> Let earth's alluring joys combine,
>   While thou art near in vain they call;
> One smile, one blissful smile of thine,
>   My dearest Lord, outweighs them all.
>
> Low at thy feet my soul would lie,
>   Here safely dwells and peace Divine;
> Still let me live beneath thine eye,
>   For life, eternal life, is thine!

AUGUST 23.

Spare not, lengthen thy cords, and strengthen thy stakes; for thou shalt break forth on the right hand and on the left; and thy seed shall inherit the Gentiles, and make the desolate cities to be inhabited.—Isa. liv. 2, 3.

How comfortable is it to the religious man to behold an increase of the true worshipers of God! and more especially in that place where his soul has dwelt among lions, and been "vexed from day to day with the filthy conversation of the wicked!" To see the banner of Christ set up there, and numbers flock unto it, as doves to their windows,—to see the kingdom of Satan weaken and contract, and the kingdom of God and His Christ strengthen and enlarge,—to see the hand of the Lord protecting and providing for His people, going before them like the pillar and cloud, refreshing them by day and by night;—this is indeed a feast of fat things. Lord, grant that I may be thankful for what I have already seen, and may behold thy glory thus displayed more and more. And while thou lengthenest our cords, do thou help us to strengthen our stakes, by holding fast the form of sound words, living as persons professing godliness, shewing that we are Christians indeed, by love to each other, and keeping the unity of the Spirit in the bond of peace! Thus shall our light shine before men, and the light of thy Gospel break forth on the right hand and on the left, and make the desolate cities to be inhabited.

> Arise, thou Son of Righteousness,
>   And bless the world with heavenly light;
> Break forth, and shew thy Gospel grace,
>   Attended with thy Spirit's might.

August 24.

If a man also strive for masteries, yet is he not crowned except he strive lawfully.—2 Tim. ii. 5; namely, in faith, by which we have the victory. And as the enemies return again and again, and are always crafty and strong, we must continually be in arms. *Until now the kingdom of heaven suffereth violence.*—Matt. xi. 12.

WITH what is all this striving, and against what is this violence to be used? Let the Christian— him who strives lawfully—tell. All hell opens every step he takes. He is determined to have his soul saved; and to help him to this, all his sins, all his evil companions, are to be fought and vanquished. But to win heaven, he must strive lawfully, that is, strive in faith. If those cannot expect to be crowned who strive, but not lawfully, what must become of those who do not strive at all? O Lord, strengthen me therefore to get the victory; for it greatly exalts thy glory if the power of mine enemies be broken; and thy grace is able to overcome the greatest power of sin, and will destroy it effectually at last, since thou hast promised that grace shall endure, and grow, and conquer, while sin is condemned to death, and is actually dying more and more, when nailed to the cross of Christ.

> Stand up, my soul, shake off thy fears,
>   And gird the Gospel armor on;
> March to the gates of endless joys,
>   Where thy great Captain Saviour's gone.
>
> What though the Prince of Darkness rage,
>   And waste the fury of his spite?
> Eternal chains confine him down
>   To fiery deeps and endless night.
>
> What though thine inward lusts rebel?
>   'Tis but a struggling gasp for life;
> The weapons of victorious grace
>   Shall slay thy sins and end the strife.

AUGUST 25.

It is not of him that willeth, but of God that shew-eth mercy.—Rom. ix. 16. *Thou hast a little strength.*—Rev. iii. 8. *But go in this thy might, etc. Surely I will be with thee.*—Judges vi. 14, 16.

A LITTLE strength is also the strength of God through Christ, the second Adam; and, consequently, stronger than the power of Satan and the first Adam should it seem ever so strong. Believers in such a state may think themselves weaker than before they had any grace, not being able now to put such a force upon themselves as formerly; because they dare not now be wrought on by pride: for they no longer swim with the stream, and experience no resistance; but swimming against the stream, feel the force of the current of lust. But it is to be remembered, that hypocrisy and proud nature, desirous of being seen, can outdo grace in many outward things, and have a better appearance in the eyes of man; for real Christians, not being willing to be worked upon by nature any longer, and yet having but little strength, cannot put such a constraint upon themselves continually, but they may be in this manner tossed to and fro; which the Lord wisely permits for their good, to convince them the more of their own insufficiency and nothingness, that they may rely on the strength of the Lord. Therefore we must not give over praying and hoping in this case; but as it is only the mercy and power of Christ which preserves and strengthens the poor and feeble, we rather ought to be more earnest in drawing near to Him with all our misery, weariness and nakedness.

> Mere mortal power shall fade and die,
>   And youthful vigor cease;
> But we that wait upon the Lord,
>   Shall feel our strength increase.

August 26.

If after they have escaped the pollutions of the world, through the knowledge of the Lord and Saviour Jesus Christ, they are again entangled therein and overcome, the latter end is worse with them than the beginning.—2 Peter ii. 20.

Some affirm that experienced Christians meet with no strong temptations, and feel no evil suggestions from within, and, of consequence, no strivings against the same: but it is quite the contrary; for beginners strive generally more against the outward pollutions of the world, whilst the experienced turn their force more against their inward and spiritual iniquities. Therefore take heed to your spirit, though your meaning be ever so good, and your assurance ever so great. Be not highminded, for fear of falling. Beware of all sins; for the least may, unawares, and by degrees, draw thee into many others, so as to be at last entangled in such a manner, that without great watchfulness it will be impossible to be disengaged; therefore, be not deceived; flee all occasions of sin. Say not within thyself, It is a light matter, it only concerns outward things, which do not belong to the essence of Christianity; for such outward liberty is a sure evidence of a false inward levity of mind. And by conforming to the world, we give a good handle to the enemy of souls to ruin us; and by sad experience, we shall be convinced in time, that our latter end is worse than the beginning.

> Oh! for a persevering power
> To keep thy just commands;
> We would defile our hearts no more,
> No more pollute our hands.
>
> Oh! for the grace that keeps our souls
> In Jesus every hour,
> We'd wash our hands in innocence,
> Nor feel the Tempter's power.

August 27.

Be kindly affectioned one to another with brotherly love; in honor preferring one another. If it be possible, as much as lieth in you, live peaceably with all men.—Rom. xii. 10, 18. *Follow peace with all men, and holiness, without which no man shall see the Lord.*—Heb. xii. 14.

There is much contest in the world about property; but believers taking Christ for their only property, whom nobody can take from them, have, in Him alone, immense treasures and lasting peace. And since wrath and anger turn into nothing but disquietness, and are punished by themselves, why dost thou suffer thyself to be easily moved by them? The least provocation, even a single word, perhaps, will stir up the corruption of thine heart, so as to change thy countenance and make thee utter dreadful words. Therefore, consider how God bears with thee, and what an abomination anger is. It is a fire from hell, the true image of the old Dragon; but being called to bear the image of God, and bring forth the fruits of the good Spirit, thou art to follow the lamb-like mind of Christ: and to that purpose, it is highly necessary, first, To avoid all occasions of strife and contention; secondly, To bridle our tongue if quarrels arise; thirdly, To suffer when we are wronged; fourthly, To pray directly, and quench the sparks of fire before they break out into a flame. This is the easiest and the only method to prevent great troubles, and lead a peaceful, happy life: for anger carries uneasiness; and love a sweet rest in itself.

> Blessed are the men of peaceful life,
> Who quench the coals of growing strife;
> They shall be called the heirs of bliss,
> The sons of God, the God of Peace.

AUGUST 28.

Having therefore, brethren, boldness to enter into the holiest by the blood of Jesus, etc., let us draw near with a true heart, in full assurance of faith, having our hearts sprinkled (with the blood of Christ, by which *He once entered into the Holy Place, having obtained eternal redemption for us, and purged our conscience from dead works, to serve the living God) from an evil conscience, and our bodies washed with pure water.*—Heb. x. 19-22.

CHRIST has for ever purged our sin by Himself; "for by one offering He hath perfected for ever them that are sanctified" (chap. x. 14); and to this sprinkling of the blood of Christ, all believers, even the weakest, are to come, in order to receive the forgiveness of sins; and the blood is said to be sprinkled, to shew the need of its application to the conscience by the Holy Spirit. In this purple fountain the believer daily washes; it is his element and life. Thus he "lives by the faith of the Son of God, who also loved him," always applying His ransom to his soul, and pleading His merits before his heavenly Father, which keeps his conscience pure and easy. Oh! may I be enabled every day, by faith, to wash in the fountain of Christ's blood!

> They find access at every hour
>   To God within the veil;
> Hence they derive a quickening power,
>   And joys that never fail.
>
> Oh! may this happy lot be mine,
>   Daily to live to Christ;
> And like the favored of the twelve,
>   To lean upon His breast.
>
> Oh! happy soul! oh! glorious state
>   Of ever-flowing grace!
> To dwell so near the Father's throne,
>   And see His holy face.

AUGUST 29.

That which may be known of God is manifest in them; for God has shewed it unto them.—Rom. i. 19. *Which when the apostles, Barnabas and Paul, heard of, they rent their clothes, and ran in among the people, crying out and saying, Sirs, why do ye these things? etc.*—Acts xiv. 14, to end.

THERE are some things declared and enjoined in the Gospel which have their foundation in the law and light of nature; such are all the moral duties which are taught therein; these, the remaining light of nature, though obscurely, yet does teach and confirm. The apostle, speaking of mankind in general, says, "That which may be known of God is manifest in them;" the essential properties of God rendering our moral duty to Him necessary, are known by the light of nature; and by the same light are men able to make a judgment of their actions, whether they be good or evil (Rom. ii. 14, 15). The same law and light which discover these things, do also enjoin their observance. Thus it is with all men before the preaching of the Gospel to them. The Gospel adds two things to the minds of men:—
1. It directs us to a right performance of these things from a right principle, by a right rule, and to a right end, so that they, and we in them, may obtain acceptance with God. Hereby it gives them a new nature, and turns moral duties into evangelical obedience. 2. By a communication of that Spirit which is joined to its dispensation, it supplies us with strength for their performance in the manner it directs.

> May God the fruits of heavenly grace
> Produce within my heart;
> And by that grace may many learn
> To choose the better part.

AUGUST 30.

*Who shall separate us from the love of Christ?
Shall tribulation, or distress, or persecution, or
famine, or nakedness, or peril, or sword? Nay,
in all these things we are more than conquerors,
through Him that loved us. For I am persuaded,
that neither death nor life shall separate us from
the love of God which is in Christ Jesus our
Lord.*—Rom. viii. 35, 37-39.

STARS shine brightest in the darkest night;
torches are better for beating; grapes come not to
the proof till they come to the press; spices smell
best when bruised; young trees root the faster for
shaking; gold looks brighter for scouring; juniper
smells sweetest in the fire; the palm-tree proves
the better for pressing; chamomile, the more you
tread it, the more you spread it. Such is the condition of all God's children: they are then most
triumphant when most tempted; most glorious
when most afflicted; most in favor of God when
least in man's, and least in their own; as their
conflicts, so their conquests; as their tribulations,
so their triumphs; true salamanders, that live best
in the furnace of persecution: so that heavy afflictions are the best benefactors to heavenly affections;
and where afflictions hang heaviest, corruptions
hang loosest; and grace, that is hid in nature, as
sweet water in rose-leaves, is then most fragrant
when the fire of affliction is put under to distil it
out.

> My life, and all its comforts too,
> From God's abundant bounty flow;
> And when He calleth back His own,
> Contented I would lay it down.
>
> Then if men scorn and Satan roar,
> Yet, strengthened by the God of power,
> His faithful witness I shall be;
> Though weak, I can do all through Thee.

AUGUST 31.

Rise up, my love, my fair one, and come away; for, lo, the winter is past, the rain is over and gone; the flowers appear on the earth; the time of the singing of birds is come, and the voice of the turtle is heard in our land, etc. Arise, my love, my fair one, and come away. O my dove, thou art in the clefts of the rock, etc.—Song of Sol. ii. 10-14.

O LORD, how often has it been winter with me, but thou hast always quickened me again! Grant that by these experiences I may be so used to thy ways, as always to expect the best from thee in everything, and to have only this one care, namely, how I may please thee as thy bride and dove, and be accepted through thee with thy Father! Let my faith be so strengthened by all thy various dealings with me, that at last I may have boldness, and find complete rest in thy wounds, my crucified Saviour, where there is room for the greatest of sinners, even for me who am the chief.

> The voice of my Beloved sounds
> Over the rocks and rising grounds;
> O'er hills of guilt, and seas of grief.
> He leaps, He flies to my relief.
>
> Gently He draws my heart along,
> Both with His beauty and His tongue;
> Rise, says my Lord, make haste, away;
> No mortal joys are worth thy stay.
>
> The Jewish wintry state is gone,
> The mists are fled, the spring comes on;
> The sacred turtle-dove we hear
> Proclaim the new, the joyful year.
>
> And when we hear our Jesus say,
> "Rise up, My love, make haste, away!"
> Our hearts would fain outfly the wind,
> And leave all earthly loves behind.

SEPTEMBER I.

Be not conformed to this world.—Rom. xii. **2.** *Love not the world, neither the things that are in the world, etc. He that doeth the will of God abideth for ever.*—1 John ii. 15, 17.

READER, whose will dost thou do? Examine thyself. Perhaps thou thinkest, to love the world and to do its will cannot be a great sin, because many reputed honest men and good Christians do the same. Nay, but for thy soul's sake consider what the Scripture says, If thou "lovest the world, the love of the Father is not in thee;" and without this love of the Father, thou hast no faith; and, being destitute of faith, thou hast no Christ, and consequently no life and salvation. Consider further, whether thou dost not love the world above either God or thy own soul. Hast thou not a hundred thoughts about the world for one of God or thy soul? Dost thou not talk a hundred times more about the world, and is not thy pursuit continually after it, to the neglect of God and thy soul? Then, the world is thine idol; thou lovest not God, and art murdering thy soul. The Lord have mercy on thee!

> I send the things of earth away;
>   Away, ye tempters of the mind,
> False as the smooth, deceitful sea,
>   And empty as the whistling wind.
>
> Your streams were floating me along,
>   Down to the gulf of black despair;
> And whilst I listened to your song,
>   Your streams had near conveyed me there.
>
> Lord, I adore thy matchless grace,
>   That warned me from the deep abyss;
> That drew me from those treach'rous seas,
>   And bade me seek superior bliss.
>
> Now to the shining realms above
>   I stretch my hands and glance my eyes;
> Oh! for the pinions of a dove,
>   To bear me to the upper skies!

September 2.

Not fashioning yourselves according to the former lusts in your ignorance; but as He who has called you is holy, so be ye holy (Note) *in all manner of conversation.*—1 Peter i. 14, 15. *Give diligence to make your calling and election sure; for the time past of our life may suffice us to have wrought the will of the Gentiles, etc.*—1 Peter iv. 3.

NONE can be so sure of salvation as to be for ever free from fears and doubts; for there is no assurance without conflicts: therefore all diligence is required to be evermore sure of it, so as to have boldness even in death. But let us take heed of presumption, since we do not know what may befall us at last; and be careful not to despise or overdrive the weaker sort of Christians, nor make our own experience a general rule for others, lest this comfortable doctrine of assurance prove a torment to them who have not yet attained it. Let all who have received a measure of grace be thankful; yet not rest in it; but press forward, fighting the good fight of faith, till they lay hold on eternal life.

How short and hasty is our life!
  How vast our souls' affairs!
Yet senseless mortals vainly strive
  To lavish out their years.

God from on high invites us home,
  But we march heedless on;
And ever hastening to the tomb,
  Stoop downward as we run.

How we deserve the deepest hell
  That slight the joys above!
What chains of vengeance should we feel
  That break such cords of love!

Draw us, O God, with sovereign grace,
  And lift our thoughts on high,
That we may end this mortal race,
  And see salvation nigh!

SEPTEMBER 3.

For the Son of Man is come to seek and to save that which was lost.—Luke xix. 10.

WHOEVER seriously seeks to be saved both from the power and punishment of sin, and seeks deliverance only through Christ, should not give way to heaviness of heart; for consider, Art thou a lost sinner? Christ's salvation is brought to such. Art thou seeking His salvation? This is a good token that Christ has sought thee, else thou wouldst not seek after Him. Whom Christ seeks He saves. Now, therefore, call upon Him diligently to set up His kingdom in thy bosom, and say to thyself, O my soul, it was the very purpose of Christ's coming into the world to save sinners circumstanced just as thou art! yea, though thy sins be as scarlet, be not thou cast down, O my soul, and be not disquieted within me; but encourage a cheerful hope in thy Covenant God, and instead of poring only upon thy sins, consider the exceeding love of Christ in dying for them; and, constrained by a sense of that love, do thy diligence to live unto Him; and for this He will enable thee by His Holy Spirit.

> The Lord of life and glory stands;
> Aloud He cries, and spreads His hands,
> He calls ten thousand sinners round,
> And sends a voice from every wound.
>
> "An ample pardon here I give,
> And bid the sentenced rebel live;
> Shew him my Father's smiling face,
> And lodge him in His dear embrace.
>
> I purge from sin's detested stain,
> And make the crimson white again;
> Lead to celestial joys refined,
> And lasting as the deathless mind."
>
> O Jesus! let me doubt no more;
> But hear, and wonder, and adore,
> Till death shall make my last remove
> To dwell for ever in thy love!

SEPTEMBER 4.

Repent ye (oh! change your minds) *and believe the Gospel.*—Mark i. 15. *From that time Jesus began to preach, and to say, Repent; for the kingdom of heaven is at hand.*—Matt. iv. 17. *Repent ye therefore, and be converted, that your sins may be blotted out, when the times of refreshing shall come from the presence of the Lord.*—Acts iii. 19.

REPENTANCE, or a godly sorrow for sin, is the doctrine of the Gospel. This is absolutely necessary to faith in the Lord Jesus Christ, and a life of union and communion with Him. Oh! reader, the Baptist calls thee to repent; Jesus calls thee to repent; the God of heaven and earth calls thee to repent; and without it thou wilt perish eternally in the flames of hell. Canst thou not give thyself the grace of repentance? Thou canst not. Oh! then pray and cry to the blessed Jesus, that His Holy Spirit may produce this saving change in thee. Pray to Him that He would give thee a living, justifying faith in His blood and righteousness, and that thy heart may be filled with real sorrow for sin, with holy indignation against it, and with a sincere and active departing from it. Oh! pray that you may walk by faith and not by sight, as seeing Him continually, who to the natural eye is invisible.

> Mistaken souls, that dream of heaven,
>   And make their empty boast
> Of inward joys and sins forgiven,
>   While they are slaves to lust!
>
> Vain are our fancy's airy flights,
>   If faith be cold and dead;
> None but a living power unites
>   To Christ, the living Head.
>
> 'Tis faith that purifies the heart;
>   'Tis faith that works by love;
> That bids our sins and lusts depart,
>   And lifts our souls above.

September 5.

What I say unto you, I say unto all, Watch.—Mark xiii. 37. See also verse 33, and chap. xiv. 38.

On a day set apart for the celebration of some great event, how anxious are the people to get in time to the place appointed! What earnestness is to be seen in their looks! As earnest should we be in watching for the hour in which our Lord shall come, that we may not be ashamed before Him. A heart deceived by sin may suggest many arguments against this holy earnestness; but they are the reasonings of folly. It is a general warning, "What I say unto you, I say unto all, Watch." Almost every day affords an instance of some one hurried into eternity on a sudden. Was not hourly watchfulness necessary, a merciful God would not permit such sudden deaths. But He hath sounded the alarm, "Ye know not what hour our Lord doth come." Give me grace, O Lord, to live always as if I heard that solemn voice sounding continually in my ears, "Awake, ye dead, and come to judgment!"

> Awake, my drowsy soul, awake,
>   And view the threat'ning scene;
> Legions of foes encamp around,
>   And treachery lurks within.
>
> Now to the work of God awake;
>   Behold thy Master near;
> The various, arduous task pursue
>   With vigor and with fear.
>
> The awful register goes on;
>   Th' account will surely come;
> And opening day, or closing night,
>   May bear me to my doom.
>
> Tremendous thought! how deep it strikes,
>   Yet, like a dream it flies;
> Till God's own voice the slumbers chase
>   From these deluded eyes.

SEPTEMBER 6.

David's Prayer :—*Now also, when I am old and gray-headed, O God, forsake me not.*—Ps. lxxi. 18. *O keep my soul, and deliver me: let me not be ashamed; for I put my trust in thee. Let integrity and uprightness preserve me; for I wait on thee.*—Ps. xxv. 20, 21.

Divine Answer :—*Hearken unto me, O house of Jacob, which are borne by me from the belly. Even to your old age I am He, and even to your hoary hairs will I carry you: I have made, and I will bear; even I will carry, and will deliver you.*—Isa. xlvi. 3, 4.

GOD never does forsake a true believer, since he is as closely united to Christ as a child to its mother whilst carried in her womb. Yea, a mother may forget her sucking child; but Jesus never forgets His ransomed people. His eyes are upon them for good continually; they are graven on the palms of His hands, and lodged in His pierced side, close to His heart. We may expect everything confidently from Him; and this confidence pleaseth Him above all things. Then, oh! may I "be careful for nothing, but in everything, by prayer and supplication, with thanksgiving, make my requests known unto Him" (Phil. iv. 6); always trusting that He will as certainly carry me through all difficulties to come as He has done hitherto; so that I may even give Him thanks for it beforehand. O Lord, grant that I may practice this better still!

> My God, my everlasting hope,
>   I live upon thy truth;
> Thine hands have held my childhood up,
>   And strengthened all my youth.
>
> Still has my life new wonders seen
>   Repeated every year;
> Behold, my days that yet remain
>   I trust them to thy care.

SEPTEMBER 7.

Trust ye not in lying words, saying, The temple of the Lord, the temple of the Lord, the temple of the Lord, are these ; but thoroughly amend your ways and your doings, etc.—Jer. vii. 4, 5. Of true prayer and worship in spirit and in truth. *God is a Spirit; and they that worship Him, must worship Him in spirit and in truth.*—John iv. 24. See also Rom. xii. 1; James i. 27.

As a contrite heart is the most pleasing temple of God, so speaking with God in words of our own, as a child does with his father, is the best book of prayer. The most cunning method by which Satan deceives many now, is the mistaking of an extensive knowledge and an assurance of their own making, not witnessed by the Spirit, for true faith ; or trusting on some outward form of worship, or having communion with others, or pretending to Gospel-experience and liberty, and thereby claiming the office of building up souls, though a true change was never wrought in their hearts ; for what can all our reading, prayers, going to church and sacrament, profit us, without this? Before all this shall be acceptable to the Lord, we must be renewed in our minds, and prove by our own words and deeds that we are the living temples of God.

> Is there a thing beneath the sun
>   That strives with thee my heart to share?
> Ah ! tear it thence, and reign alone,
>   The Lord of every motion there ;
> Then shall my heart from earth be free
> When it has found repose in thee.
>
> Oh ! hide this self from me, that I
>   No more, but Christ in me may live.
> My vile affections crucify ;
>   Let not one darling lust survive ;
> In all things may I nothing see,
> Nothing desire or seek but thee.

SEPTEMBER 8.

David's Prayer :—*Forsake me not, O Lord ; O my God, be not far from me.*—Ps. xxxviii. 21.

Divine Answer :—*My kindness shall not depart from thee, neither shall the covenant of my peace be removed, saith the Lord that has mercy on thee. O thou afflicted! I will lay thy stones with fair colors, and lay thy foundations with sapphires; etc.*—Isa. liv. 10-15.

Such as have never felt spiritual distress, cannot relish this word of promise ; but they who have been brought out of great misery by this sweet word, or any other word of promise applied to their hearts by the Holy Ghost, will henceforth take hold of it and prize it ; yea, they should firmly believe, even without a present feeling of its comfort, that God will certainly perform the promise He has once sealed upon them. He is a God that changeth not, and a God in covenant with His people, and His covenant is everlasting ; therefore He will not forsake His people, but order all things for their good, and conduct them safely through their pilgrimage, though violent enemies assault them, and mighty tempests fall upon them. His faithfulness stands engaged for this.

> Firm are the words His prophets give,
> Sweet words, on which believers live ;
> Each of them is the voice of God,
> Who spoke and spread the skies abroad.
>
> Oh ! for a strong, a lasting faith,
> To credit what th' Almighty saith ;
> T' embrace the message of His Son,
> And call the joys of heaven our own.
>
> Then should the earth's old pillars shake,
> And all the wheels of nature break ;
> Our steady souls should fear no more
> Than solid rocks when billows roar.

September 9.

Trust in the Lord with all thine heart; lean not unto thine own understanding. In all thy ways acknowledge Him, and He shall direct thy paths. Be not wise in thine own eyes: fear the Lord, and depart from evil.—Prov. iii. 5-7. *Be not wise in your own conceits,*—Rom. xii. 16; *for the wisdom of this world is foolishness with God.*—1 Cor. iii. 19. See also Isa. v. 21.

Whoever desires to know the will of the Lord, and prayeth earnestly for instruction, shall certainly know His will. But he must not be wise in his own conceit, nor lean to his own understanding, nor expect that the wisdom or learning of this world will explain the things of God. He must not seek to reconcile the word to his lusts, but combat his lusts by the word. In short, he must come to Jesus for instruction with the same simplicity of mind as a child comes to learn its letters; and not come for a month or a year, but sit all his life at the feet of Jesus, to receive instruction from Him. Lord, make me jealous of myself, enable me to go in and out with prayer, and keep me from all errors that may hurt my soul.

> Thus saith the wisdom of the Lord,—
> Bless'd is the man that hears my word;
> Keeps daily watch before my gates,
> And at my feet for mercy waits.
>
> The soul that seeks me shall obtain
> Immortal wealth and heavenly gain;
> Immortal life is his reward,
> Life and the favor of the Lord.
>
> But the vile wretch that flies from me
> Doth his own soul an injury;
> Fools that against my grace rebel,
> Seek death, and love the road to hell.

SEPTEMBER 10.

So we preach, and so ye believed.—1 Cor. xv. 11.

THE method of the Gospel is this: First, it proposeth things which are peculiarly its own. So the Apostle sets down the constant entrance of his preaching (1 Cor. xv. 3). It reveals its own mysteries, laying them as the foundations of faith and obedience; and it also inlays them in the mind, thereby conforming the whole soul unto them (Rom. vi. 17; Gal. iv. 19; Tit. ii. 11, 12; 1 Cor. iii. 11; 2 Cor. iii. 18). This foundation being laid, it then grafts all duties of moral obedience on the stock of faith in Christ Jesus. Where this foundation is not laid through ignorance, or rejected through prejudice, the Gospel has nothing to do with such men; it neither renews their souls, nor produces any genuine fruit of obedience. Thus the Apostle Paul, in all his epistles, teaches first the mysteries of faith that are peculiar to the Gospel, and then descends unto those moral duties which are regulated thereby; so we must first hear the Gospel, and be acquainted with its discoveries, before we can believe aright: and when our faith is rightly founded, it is to shew itself in the practice of all those good works that are required of us in the Scriptures. "As many as walk according to this rule, peace be on them, and mercy, and upon the Israel of God."

> Let all thy precepts good and right,
> And laws which in thy word are found,
> And the strong faith which gives these weight,
> Be always in me and abound.
>
> And, oh! reveal thy Gospel-truth,
> And plant it in my mind, O Lord,
> So will my spirit be renewed,
> And yield obedience to thy word.

September 11.

How can I do this great wickedness, and sin against God?—Gen. xxxix. 9.

Joseph was a slave, and in a strange country; he was tempted by a wanton and revengeful mistress; had he complied, he would have been sure of secrecy and rewards; but if he resisted, he might expect her keenest resentment, if not the loss of his life. Yet all these could not influence him; he chooses to submit to every inconvenience and danger, rather than be guilty of so foul a crime and sin against God. From hence we may learn, that the fear of God is a most effectual preservative against all criminal indulgences. It was this that restrained Joseph, and will, where it is possessed, have the same effect on all mankind, upon all occasions, and in every scene of life. It strikes every passion, every spring of human actions, and includes in it all the most powerful motives by which the conduct of mankind is determined. If interest be the principal thing that sways us, that surely cannot be so certainly promoted as by securing the favor of God, and avoiding His displeasure. If we are governed by our fears, He is the most formidable being in the universe to a mind that has perverted its faculties and transgressed the laws of its nature; if by hope, He is the Supreme God; if by love, He is the most amiable and perfect Excellence; if by gratitude, He is the Author of all our happiness.

> Give me, O Lord, such godly fear
>   As feels thy presence nigh;
> And looks to thee when sin is near,
>   And makes the Tempter fly.
>
> Nor let me e'er thy name forget,
>   In sad nor happy hour,
> But through temptation's keenest state
>   Be guided by thy power.

SEPTEMBER 12.

I have found the book of the law in the house of the Lord. Because thy heart was tender, and thou hast humbled thyself before the Lord, etc.— 2 Kings xxii. 8, 19.

THE priests, probably to save themselves the trouble of writing, and the people of reading the book at large, had furnished themselves with abstracts of the law, leaving out, or slightly mentioning some parts thereof, and particularly the threatenings,—which Josiah was so much affected with, as being new to him. The book of God's law seems in our day to be lost; a sealed book to most of the congregations that profess themselves Christians; imperfect accounts of it are given, which hide the promised blessings and threatened curses of God. When this book by spiritual light is found, and, on reading or hearing thereof, conviction reaches the conscience, it is a great instance of God's favor, a token for good, and must be faithfully acknowledged as such. Reader, art thou truly apprehensive of the weight of God's wrath, and solicitous to obtain His favor? Seek then earnestly, upon thy knees, and in the house of the Lord, redemption from the curses of the law; pray that Jesus may be revealed to thee,—the blood of the Lamb of God alone can take away the guilt of sin; having found the law, rest not till thou find the Gospel also, and arrive at a comfortable assurance of thine interest in its blessings. Josiah's heart was tender, he wept, and was encouraged; follow his sorrow, and thou wilt partake of his blessings; and make the law of God thy delight and counsellor.

> The precious word of God is hid,
>   Or sealed everywhere;
> But when the Spirit light imparts,
>   'Tis found and read with care.

September 13.

Draw me, we will run after thee. The King hath brought me into His chambers; we will be glad and rejoice in thee; we will remember thy love more than wine: the upright love thee.—Song of Sol. i. 4. *In thee the fatherless findeth mercy.*—Hosea xiv. 3. See also Ps. cii. 13.

The needle's point in the seaman's compass never stands still, but quivers and shakes till it comes right against the North Pole. The wise men of the East never rested till they were right against the star which appeared unto them: and the star itself never stood still till it came right against that other Star, which shone more brightly in the manger than the sun did in the firmament. And Noah's dove could find no rest for the sole of her foot all the while she was fluttering over the flood, till she returned to the ark with an olive branch in her mouth. So the heart of every true Christian, which is the turtle-dove of Jesus Christ, can find no rest all the while she is hovering over the waters of this world; till, with the silver wings of a dove, and the olive branch of faith, it flies to Jesus, the true Noah and rest of our souls, who puts forth His hand out of the ark, and taking the dove in, receiveth it to Himself.

> Vain are the things of time,
>   There's nought of pleasure here,
> E'en our most sunny clime
>   Is dark, and wild, and drear;
> God only is our refuge sure,
> The source of pleasure full and pure.
>
> In vain I seek for rest
>   In all created good;
> It leaves me still unblest,
>   And makes me cry for God.
> And sure at rest I cannot be
> Until my heart find rest in thee.

September 14.

What think ye of Christ?—Matt. xxii. 42.

And ought we not to put this question to our souls, when our happiness forever depends upon Him, and when without Him we are undone to eternity? How ought we then to think of the Lord Jesus Christ? Surely, as the Scripture represents Him to be, "the chief among ten thousand, and altogether lovely." We ought to think of Him in His person, as the great God incarnate; in His work and His offices, as the Saviour of Israel. We ought to think of Him as one in whom justice is satisfied, love and righteousness are manifested, and sinners are saved. Oh! how highly have God's people ever thought of Christ Jesus! and how exulting do the saints now in heaven think of Him! But what think we of Christ when burdened with sin, when oppressed with affliction? When we cannot entertain a good thought of ourselves, can we then think of Christ as highly as heretofore? Alas! how very weak is our faith at the best? Lord, strengthen our faith, inflame our love, enlarge our views, support us in trials, guide us by thy counsels, and receive us into glory, that we may sing thy praise to all eternity. Amen.

> Now living waters flow
> To cheer the humble soul;
> From sea to sea the rivers go,
> And spread from pole to pole.
>
> Now righteousness shall spring,
> And grow on earth again;
> Jesus Jehovah be our king,
> And o'er the nations reign.
>
> Jesus shall rule alone,
> The world shall hear His word;
> By one blessed name shall He be known,
> The Universal Lord.

September 15.

Our conversation, or our citizenship, *is in heaven.*
—Phil. iii. 20. Therefore *rejoice, because your names are written in heaven.*—Luke x. 20. *And set your affection on things above, not on things on the earth.*—Col. iii. 2.

A CHRISTIAN being only a traveler through the world, must expect a traveler's fare—bad roads sometimes, bad weather, and bad accommodations; but since his journey's end and city is heaven, all his actions, sufferings, prayers, trade and conversation, turn that way. His actions, for whatsoever is bound on earth is bound in heaven; his sufferings, for those who overcome shall receive a crown of glory; his prayers, for grace is the answer to prayer; his trade, for whatsoever is of the world is sin; his conversation, for whatsoever is earthly is abomination, and worketh a lie. O Lord, grant that mine eyes may be always fixed upon this mark, so as to regulate all my doings accordingly,—asking myself in everything, whether it be fit for heaven, and agreeable to the mind of the heavenly Bridegroom, and to the manners of the heavenly citizens?

> Lord, bid my soul fly up and run
> Through every heavenly street;
> And say, There's nought below the sun
> That's worthy of thy feet.
>
> So shall we mount on sacred wings,
> And tread the courts above:
> Nor earth, nor all her mightiest things
> Shall tempt our meanest love.
>
> The glorious tenants of the place
> Stand bending round the throne;
> And saints and seraphs sing and praise
> The infinite Three-One.
>
> Jesus, oh! when shall that dear day,
> That joyful hour appear,
> When I shall leave this house of clay,
> To dwell among them there?

SEPTEMBER 16.

To Him give all the prophets witness, that, through His name, whosoever believeth in Him shall receive remission of sins.—Acts x. 43; and iv. 12. *This name is as ointment poured forth*, the fullness of His grace.—Song of Sol. i. 3. *It is a strong tower: the righteous runneth into it, and is safe.*—Prov. xviii. 10.

In this name we should draw nigh to the Father in prayer, and not approach Him with a strange fire of our own, kindled from the fancied merit of devotion, and He will draw nigh to us again. "Draw nigh to God, and He will draw nigh to you" (James iv. 8). He will certainly grant our petitions, "and we shall receive, that our joy may be full" (John xvi. 24). "For the Lord is good, and ready to forgive, and plenteous in mercy unto all them that call upon Him" (Ps. lxxxvi. 5). And all these promises are Yea and Amen in Christ; so that every believer may say, "The Lord will receive my prayer" (Ps. vi. 9); "Blessed be God, who hath not turned away my prayer, nor His mercy from me;" for "He hath dealt bountifully with me" (Ps. lxvi. 20; and xiii. 6). Lord, may this be the language and the exercise of my heart; and do thou grant me to believe more firmly in thy name!

> Lift up your eyes to th' heavenly seat
>   Where your Redeemer stays;
> Kind Intercessor! there He sits,
>   And loves, and pleads, and prays.
>
> Petitions now, and praise may rise,
>   And saints their offerings bring;
> The Priest, with His own sacrifice,
>   Presents them to the King.
>
> Jesus alone shall bear my cries
>   Up to the Father's throne;
> He, dearest Lord, perfumes my sighs,
>   And sweetens every groan.

September 17.

In thy presence is fullness of joy; at thy right hand there are pleasures for evermore.—Ps. xvi. 11.
And I saw the New Jerusalem, descending out of heaven from God, prepared as a bride adorned for her husband.—Rev. xxi. 2-4, 10, 12.

O MY dear Saviour, look upon me in mercy! Thou seest what earthly desires and unmortified tempers are yet found in me; and though I cry unto thee daily, mine enemies still prevail over me. Yet thou art almighty to save, and hast promised to cast out none that come unto thee. Let me then experience the power of thy grace, in raising me up to more newness of life, in stirring up prayer and strengthening faith, in creating hungerings after righteousness, and thirstings after God, and in bestowing a right heavenly mind upon me, that my soul may be as a bride prepared and adorned for her husband. Give me also a frequent taste below of those pleasures which are at thy right hand for evermore, that my heart may be kept waiting and eagerly looking for thy coming, and that, united unto thee in faith, my life may be spent in thy favor and unto thy glory.

> Oh! the delights, the heavenly joys,
>   The glories of the place,
> Where Jesus sheds the brightest beams
>   Of His o'erflowing grace.
>
> Archangels sound His lofty praise
>   Through every heavenly street;
> And lay their highest honors down
>   Submissive at His feet.
>
> Lord, how our souls are all on fire
>   To see thy blest abode!
> Our tongues rejoice in tunes of praise
>   To our incarnate God.
>
> And while our faith enjoys this sight
>   We long to leave our clay;
> And wish thy fiery chariots, Lord,
>   To fetch our souls away.

SEPTEMBER 18.

Watch and pray; let us be going.—Matt. xxvi. 41, 46. *Remember Lot's wife.*—Luke xvii. 32. *This is the way, walk ye in it.*—Isa. xxx. 21. *He that hath begun a good work in you will perform it until the day of Jesus Christ.*—Phil. i. 6.

To be kept from self-righteousness on the one hand, and from false liberty on the other, is the right Christian way. But how shall I find it? Oh! my dear Jesus, thou art the way! Teach me then to walk in thy strength, to live in thy faith, to gaze much upon thee, to cleave firm unto thee, and abide ever in thee: so shall I experience the liberty of thy Gospel, which yieldeth no license for sin, but bringeth joyful deliverance from its power; for when my heart resteth on thee, it cannot rest in the flesh, and seek to fulfill its lusts; but being delighted with thy beauty and glorious love, all other things vanish, and I am kept watchful, close and fervent: I live a life of godly holiness hid with thee. Send forth the Spirit and prepare my heart thus to abide in thee, and to turn and bring me back when I turn to the right hand or to the left.

> When my forgetful soul renews
>   The savor of thy grace,
> My heart presumes I cannot lose
>   The relish all my days.
>
> But, ere one fleeting hour is past,
>   The flatt'ring world employs
> Some sensual bait to seize my taste,
>   And to pollute my joys.
>
> Then I repent and vex my soul,
>   That I should leave thee so;
> Where will those wild affections roll
>   That let a Saviour go?
>
> Shew my forgetful feet the way
>   That leads to joys on high;
> There knowledge grows without decay,
>   And love shall never die.

September 19.

Walk before me, (as in my presence,) *and be thou perfect.*—Gen. xvii. 1. *Fear God, and keep His commandments; for this is the whole duty of man. For God shall bring every work into judgment, with every secret thing, whether it be good, or whether it be evil.*—Eccles. xii. 13, 14. *I say unto you, That every idle word that men shall speak, they shall give account thereof in the day of judgment.*—Matt. xii. 36.

CONSEQUENTLY all such things as are now called indifferent in their nature will also be brought to God's bar, and not be called indifferent there, but judged as actually good or actually evil. Oh! the prodigious harm that is done by this false doctrine of innocent things! It opens the door to innumerable sins; for though our conscience often tells us that we should not do such things as are not actually good, yet presently innocence is pleaded, it is called a harmless thing, which, though it could not be said to be good, yet it was not evil neither, but quite indifferent in its nature; by which thousands are drawn into the snares of the devil. O Lord, grant that all my works may be done unto thee, and in thy presence, agreeably to thy commandments; that even my leaves may not wither, and whatsoever I do may prosper and abide for ever; and that while here I may be fitted, by the sanctifying influences of the Spirit, for the holy and blessed communion of heaven that is hereafter to those who keep thy law.

> Within thy circling power I stand;
> On every side I find thy hand;
> Awake, asleep, at home, abroad,
> I am surrounded still with God.
>
> Oh! may these thoughts possess my breast,
> Where'er I rove, where'er I rest;
> Nor let unruly passions dare
> Consent to sin, for God is there.

September 20.

Verily, verily, I say unto thee, Except a man be born again, he cannot see the kingdom of God.—John iii. 3. *Therefore if any man be in Christ, he is a new creature: old things are passed away; behold, all things are become new.*—2 Cor. v. 17. *Not by works of righteousness which we have done, but according to His mercy He saved us, by the washing of regeneration, etc.*—Titus iii. 5, 6. See also James i. 18, and 1 Peter i. 23.

Consequently no outward form of religion will do; but we must be renewed by the Spirit of God, and have our hearts changed, else we cannot enter into the kingdom of God. Christ (by saying, Verily, verily) has confirmed this twice by an oath. How is it possible, then, that mere honest and moral men can be saved? Will Christ break His double oath! No, surely. Now, since outward gross vices only are blamed in conversation or preaching, a moral man slips through the law without censure; and the careless think they can leave off their open sins one time or another; and so none are duly concerned to be thoroughly converted; but the new birth and the real change of the heart being insisted upon, and Christ held forth in this only true way, every one who will be saved must be turned.

> The second Adam shall restore
>   The ruins of the first;
> Hosanna to that sov'reign power
>   That new-creates our dust.
>
> When from the curse He sets us free,
>   He makes our natures clean;
> Nor would our Saviour come to be
>   The minister of sin.
>
> His Spirit purifies our frame,
>   And seals our peace with God;
> Jesus and His salvation came
>   By water and by blood.

September 21.

Why art thou cast down, O my soul? and why art thou disquieted within me? Hope thou in God; for I shall yet praise Him, who is the health of my countenance, and my God.—Ps. xlii. 11. *For I reckon, that the sufferings of this present time are not worthy to be compared with the glory which shall be revealed in us.*—Rom. viii. 18.

Believers, we are here assured, may be in great distress; but though much perplexed, and often discouraged, they are secretly lifted up by faith, and brought off conquerors. If God had commanded us to pray and hope only till a certain time mentioned, and His help had failed to come within that time, we might justly despair. But since He requires us to hope even to the end, or last moment of life, this should keep us from impatience and despair; for though He should tarry even to the end, believers will certainly experience Him then to be faithful to His promise. He may try our faith and patience to the utmost, but He cannot break His own word. Dear Lord, whatever load thou art pleased to lay upon me, enable me to wait in faith and prayer till the joyful hour of deliverance comes,—knowing that thou layest on no burden disproportioned to the grace thou art giving.

> 'Tis God that lifts our comforts high,
>   Or sinks them in the grave;
> He gives, (and blessed be His name,)
>   He takes but what He gave.
>
> Peace, all our angry passions then;
>   Let each rebellious sigh
> Be silent at His sov'reign will,
>   And every murmur die.
>
> If smiling mercy crown our lives,
>   Its praises shall be spread;
> And we'll adore the justice, too,
>   That strikes our comforts dead.

SEPTEMBER 22.

Be not soon shaken in mind.—2 Thess. ii. 2. *I determined not to know anything among you, save Jesus Christ, and Him crucified.*—1 Cor. ii. 2. *In whom are hid all the treasures of wisdom and knowledge.*—Col. ii. 3. *But we preach Christ crucified. The testimony of Christ was confirmed in you.*—1 Cor. i. 23, 6.

O MY dear Saviour! enable me to rest humbly and quietly in thee, avoiding all such novelties as might breed presumption, distract my thoughts, and cause my heart to swerve from thee. Whoever has tasted the sweetness of thy Word will be satisfied with it; and better it is to improve in the life of faith and power of godliness, than in new words, forms and professions. May the Lord quicken me by the old truths, and humble my heart evermore, so as to receive them better, and to abide in that which I have heard from the beginning. Novelty is the bane of souls, by which we are often grievously tormented and distracted. It is work enough for a meek and quiet soul to keep within the bounds of a settled mind, and effectually to centre in God. How can such enjoy true rest, who from a vain curiosity to know everything, are ever running after new doctrines, or prying into every man's business? Lord, save me from this unsettled mind, and make me determined to know nothing but Jesus Christ and Him crucified, and to have His testimony confirmed in my heart! Amen.

> Oh! that the Lord would guide my ways
>   To keep His statutes still;
> Oh! that my God would grant me grace
>   To know and do His will!
>
> My soul has gone too far astray,
>   My feet too often slip;
> Yet since I've not forgot thy way,
>   Restore thy wand'ring sheep.

SEPTEMBER 23.

David's Prayer :—*Wash me thoroughly from mine iniquity, and cleanse me from my sin.*—Ps. li. 2.
Divine Answer :—*The blood of Jesus Christ, the Son of God, cleanseth us from all sin.*—1 John i. 7. See also 1 Cor. vi. 11.

UNDER the ceremonial law all things were purged with blood; and without shedding of blood there was no remission; thus it is impossible that any one sin, even the least sinful motion, should be taken away, except by the blood of Jesus Christ. May this teach me the heinousness of sin in the sight of the great Jehovah, and may it tend to keep my heart humble and my conscience tender; for how dreadful must the stain of sin be, since nothing but the blood of Christ can wash it out! Blessed be God for opening this fountain, and keeping it open day and night, for the vilest sinners to wash in. May my polluted soul be daily washed in this fountain, and receive both peace and strength from it; and, arrayed in the robes of Christ's righteousness, may I be prevented from doing anything dishonorable to thy name!

> My dying Saviour and my God,
>   Fountain for guilt and sin,
> Sprinkle me ever with thy blood,
>   And cleanse and keep me clean.
>
> Wash me, and make me thus thy own;
>   Wash me, and mine thou art;
> Wash me, but not my feet alone,—
>   My hands, my head, my heart.
>
> Th' atonement of thy blood apply,
>   Till faith to sight improve;
> Till hope shall in fruition die,
>   And all my soul be love.
>
> For ever here my rest shall be,
>   Close to thy bleeding side;
> 'Tis all my hope and all my plea,
>   "For me the Saviour died."

September 24.

Examine yourselves, whether ye be in the faith.—
2 Cor. xiii. 5. See also 1 Cor. ii. 28.

But is there any need of such self-examination, when yet we preach Christ, and stay ourselves on His name? Alas! it is possible both to preach and profess Him, yea, to have a seeming confidence in Him, and call Him our Rock, and talk of His grace, and yet be lovers of sin, and haters of holiness; and thereby shew we have no interest in Him, but are in the road of destruction. Thus Jesus hath told us, Matt. vii. 22, 23. Let us examine ourselves. Is our faith in Him accompanied with much self-abhorrence in the views of our sinfulness and pollution before Him! Do we prize Him, not only for His favor to us, but for His own goodness, His grace, and His excellence? Do we love Him so as to love nothing in comparison of Him,—neither self, nor the world, nor our ease, nor advantage? Then, surely, we are His, and He also is ours. These graces are the fruits of His Spirit within us; they are proofs of our faith and of our union with Him; and if we are united by the Spirit to Jesus, He will certainly own us before men and angels; He will never forsake us in time or eternity. But how dreadful will their case be, who deceive themselves here, and habitually give themselves unto sin and iniquity, whilst yet they make mention of Jesus Christ with their lips! Keep us, Lord, we beseech thee, from such sad delusion! Oh! give us to remember all our past provocations, and to know, to love, and serve thee in sincerity!

> Is Christ your only trust and guide,
> And dearer far than all beside?
> And pants your heart for holiness?
> Then sure you are a child of grace.

September 25.

What lack I yet?—Matt. xix. 20. *Yet lackest thou one thing.*—Luke xviii. 22. *For one thing is needful.*—Luke x. 42.

This one thing needful is to have Christ; but He must first serve and treat us with His grace before we can draw strength from Him to serve Him again. We must be taught to see Him our food, and to hunger for Him, before we can feed upon Him, or do anything for Him. And as Christ is the author of faith, He gives it increase out of His fullness; and faith, being somewhat strengthened, begins to work for Him, though it be but faintly. However, we become Christians, and remain in a perfect state of salvation, not by what faith works, but by what it receives; for though a feeble faith will perform feeble works, it can receive a whole and perfect Christ, which is the one thing needful. Grant, dear Lord, that I may possess the one thing needful, that He may dwell in my heart, rooting and grounding me in love.

> Oh! may I never want the seal
> Of Christ my dying soul to heal;
>   He is my sure defence;
> The one thing needful I must get,
> Ere death's dark clouds around me set,
>   And my freed soul fly hence.
>
> I'll hear of nothing else beside
> My Jesus, and Him crucified;
>   In Him is all I want:
> His blood, His meritorious blood,
> Alone is rich, alone is good;
>   For that alone I pant.
>
> Sure none refuse to join this song,
> To praise our Saviour all along
>   Their pilgrimage below;
> To sing, "There's none, there's none beside,
> But Jesus and Him crucified,
>   Needful for us to know."

SEPTEMBER 26.

Joseph is a fruitful bough; the archers have sorely grieved him, and shot at him; but his bow abode in strength, and the arms of his hands were made strong by the hands of the mighty God of Jacob: (from thence is the Shepherd, the Stone of Israel.)—Gen. xlix. 22-24.

JOSEPH is an eminent type of the Messiah: let us trace the resemblance. Joseph was in a peculiar manner beloved by his father; Christ is the dear Son of His Father's love. Jacob made for Joseph a coat of many colors; God prepared a body in human nature for Christ, filled and adorned with the various gifts and graces of the Spirit without measure. Joseph was hated by his brethren, and they could not endure to think he should have the dominion over them; the Jews, Christ's brethren according to the flesh, hated Him, and would not have Him to reign over them. Joseph was sent by his father a long journey to visit his brethren, and know their welfare; Christ was sent from the bosom of the Father, to seek and to save the lost sheep of the house of Israel. Joseph's brethren conspired to take away his life; the Jews said, "This is the heir, let us kill Him," and they consulted to take away His life. Joseph was sold for twenty pieces of silver at the motion of Judah; and Christ, by one of the same name, was sold for thirty pieces. Joseph was delivered to strangers, and Christ to the Gentiles. Joseph being reckoned dead by his father, and yet alive, may be an emblem of Christ's death and resurrection from the dead.

> O Jesus! I in Joseph see
> How archers shot and grieved thee;
> Into the grave like Joseph cast,
> And raised, like him, a Prince at last.

SEPTEMBER 27.

What things were gain to me, those I counted loss for Christ; yea doubtless, and I count all things but loss for the excellency of the knowledge of Christ Jesus my Lord; for whom I have suffered the loss of all things, and do count them but dung, that I may win Christ, and be found in Him as my righteousness.—Phil. iii. 7-9.

This was the life and constant mind of St. Paul. The words, "in Him," "in Christ," "in the Lord," "I am Christ's," etc., occur continually. I choose them also for my staff, and my song in the wilderness; they shall be my great tower, my strong fortress, my sweet paradise, mine only element and life. Here may I take up mine abode for ever, and the Lord keep me steadfast! "It is good for us to be here;" for this is Pisgah, the mount of the Lord, where Jesus, being transfigured, reveals His glory to His disciples. Here we should build our tabernacle; and here may death find me at last. Help me, O thou Spirit of the Lord, to be a true believer in Christ Jesus, "not having mine own righteousness," nor trusting to anything that I have done or am able to do, but casting away as worthless all that the world calls excellent, I may cleave to Christ and be found in Him. Oh! may I be able to make Christ my resting-place and my refuge at all times!

> Had I ten thousand gifts beside,
> I'd cleave to Jesus crucified,
>   And build on Him alone;
> For no foundation is there given
> On which I'd place my hopes of heaven,
>   But Christ the corner-stone.
>
> Possessing Christ, I all possess,—
> Wisdom, and strength, and righteousness,
>   And holiness complete;
> Bold in His name, I dare draw nigh
> Before the Ruler of the sky,
>   And all His justice meet.

SEPTEMBER 28.

The Penitent's Prayer:—*What must I do to be saved?*—Acts xvi. 30.

Divine Answer:—*Believe on the Lord Jesus, and thou shalt be saved, and thy house.*—Acts xvi. 31.

FAITH is not a confidence of our own making; but it is God that works it in a broken and repenting heart. This faith purifies the heart, crucifies the old Adam, overcomes the world, changes us in heart, mind, and all the powers and faculties of the soul, which is the true Protestant faith; and not that we only think and say, "I believe." By this we must try our faith. All true believers have received it, under a sense of godly sorrow, and with brokenness of heart. If we feel something of this, and apply to Christ by prayer for faith and grace, we have a sure mark of faith already; for if we did not believe, we would not pray. And he that daily applies to the blood of Christ for cleansing, has true faith and hope already, though he is but weak, and does not taste any joy. The Lord grant to all our souls that repentance unto life, and that faith in Jesus Christ, which are the saving graces of the Spirit, that in due time, when the end is come, we may receive a crown of glory to wear for ever in the presence of the Prince of Life, and of God Himself.

> Ye dying souls, that sit
>   In darkness and distress,
> Look from the borders of the pit,
>   To Christ's recovering grace.
>
> Sinners shall hear His sound;
>   Their thankful tongues shall own,
> Their righteousness and strength is found
>   In Christ the Lord alone.
>
> In Him shall Israel trust,
>   And see their guilt forgiven;
> God will pronounce the sinners just,
>   And take the saints to heaven.

SEPTEMBER 29.

Abstain from all appearance of evil, that ye may be blameless and harmless, the sons of God, without rebuke, in the midst of a crooked and perverse nation, among whom ye shine as lights in the world.—Phil. ii. 15. See also Eph. v. 8.

BE as the sun in the firmament—he giveth light to all; so let your light shine before all men. By doing so some may walk in it, and God will be glorified. Be no slaves to the flesh; but on the contrary, shew a willing and holy service to the most high God! Bless those that are against you. Lord, I desire to shine in good works, the genuine fruits of faith; therefore will I give myself up to thee, to purge me, that I may bring forth more fruit. Looking upon myself as thine, I would not only abstain from evil, but from the very appearance of it. Some are satisfied with knowing they are blameless, and care not what others think of them; but for the gospel's sake I desire to appear blameless before others, lest some offence should come through me; which, as far as in me lieth, I would prevent. Thy children, O God, are as lights in the world. Oh! pour thy grace, that heavenly oil, into my lamp, and so trim it that it may give light unto all around, that they may be led to glorify thy holy name.

O Lord, my stubborn will subdue;
Create my ruined frame anew!
 Dispel my darkness by thy light;
Into all truth my spirit guide,
But from mine eyes for ever hide
 All things displeasing in thy sight.

Be heaven now my soul's abode!
Hid be my life with Christ in God;
 My spirit, Lord, be one with thine;
Let all my works in thee be wrought,
And filled with thee be all my thought,
 Till in me thy full likeness shine.

SEPTEMBER 30.

Let him that is athirst come; and whosoever will, let him take of the water of life freely.—Rev. xxii. 17.

IF there be a sense of sin, and want of spiritual blessings, and a willingness to be saved by grace, though you know not that it is Christ's secret power that makes you willing, yet being athirst and willing, you are invited: do not puzzle and perplex yourselves with such questions as these: Am I elected? Have I a right? Am I prepared? —but come upon the invitation, and take pardon, peace, righteousness, and every gospel blessing, as free gifts to the needy. If one ready to perish with hunger and thirst were invited to a feast, and assured of welcome, and he should stand hesitating, Have I a right? Am I worthy?—would it not seem preposterous in him thus to demur, when his necessities were pressing upon him, and a plentiful table before him? The weary, the hungry, the thirsty, the guilty, the worthless, the vilest, are invited to believe in Jesus, who came only to save sinners, and hath assured them in His word, that those who thus come to Him, "He will in nowise cast out."

> The Spirit in the Word,
>   And in His motions cries,
> "Come to the Fountain-head of life,
>   And come for large supplies.
>
> "Let him who feels his thirst,
>   Nor can endure its rage,
> Come to salvation's copious springs,
>   And all his pains assuage.
>
> "And whosoever will
>   Is welcome to receive
> The streams of everlasting life
>   That Heaven will freely give."
>
> Jesus, is this thy voice?
>   We bless thy gracious call,
> And flee with joyful haste to thee,
>   Our Saviour and our All.

October 1.

Weep not; behold, the Lion of the tribe of Judah, the Root of David, has prevailed.—Rev. v. 5. He rose triumphantly, *and destroyed the works of the devil; therefore sin shall not have dominion over us.*—Rom. vi. 14. *For the law of the Spirit of life in Christ Jesus hath made me free from the law of sin and death.*—Rom. viii. 2.

MANY complain that, though they will not turn back, yet they have no power to advance farther. If this should be thy case, my reader, remember that the enemy of souls will discourage thee. Go on praying, and venture it evermore upon the Lord. Consider how He awakened you at first, how often He has heard your prayers afterward, and assisted you in many hard struggles. Surely He will help you now also. If that will not do, begin, as it were, afresh; acknowledge yourself guilty in every respect; and, as the chief of sinners, plead for mercy, and be instant in your humble supplications; looking, at the same time, upon God as a reconciled Father through Christ, who is willing to receive you, pardon, and bless you in spite of all your misery: then you will soon make a better progress. To despair of our own strength is good; but we must never despair of the power of Christ, who is risen from the dead, but be sure to overcome with Him at last. He will certainly help you in the due and best season.

> Hell and thy sins resist thy course,
>   But hell and sin are vanquished foes;
> Thy Jesus nailed them to the cross,
>   And sung the triumph when He rose.
>
> He dies, and in that dreadful night
>   Did all the powers of death destroy;
> Rising, He brought our heaven to light,
>   And took possession of the joy.

October 2.

Whom the Lord loveth He chasteneth, and scourgeth every son whom He receiveth. If ye endure chastening, God dealeth with you as with sons: for what son is he whom the Father chasteneth not? He chasteneth us for our profit.—Heb. xii. 6-10.

To these chastenings belong outward afflictions, which are precious means, and sanctified to believers. And this is a clear proof that we should receive such chastenings with gladness, and that we should not repine under them. They evidence the fatherly care and love of God, and are designed to try our faith, and purge our souls from the drossy matter of earth that is mixed up with them; and from them we must learn that chastisements will be the means of good to us if we use them aright. Oh! my dear heavenly Father, thou art only pleased with a true child-like confidence; but I am still of a distrusting heart when anything comes upon me on a sudden. Help me always to entertain the kindest thoughts of thee, and to fear no adversity; looking on it as a token of love and not of hatred, and really believing it to be intended as a blessing for my good. Whatever thy providence may order, let me only be convinced of thy fatherly affection, and fall in with thy wholesome and loving designs.

> Though for my sin I justly feel
>   Thy discipline, O God,
> I wait thy gracious moment still,
>   Till thou remove thy rod.
>
> For I have found 'tis good for me
>   To bear my Father's rod;
> Affliction makes me learn thy law,
>   And live upon my God.
>
> This is the comfort I enjoy
>   When new distress begins;
> I read thy word, I run thy way,
>   And hate my former sins.

OCTOBER 3.

The entrance of thy word gives light; it giveth understanding to the simple.—Ps. cxix. 130. *Order my steps in thy word; and let not any iniquity have dominion over me.*—Ver. 133. *The Scriptures testify of me* (Christ).—John v. 39.

WE may have a clear sight and a real taste of the Gospel, and yet be soon deprived of the comfort of it again, if we do not walk in godly simplicity and poverty of spirit; for Christ will have none but humble and child-like disciples. But if we abide in Christ, by a close and humble walk with Him, we shall come to great and lasting assurance; for neither a sweet sense of Christ, nor even faith itself in Christ, is the ground of our salvation; but Christ alone received into the heart as the Saviour. Faith does not save, but enables us to receive the Saviour, and with Him salvation. Neither does a sweet sense of Christ save us; it only shews the Saviour is present with us. Now, the weakest true believer does receive Christ as well as the strongest, though he reap no present comfort from his faith. We must first believe, before we can feel, and be thankful for our feelings, but not trust in them.

> Thy mercies fill the earth, O Lord,
>   How good thy works appear!
> Open mine eyes to read thy word,
>   And see thy wonders there.
>
> When once it enters to the mind,
>   It spreads such light abroad,
> The meanest souls instruction find,
>   And raise their thoughts to God.
>
> 'Tis like the sun, a heavenly light,
>   That guides us all the day;
> And through the dangers of the night
>   A lamp to lead our way.
>
> Since I'm a stranger here below,
>   Let not thy path be hid,
> But mark the road my feet should go,
>   And be my constant guide.

OCTOBER 4.

Turn away mine eyes from beholding vanity, and quicken thou me in thy way.—Ps. cxix. 37.

IF you were to see a man endeavoring all his life to satisfy his thirst, by holding up one and the same empty cup to his mouth, you would certainly despise his ignorance; but if you should see others ridiculing the dull satisfaction of one cup, and thinking to satisfy their own thirst by a variety of gilt and golden empty cups, would you think that these were the wiser or ever the happier, or better employed, for their finer parts? Now, this is all the difference that you can see in the happiness of this life. The dull and heavy soul may be content with one empty appearance of happiness, and be continually trying to hold one and the same empty cup to his mouth all his life. But then, let the talented men of the world lay all their heads together, and they can only shew you more, and various empty appearances of happiness; give them all the world into their hands, they can only make a great variety of empty cups; for search as deep as you will, there is nothing to be found here nobler or greater than eating and drinking, rich dress and applause, unless you look for it in the wisdom and laws of religion. Reader, reflect upon the vanity of all orders of life who live without godliness, and see how all the ways of the world are only so many different ways of error and blindness, that you may be earnest at a throne of grace to be turned from the creature, and seek for happiness in the Creator.

> No peace or lasting rest
>   Earth's flattering joys impart;
> The portion of a beast
>   Will not content my heart.
> The God of spirits only can
> Fill up the vast desires of man.

October 5.

David's Prayer:—*Give ear to my prayer, O God, and hide not thyself from my supplication.*—Ps. lv. 1.

Christ's Answer:—*Verily, verily, I say unto you, Whatsoever ye shall ask the Father in my name, He will give it you.*—John xvi. 23. *For the Father Himself loveth you.*—Ver. 27. He has promised:—*Before they call, I will answer; and whilst they are speaking, I will hear.*—Isa. lxv. 24. *Therefore I say unto you, What things soever ye desire, when ye pray, believe that ye receive them, and ye shall have them.*—Mark xi. 24.

He that converses much with God in prayer, and has some child-like confidence in His word, shall certainly be heard; and these answers of prayer are undeniable evidences of the truth, faithfulness and love of God, and greatly strengthen his faith; and at last bring him to be intimately acquainted with God. The more we receive, the more we are enlightened to see how much there is still wanting. This stirs up to more frequent prayer, and to more fervent desires; and the more we desire and believe that we shall receive it, the more shall be granted. Unbelief receives nothing (Matt. xiii. 58); but faith opens all the treasures of God, and never goes away empty.

> Because on me they set their love,
> I'll save them, saith the Lord;
> I'll bear their joyful souls above
> Destruction and the sword.
>
> In me they every grace shall find
> For sorrow, joy, or care;
> Their broken hearts I will upbind,
> Unloose their every snare.
>
> My grace shall answer when they call;
> In trouble I'll be nigh;
> My power shall help them when they fall,
> And raise them when they die.

October 6.

If I yet pleased men, I should not be the servant of Christ.—Gal. i. 10. *Let every one of us please his neighbor for his good to edification.*—Rom. xv. 2. Fear or love of men, and hypocrisy, very often are nearly allied: *A man that flattereth his neighbor, spreadeth a net for his feet.*—Prov. xxix. 5. *But he that rebuketh a man, afterwards shall find more favor than he that flattereth with his tongue.*—Chap. xxviii. 23.

We are ever inclined to extremes, even then when God has begun His work in our soul. At one time we are apt to run into a false activity for the conversion of others, trusting too much to our own sufficiency and strength; at other times, perhaps, we fall into much remissness, and inactivity for the salvation of others. May the Lord therefore always guide me to steer the middle course, so as to walk in all singleness and humility of heart, as well as in true fervency of spirit, faith and love, that it may be said, "I believe, therefore do I speak." Grant, O my dear Saviour, that I may shine as a light, and be useful to all about me; never seeking my own, but only the salvation and good of others, with unfeigned love! Oh! that thy love may constrain me in all things! Amen.

> My own glory still I seek,
>   Still I covet human praise;
> Still, in all I do or speak,
>   Thee I wrong, and rob thy grace.
>
> And must that which is so good
>   Evil prove to sinful me?
> Poison shall I draw from food,
>   Sin from grace, and pride from thee?
>
> Oh! forbid it, humble love!
>   Hide me, O my Father, hide!
> Far away this snare remove;
>   Save me from the sin of pride!

October 7.

Hereby we know that we are of the truth, and shall assure our hearts before Him.—1 John iii. 19.
Every one that is of the truth heareth my voice.—John xviii. 27.

The evidence of our assurance of eternal happiness is that which every soul that makes any serious reflections on matters of religion pants after: it is therefore necessary to know upon what foundation this blessed evidence is built, and from what principles it arises; and those, I think, are chiefly faith, love and obedience; since no man can have this assurance who does not feel in himself the principle of obedience; nor can he have obedience without the principle of love, nor love without the principle of faith: for it is a notorious contradiction to imagine that any one can be assured of God Almighty's pardon, without obeying Him; of His favor, without loving Him; or of the eternal enjoyment of Him, without a firm and steadfast belief in Him. But here many mistake the nature of these things; true belief in God represents Him to the mind as infinite in glory, and power, and wisdom, and goodness, and in all perfections; with such charms, such beauty, such loveliness, as to captivate and ravish the affections of the soul, and smite it with a Divine love: true love reigns triumphant in the soul, engrosses all its affections, strips other objects of their charms, nay, makes them appear vile and contemptible in comparison with the supreme good: true obedience strives to please God, to resemble Him, to render itself acceptable to Him, and ardently desires the enjoyment of Him.

> Faith only gives me peace with God;
>   But if my faith be true,
> It surely shews itself by love,
>   And kind obedience too.

OCTOBER 8.

He that shall endure unto the end, the same shall be saved.—Matt. xxiv. 13. *Behold, I come quickly: hold that fast which thou hast, that no man take thy crown.*—Rev. iii. 11. *Wherefore, let him that thinketh he standeth take heed lest he fall.*—1 Cor. x. 12.

He that stands in faith, and by nature is of a cheerful temper, must not magnify the measure of his own faith, nor undervalue that of weaker souls; for such conduct would declare that he is even now fallen into pride, and a contempt of his brother; therefore, however fast we may seem to stand, let us be wary and watchful. We are never so near a fall as when we grow self-confident. He who knows the nature and power of temptations will not discourage the weak, nor insist too much upon particular enjoyments and sensible assurances, which are not the constant witness and marks of faith. The Holy Spirit Himself is the earnest and seal of adoption; who is to be known, not only by this joy, but by all His other fruits and operations. To trust too much upon feeling disturbs our peace as soon as it is gone; but to rely on the Word of God preserves a settled assurance.

> Jesus! shall I never be
> Firmly grounded upon thee?
> Strong in faith I seem this hour;
> Stript the next of all my power.
>
> Plant, and root, and fix in me
> All the mind that was in thee;
> Settled peace I then shall find,
> When I am renewed in mind.
>
> Grant that every moment I
> May believe and feel thee nigh;
> Steadfastly behold thy face,
> 'Stablished with abiding grace.

OCTOBER 9.

If any man have not the Spirit of Christ (but the spirit of this world), *he is none of His. For as many as are led by the Spirit of God, they are the sons of God.*—Rom. viii. 9, 14. See also ver. 7, 8.

Not gross wickedness only, but even a carnal mind, is enmity against God. "Know ye not that the friendship of the world is enmity with God? whosoever therefore will be a friend of the world is the enemy of God" (James iv. 4). "For many walk, of whom I have told you often, and now tell you even weeping, that they are the enemies of the cross of Christ: whose end is destruction, whose god is their belly, and whose glory is in their shame, who mind earthly things" (Phil. iii. 18, 19). But how do I know that I have the Spirit of Christ?

Answer:—I have prayed for Him earnestly; this cannot be in vain. "If ye then, being evil, know how to give good gifts unto your children: how much more shall your heavenly Father give the Holy Spirit to them that ask Him?" (Luke xi. 13). He works also hatred and sorrow of sin; rebukes, comforts, and drives me to Christ and to prayer. This is his abiding witness, built upon the Word of God, which no man of this world can have, but even the weakest believer enjoys.

> Holy, true, and righteous Lord,
>   I seek to know and do thy will;
> Be mindful of thy gracious word,
>   And stamp me with thy Spirit's seal.
>
> My conscience purge from every blot;
>   My idols all be cast aside;
> Rebuke each vain and sinful thought,
>   And crucify both self and pride.
>
> Within me thy good Spirit place,
>   Spirit of health, and love, and power;
> And grant me such victorious grace,
>   That inbred sin may reign no more.

OCTOBER 10.

Whosoever hath, to him shall be given, and he shall have more abundantly.—Matt. xiii. 12. *For the water that I shall give him shall be in him a well of water springing up into everlasting life.*—John iv. 14. *He that is righteous, let him be righteous still; and he that is holy, let him be holy still.*—Rev. xxii. 11.

Of the remarkable increase of the kingdom of God, even from the least beginning, see also Matt. xiii. 31–33; and that beautiful figure, Ezek. xlvii. 1–12. This well being opened, it highly concerns us to draw living water out of it daily by fervent prayer, and then it will spring up freely. But, reader, if you begin to be slothful, and distracted with worldly cares, not abiding closely with Christ, nor calling diligently on Him, your spirit will soon be dried up, and you will scarcely be able, with anxious groans, to draw a single drop from this well. Therefore, take heed to your spirit, and if you desire your own comfort and God's glory, keep near the well's mouth, and be drawing its water continually by prayer, and drinking it sweetly by faith.

> Glory to God that walks the sky,
>   And sends His blessings through;
> That tells His saints of joy on high,
>   And gives a taste below.
>
> Cheerful I feast on heavenly fruit,
>   And drink the pleasures down,—
> Pleasures that flow hard by the foot
>   Of the eternal throne.
>
> But, ah! how soon my joys decay!
>   How soon my sins arise,
> And snatch the heavenly scene away
>   From these lamenting eyes!
>
> When shall the time, dear Jesus, when
>   The shining day appear,
> That I shall leave these clouds of sin,
>   And guilt and darkness here?

October 11.

Cast ye the unprofitable servant into outer darkness, etc.—Matt. xxv. 30. Read the whole of the parable.

Look at this man to whom his Lord had given one talent; he could not bear the thought of using his talent according to the will of Him from whom he had it, and therefore he chose to make himself happier in a way of his own. "Lord," said he, "I knew thee, that thou wast a hard man," etc. But his Lord having convicted him out of his own mouth, dispatched him with this sentence, "Cast the unprofitable servant into outer darkness," etc. Here you see how happy this man made himself by not acting wholly according to his Lord's will. It was, according to his own account, a happiness of murmuring and discontent: "I knew thee," says he, "that thou wast a hard man;"—it was a happiness of fears and apprehensions: "I was," says he, "afraid;"—it was a happiness of vain labors and fruitless travels: "I went," said he, "and hid thy talent;"—and after having been awhile the sport of foolish passions and fears, he is rewarded with darkness, eternal weeping, and gnashing of teeth. Look at the man with his five talents:—"Lord, thou gavest me five talents," etc. Here you see a man intent on improving his talents; he hath no uneasy passions, murmurings, vain fears, and fruitless labors, like the other; but his work prospers in his hands, his happiness increases upon him, the blessing of five becomes doubled, and he is received with a "Well done, good and faithful servant, enter thou into the joy of thy Lord."

> With careful hand may I employ
> The talents God has given;
> Yet not my profit, but my faith,
> Must bring my soul to heaven.

OCTOBER 12.

Through desire, a man having separated himself, seeketh and intermeddleth with all wisdom.—Prov. xviii. 1. *The fruit of the Spirit is love, joy, peace, long-suffering, gentleness, etc.*—Gal. v. 22, 23.

THROUGH pride and self-will, a man having separated himself from the written word of God and the Spirit of the Lord Jesus Christ, seeks to set up and pull down, and to establish everything according to his own wisdom, self-interest, or ambition, instead of humbly following the truth as it is in Jesus. Self-will never becomes a Christian, and much less a reviling those who differ from us. The Lord was not in the strong wind, nor in the earthquake, nor in the fire; but in the still small voice (1 Kings xix. 11, 12). He that taketh offence at everything that differs from him, shews great weakness. It is written "Destroy it not" (Isa. lxv. 8). Though the grape be young, there is wine in the cluster. All spiritual exercises are good; brotherly love renders them beautiful and lovely. The Spirit of the Lord Jesus Christ breathes love to him, holy joy in his salvation, and a divine and peaceable temper, with long suffering and gentleness toward the weakness and infirmities of all around us. The fruit of the Spirit is real goodness in heart and life, a steadfast faith in a precious Jesus, a partaking of His divine meekness, temperance, etc. By these things let us daily try our own spirit, instead of sitting in judgment on the spirit of others.

> Lo! what an entertaining sight
>   Are brethren that agree;
> Brethren whose cheerful hearts unite
>   In bands of piety!
>
> When streams of love, from Christ the spring,
>   Descend to every soul,
> And heavenly peace, with balmy wing,
>   Shades and bedews the whole.

October 13.

By this shall all men know that ye are my disciples, if ye love one another.—John xiii. 35. *And the multitude of them that believed were of one heart and of one soul.*—Acts iv. 32.

"God is Love; and every one that loveth is born of God;" if we love one another as brethren in Christ, and love all saints as saints, not because they are of this or that party; and if we love not in word only but in deed, and shew the truth of our love by works and labors of love,—this is a solid proof to ourselves and to others that we are real disciples of Jesus. It is a clear testimony that we have truly learned Christ, and that we have His Spirit and His love shed abroad in our hearts; that we are of the family and household of faith, and shall enjoy all the family privileges. This is a better evidence, and more convincing to all around us of what we are, than all knowledge, gifts, attainments, and outward privileges whatever. O God of love, cause me to love thee, and all thine; the poor, the weak, and the feeble, as well as the strong; for all are thine!

Let party names no more
  The Christian world o'erspread;
Gentile and Jew, and bond and free,
  Are one in Christ their Head.

Among the saints on earth
  Let mutual love be found;
Heirs of the same inheritance,
  With mutual blessings crowned.

Let envy and ill-will
  Be banished far away;
Those should in strictest friendship dwell
  Who the same Lord obey.

Then will the Church below
  Resemble that above,
Where streams of pleasure ever flow,
  And every heart is love.

OCTOBER 14.

Watch therefore; for ye know not what hour your Lord doth come.—Matt. xxiv. 42.

To watch is the wise exercise of a gracious soul, who is sensible of his own weakness, loves his Saviour, and fears to grieve His Spirit; who is well acquainted with the depth of corruption in his fallen nature; is well apprised of the invisible powers of darkness, and hearkens to the voice of his kind and adorable Shepherd. This watchfulness discovers an awakened attention to our spiritual concerns, and has the love of Christ for its motive, and is attended with a constant dependence on Christ for protection from dangers, and for strength against all enemies, together with supplies of grace in every time of need. If our religion be only in outward profession, it may pass without watching; but if it be true grace in the heart from Jesus Christ, that sacred treasure will need to be guarded by circumspect watchfulness. The exhortation is to all God's children, necessary in every condition, in every stage of a Christian's life; in youth, manhood, old age; in prosperity and adversity, in the seasons of consolations, and in the times of temptation; in company, and alone. O blessed Jesus, help me to watch and pray; let me be always ready; keep me in thy love, and preserve me by thy power, till my change shall come.

> Lord, help me to watch,
>   And help me to pray;
> For foes lie at catch
>   By night and by day.
>
> The world and the devil
>   Are spreading their net;
> My heart, too, is evil,
>   And full of deceit.

October 15.

David's Prayer:—*As a hart panteth for the water brooks, so panteth my soul after thee, O God. My soul thirsteth for God, for the living God.*—Ps. xlii. 1, 2.

Divine Answer:—*Ho! every one that thirsteth, come ye to the waters, and he that hath no money: come ye, buy and eat; yea, come, buy wine and milk without money, and without price. Hearken diligently unto me, and eat ye that which is good, and let your soul delight itself in fatness.*—Isa. lv. 1, 2.

There is a great difference between a legal and a faint-hearted soul: the former is puffed up with self-righteousness; the latter humbly thirsts after Christ's righteousness; therefore he is not under the law, but has grace already. It is only the child, or the new man actually born, that can cry and thirst. And though he cannot so fully believe it, yet to have grace is one thing, and to feel and enjoy it is another. Therefore let not the weak be confounded, which is done very easily, the enemy himself contributing to it as much as he can; but let it be declared, even to the weakest, that they have saving grace when they are brought to be earnestly panting and made truly willing to receive all without price (Matt. v. 3).

> Eternal wisdom has prepared
>   A soul-reviving feast,
> And bids our longing appetites
>   The rich provisions taste.
>
> Jesus, the God, invites us here
>   To this triumphant feast,
> And brings immortal blessings down
>   For each redeemed guest.
>
> O! glorious God, what can we pay
>   For favors so divine?
> We would devote our hearts alway
>   To be for ever thine.

OCTOBER 16.

David's Prayer:—*How long shall I take counsel in my soul, having sorrow in my heart daily?*—Ps. xiii. 2.

Divine Answer:—*Be careful for nothing; but in everything by prayer and supplication, with thanksgiving, let your requests be made known unto God.*—Phil. iv. 6. *Commit thy way unto the Lord; trust also in Him, and He shall sustain thee.*—Ps. xxxvii. 5; lv. 22. *For He has done wonderful things; His counsels of old are aithfulness and truth.*—Isa. xxv. 1.

"BE careful for nothing," is a wall against a thousand troubles. But if we give room to any care and unbelief, it is like a leaven that spreads through all our actions. Therefore we ought never to despair in our lawful calling, but rely in all things on the good providence and faithfulness of God; firmly believing that He will never fail to carry us through the most difficult and intricate circumstances, though there should be ever so little appearance for it in our own eyes. But, alas! Lord, how often do our hearts misgive us, and we either murmur at thy providence, or we trust to ourselves! how seldom have we cast all our care upon thee, and, in humble faith, implored thy direction! Oh! help us to commit our way unto thee.

> He that can dash whole worlds to death
>   And make them when He please,
> He speaks, and that Almighty breath
>   Fulfills His great decrees.
>
> His very Word of grace is strong,
>   As that which built the skies;
> The voice that rolls the stars along
>   Speaks all the promises.
>
> He said, "Let the wide earth be spread;"
>   And heaven was stretched abroad;
> "Abram, I'll be thy God," He said;
>   And he was Abram's God.

October 17.

It is done.—Rev. xxi. 6.

When Jesus bowed the head, and gave up the ghost, He said, "It is finished!"—the work of obedience and suffering, which I had undertaken, is finished. When all the redeemed are gathered, He who sitteth on the throne, beholding those He purchased with His blood, thus expresseth himself, "It is done!"—the means and helps appointed for training you up and preparing you for glory, are now laid aside,—that "which is perfect is come, and that which was in part is done away." What depth of wisdom, what order in the plan of salvation, and in the tendency of its various parts to perfect the glorious work of redeeming love, agreeably to the eternal counsel of peace! (Rom. viii. 29, 30). "This is the doing of the Lord, and is it not marvelous in our eyes?" When receiving the Spirit that is of God, do I not see and admire my dear Immanuel in the whole of the plan; in Him the beginning and finishing of this grand design? Am I a part of the plan? is not His eye upon me, His hand about me? Oh! amazing wisdom and love! shall no part be neglected?—can nothing fail in the Redeemer's hand?—shall even the weakest be supported?—shall none be lost?—shall all His have eternal life? Why then should I fear? The mighty One will do His works in me and for me. Is the prospect by faith of this finished work pleasant and transporting?—what must the immediate blessed vision be! O my God, keep me by thy power to everlasting salvation.

> When all the saints are gathered home,
>   And time its course has run,
> What shouts the ransomed souls will give,
>   When Jesus cries, "'Tis done!"

OCTOBER 18.

We must through much tribulation enter into the kingdom of God.—Acts xiv. 22. Therefore, *let us run with patience the race that is set before us.*—Heb. xii. 1. *Ye have not yet resisted unto blood, striving against sin.*—Verse 4.

SOME licentious professors think there is no need to strive against sin, and some would seem so holy as to be above it; but here we are plainly told of a striving against it. What St. Paul speaks of the conflict between the flesh and the Spirit, is to the same purpose: "For the flesh lusteth against the Spirit, and the Spirit against the flesh; and these are contrary the one to the other; so that ye cannot do the things that ye would" (Gal. v. 17). The most experienced Christians are witnesses to it. The Word of God is said to be a sword, our prayers the wrestling, and our faith the victory. Thus our whole race consists in strivings and conquests. There is always an enemy to be conquered first, before we can make a considerable progress in anything that is good; and none of our enemies are very easily to be overcome; but some are very stubborn; therefore courage and patience are required; and thus we may be sure to have the victory at last.

> In Jesu's strength seek, O my soul,
>   Thy glorious warfare to pursue;
> He only can thy sins control,
>   And give thee vict'ries ever new.
>
> The land of triumph lies on high,
>   There are no fields of battle there;
> Lord, make me conquer till I die,
>   And finish well the glorious war.
>
> Assist me with supplies of grace,
>   To bring thy gospel good renown;
> And let me, when my labors cease,
>   Receive through Christ the promised crown.

October 19.

We are justified freely by His grace, through the redemption that is in Christ Jesus; whom God hath set forth to be a propitiation through faith in His blood, to declare His righteousness for the remission of sins that are past.—Rom. iii. 24, 25. See also John iii. 16.

How sweet are the words, "By grace (without merit) ye are saved!" Here is an overflowing fountain of comfort and divine strength. But how little are the generality of vain and worldly people, who still feed upon husks, acquainted with these words! How little are they relished by our self-righteous moral Christians! But, oh! how deliciously does a poor hungering sinner fare upon them! There is hardly anything less known and understood, as to the power and experience, than the mystery of Christ's suffering and dying for us, and justification by faith in Him; though it is the only paradise and element of believers, and the greatest jewel restored by the Reformation. Such talking and representations of sin as only strike the imagination, are not sufficient; but we must also feel the mortal wounds of sin, by which the flesh is mortified, and be actually healed by the stripes of Christ.

> God, the great God that rules the skies,
>   The gracious and the just,
> Makes His own Son a sacrifice;
>   And here lies all our trust.
>
> Here rest, my faith, and ne'er remove;
>   Here let repentance rise,
> While I behold His bleeding love,
>   His dying agonies.
>
> With shame and sorrow, here I own
>   How great my guilt has been;
> This is my way t' approach the throne,
>   And God forgives my sin.

October 20.

See that ye fall not out by the way.—Gen. xlv. 24.

Joseph, having shewn himself fully reconciled to his brethren, dismisses them with this needful caution, "See that ye fall not out by the way." He knew that they were but too apt to be quarrelsome. One might say, "It was you that first upbraided him with his dreams;" another, "It was you that said, "Let us kill him," etc. Thus their journey to their father's house would be very uncomfortable, if this spirit of quarreling and upbraiding once got possession of them. Fellow-Christians, what a lesson is here for us! What says our Lord Jesus to us? Love one another, live in peace: whatever occurs, "Let us not fall out by the way." Are we not all brethren? Have we not all one Father? Are we not all subjects of free and sovereign grace? Are we not all agreed in essential points? Are we not all sinners by nature and practice? Have we not all one object of faith? Are we not all traveling the same road? Oh! then, why should we fall out by the way? Suppose we be of different denominations, yet holding the same Head, why cannot we love as brethren? Let not the strong despise the weak, nor the weak judge the strong. Suppose our way should part a little as to externals; yet all setting out from the same spiritual Egypt, all under the same Leader, why may we not all hope to meet at last in the true Canaan? Satan, false professors, and the ungodly world, are unanimous in their opposition to us: let us be united, that they prevail not against us (Phil. ii. 1, 2).

> Our Jesus is the Prince of Peace,
> Who made God's quarrel with us cease;
> And now He bids the children come,
> But quarrel not as they go home.

OCTOBER 21.

The sinner's Prayer:—*Where shall I find rest?*
Divine Answer:—*Thus saith the Lord, Stand ye in the ways and see; and ask for the old paths, where is the good way, and walk therein, and you shall find rest for your souls.*—Jer. vi. 16. *Come unto me, all ye that labor and are heavy laden, and I will give you rest. Take my yoke upon you, and learn of me; for I am meek and lowly in heart: and ye shall find rest unto your souls. My yoke is easy, and my burden is light.*—Matt. xi. 28-30.

IN our own ways there is nothing but trouble; but giving ourselves entirely up to be guided by God at His own pleasure, we may always be easy, since we know that by every step He brings us nearer to heaven. The only way to rest is the way of repentance and faith; in which we consider ourselves from the beginning, even to the end of our Christian life, as utterly lost and condemned by the law, but as perfectly reconciled and justified through Christ. Thus to abide in Him, to let Him work alone, and be truly resigned to His ways, will certainly have the desired effect; whilst, by the righteousness and workings of our own hearts, we can never attain to it, and, which is worse, may be lulled into a false rest.

> Lord, I believe a rest remains,
>   To all thy people known,
> A rest, where pure enjoyment reigns
>   And thou art loved alone.
>
> A rest, where all our soul's desire
>   Is fixed on things above;
> Where grief, and pain, and fear expir
>   Cast out by perfect love.
>
> This is the feast of saints on high,
>   But I may taste below;
> And sweeter tastes God will supply,
>   As into Christ I grow.

October 22.

Ye are complete in Him.—Col. ii. 10. *The Scriptures are able to make thee wise unto salvation through faith which is in Christ Jesus. That the man of God may be perfect, thoroughly furnished unto all good works.*—2 Tim. iii. 15, 17. *And of His fullness have all we received, and grace for grace.*—John i. 16.

THINK, O believer, with wonder and amazement, reflect with gratitude and love, that, whilst thou art deploring the common ruin of human nature, and mournfully feeling its sad effects upon thy own soul, thou mayest yet look through all thine imperfection, frailty, and unworthiness, to thy glorious Representative, and see thyself complete in Him. The law which would condemn thee, He has completely satisfied: the obedience which it requires, in order to thine acceptance with God, He has completely paid; and that eternal life, from which thy sinful imperfections must have for ever barred thee, is now become thine inalienable inheritance, as the reward of His righteousness, who lived and died for thee. Go forth, then, and glorify Him in heart and life. The more thou believest in Him, the more wilt thou love Him; and the more thou lovest Him, the better wilt thou serve Him; and till He shall remove thee from this vale of sin and sorrow, let thy song in the house of thy pilgrimage be this, "Complete in Him!"

> To all my vileness, Christ is glory bright;
> To all my mis'ries, infinite delight;
> To all my ignorance, wise without compare;
> To my deformity, the eternal fair.
>
> Sight to my blindness, to my meanness wealth;
> Life to my death, and to my sickness health;
> To darkness light, my liberty in thrall;
> What shall I say?—My Christ is All in All!

OCTOBER 23.

Will ye speak wickedly for God? and talk deceitfully for Him?—Job xiii. 7. *Thy word is truth.*—John xvii. 17.

WHEN Moses saw an Egyptian and an Israelite striving together, he killed the Egyptian and saved the Israelite (Exod. ii. 12). But when he saw two Israelites striving together, he labored to reconcile them, saying, "Ye are brethren, why do ye strive?" So when we read, or see the Apocryphal Books, or Heathen Story, or Popish Traditions, contradicting the Scriptures,—as, for instance, Jacob curseth the wrath and anger of Simeon and Levi, for murdering the Shechemites (Gen. xlix. 7); and Judith blessed God for killing them (Judith 9),—here, and in such like places, let us kill the Egyptian, but save the Israelite,—set a value on the Scriptures, but slight the Apocrypha. But when we meet with any appearance of seeming contradiction in the canon of Scripture, as where it is said, "God tempted Abraham" (Gen. xxii. 1) and, "God tempteth no man" (James i. 13)—here now, and in many other places, we must be reconcilers, and distinguish between a temptation of trial, which is from God, and a temptation of seduction, which is by the devil; and these two, seemingly differing friends, will appear to be brethren, and agree well.

> The Spirit breathes upon the word,
>   And brings the truth to sight;
> Precepts and promises afford
>   A sanctifying light.
>
> A glory gilds the sacred page,
>   Majestic like the sun;
> It gives a light to every age,
>   It gives, but borrows none.
>
> The hand that gave it still supplies
>   The gracious light and heat;
> His truths upon the nations rise,
>   They rise, but never set.

OCTOBER 24.

And Joshua blessed him, and gave unto Caleb Hebron for an inheritance.—Joshua xiv. 13.

THE spies that went up to view the promised land, all except Caleb and Joshua, made a formiddable report of the gigantic inhabitants of Hebron, saying, "We are not able to go up against the people, for they are stronger than we." Caleb (answering well to his name, which signifies all-heart) stilled the people before Moses, and said, "Let us go up at once and possess it, for we are well able to overcome." We are told he had another spirit with him, and followed God fully. Moses, therefore, was commissioned to make him a grant of all the land whereon his feet had trodden, which was the mountain of Hebron. Caleb was eighty-five years old when he reminded Joshua of his promise; he was forty when Moses sent him to spy out the land; forty-seven years the Lord had saved him in the wilderness, and amid the perils of war. Joshua blessed him, acknowledged his claim and deserts, besought God to prosper him, and gave him the country;—thus was his fidelity and uprightness rewarded. Reader, are you like-hearted with Caleb? Are you longing after Hebron?—that is, communion with God. Are you eager to fight against your spiritual foes—those sons of Anak—lusts, passions, the devil, and the world? If so, remember the promise, "As your day is, so shall your strength be found." Keep up fellowship with God, and no enemy shall be too strong for you; follow God fully; eye the Captain of your salvation; fight in His name and strength, and you shall conquer every foe.

> All heart, like Caleb, may I be
> Against each spiritual foe;
> And, like him, trusting in the Lord,
> To fight and conquer go.

October 25.

At midnight the Lord smote all the first-born in the land of Egypt, from the first-born of Pharaoh that sat on his throne, unto the first-born of the captive that was in the dungeon.—Exod. xii. 29.

The death of every first-born of the Egyptians carried so lively a resemblance, and bore so natural a relation to their sin in destroying every male of the Israelites, that they must needs perceive it was inflicted as a punishment for that very cruelty; and consequently, must conclude, that the God of Israel took particular notice of human transactions, and, sooner or later, rewarded every man according to his works. The gradual increase of the judgments inflicted on Egypt is somewhat remarkable, and equally expressive of the mercy and justice of God. The four first plagues were loathsome rather than fatal to the Egyptians; but after that of the flies, came the murrain, which chiefly spent its rage upon the cattle; the biles and blains reached both man and beast, though there was still a reserve for life; the hail and locusts extended, in a great measure, even to life itself,—the first by an immediate stroke, and both, consequently, by destroying the fruits of the earth; that of darkness added consternation to their minds, and lashes to their consciences; and when all this would not reclaim, at length came the decisive blow,—first, the slaying of the first-born, and then the drowning of the incorrigible tyrant, and all his host. "Great and marvelous are thy works, O Lord God Almighty! just and true are thy ways, thou King of saints!"

> Let no proud sinner grow secure
> Who has through dangers past;
> If former judgments turn thee not,
> Thy life shall go at last.

OCTOBER 26.

Solomon's Prayer:—*Draw me, we will run after thee.*—Song of Sol. i. 4.

Divine Answer:—*I have loved thee with an everlasting love; therefore with loving-kindness have I drawn thee.*—Jer. xxxi. 3. See also Rom. viii. 39.

MANY and various are the ways the Almighty takes in bringing His children to Himself, and to a knowledge of the things of their peace. Sometimes He draws by the silken bands of love; sometimes by the still small voice of His Spirit; sometimes by the knotted cords of pain and sickness; sometimes He drives them by the storm and tempest of His broken law; but most effectually in giving His Son to die for them. Reader, pray always to Him to make you sensible of the secret, tender drawings of His love, and willing to follow them directly. This praying always is very needful, because we are always in want, and without being instant and earnest; we cannot receive much. Therefore it is not a hard command, but a great benefit and privilege; as if God should say, "You are a poor child, always wanting something; but you may always pray to me, and I will always hear, and assist, and draw thee after me."

> Oh! draw me, Saviour, after thee,
>   So shall I run and never tire;
> With gracious words still comfort me,
>   And be my hope and whole desire.
> No lust can stir, or guilty fear,
> Nor worldly wish, if thou art there.
>
> Oh! that I, as a little child,
>   May follow thee, nor ever rest,
> Till sweetly thou hast poured thy mild
>   And lowly mind into my breast;
> Nor ever may we parted be,
> Till I become one spirit with thee.

October 27.

Them that honor me I will honor; and they that despise me shall be lightly esteemed.—1 Sam. ii. 30.

This is part of the prophet's message to Eli when he honored his sons above God. He had indeed reproved them, saying, "Why do ye these things? for I hear of your evil doings by all the people;" but he did not exert his authority in punishing them as they deserved when they slighted his reproof. This was accounted by God as winking at their sin. He therefore acquaints him, that Hophni and Phinehas, as they had sinned together, should die together, and his posterity be cut off in the flower of their age, and from the high priesthood. Eli was not much affected with this prophecy, till the threatening was repeated by Samuel, an artless child, who did not know the voice of the Lord till Eli instructed him. It appeared then much more terrible than from the mouth of the prophet, and led him humbly to acknowledge the justice of God, and to submit to the sentence with a truly penitent heart. This is written for our admonition. Are we valiant for the truth, regarding neither father, nor mother, nor the most tender relation, where the interest and honor of our God are concerned? Parents, let this be a warning to you to train up your children in the fear of the Lord: "For the arms of the wicked shall be broken; but the Lord upholdeth the righteous" (Ps. xxxvii. 17).

> The Lord Jehovah calls,
>   Be every ear inclined;
> May such a voice awake each heart,
>   And captivate each mind.
>
> Oh! harden not your hearts,
>   But hear His voice to-day;
> Lest, ere to-morrow's earliest dawn,
>   He call your souls away.

October 28.

Abraham against hope believed in hope.—Rom. iv. 18.

Abraham's faith seemed to be in a thorough correspondence with the power and constant faithfulness of Jehovah. In the outward circumstances in which he was placed, he had not the greatest cause to expect the fulfillment of the promise. Yet he believed the word of the Lord, and looked forward to the time when his seed should be as the stars of heaven for multitude. O my soul, thou hast not one single promise only, like Abraham, but a thousand promises, and many patterns of faithful believers before thee: it behooves thee, therefore, to rely with confidence upon the word of God. And though the Lord delayeth His help, and the evil seemeth to grow worse and worse, be not weak, but rather strong, and rejoice, since the most glorious promises of God are generally fulfilled in such a wondrous manner, that He steps forth to save us at a time when there is the least appearance of it. He commonly brings His help in our greatest extremity that His finger may plainly appear in our deliverance. And this method He chooses, that we may not trust upon anything that we see or feel, as we are always apt to do, but only upon His bare word, which we may depend upon in every state.

> How large the promise! how divine!
>   To Abra'm and his seed;
> "I'll be a God to thee and thine,
>   Supplying all their need."
>
> The words of this extensive love
>   From age to age endure;
> The Angel of the Covenant proves,
>   And seals the blessing sure.
>
> Our God, how faithful are His ways,
>   His love endures the same;
> Nor from the promise of His grace
>   Blots out the sinner's name.

October 29.

Immediately I conferred not with flesh and blood.—Gal. i. 16. *For the king's commandment was urgent;* much more the commandment of the King of kings.—Dan. iii. 22. Therefore, *be not slothful in business,* but *fervent in spirit, serving the Lord.*—Rom. xii. 11.

The speediest and easiest method to accomplish our desire of overcoming the evil and doing the good, is an immediate compliance with our first convictions, without conferring with flesh and blood. If we delay the work, we give room to other people without, and to Satan and to our sinful hearts from within, to persuade us to the contrary; by which the flesh can easily renew its strength, and the spirit will be weakened. And what will be the consequence of this, but that either we miscarry in our design, or that the conflict will be afterward so much sharper, and the good work, if not stifled, dropt entirely; yet if it be done, it will not be done so completely, and with such singleness of heart, as it should be. But if we narrowly watch our hearts, and directly engage with even the least opposition when it stirs, then our enemies will not be so strong, and we shall have no reason to despair.

> Jesus, mighty to renew,
> Work in me to will and do;
> Turn my nature's rapid tide;
> Stem the torrent of my pride.
>
> Take away my darling sin,
> Make me willing to be clean;
> Make me willing to receive
> What thy goodness waits to give.
>
> Then my soul shall praise thy grace;
> Then with gladness run my race;
> And, when all my course is done,
> Receive the prize thy cross has won.

OCTOBER 30.

Yield not your members as instruments of unrighteousness unto sin; but yield yourselves unto God, as those that are alive from the dead, and your members as instruments of righteousness.—Rom. vi. 13. *Present your bodies a living sacrifice, holy, acceptable unto God.*—Rom. xii. 1.

IF God has my members as weapons and instruments in His hands, I shall certainly be able not only to work, but also to conquer, since He understands full well how to manage them. May the Lord only give me grace not to wind myself out of His hands, else I must needs be like a dead, useless carcass; for how can a pen write alone, without being in the hand of a writer? It is true, indeed, it is very hard, nay, impossible, to be really good, and to do all that is good, if we undertake it alone; but God himself living and working in us, and we truly delighting in Him, it is very easy and pleasant. Therefore, care is only to be taken that our hearts may be always the working-place, and our members the instruments of God, in which, and through which, He can perform everything himself.

> Now God I serve; to Him alone
> My thankful homage pay;
> My only master Christ I own,
> And Him will I obey.
>
> To Him my members I present,
> Which He will not refuse;
> The meanest, basest instrument,
> His glory deigns to use.
>
> Come then, my soul, to God the Lord,
> In holy ardor come;
> Obey the precepts of His Word,
> Until He calls thee home.
>
> A slave to sin too long thou wast,
> But Christ has set thee free;
> Anthems of praise forever burst
> To Him who ransomed thee.

October 31.

The fear of man bringeth a snare.—Prov. xxix. 25.
Be not conformed to this world.—Rom. xii. 2.
If any man love the world, the love of the Father is not in him.—1 John. ii. 15.

How many people swell with pride and vanity for such things as they would not know how to value at all but that they are admired in the world! How fearful are many of having their houses poorly furnished, or themselves meanly clothed, for this only reason, lest the world should make no account of them, and place them amongst low and mean people! How often would a man have yielded to the haughtiness and ill-nature of others, and shewn a submissive temper, but that he dares not pass for such a poor-spirited man in the opinion of the world! How many wish to be real Christians, and would practice Christian temperance and sobriety, were it not for the censure the world passes upon such a life! Others have frequent intentions of living up to the rules of Christianity, from which they are frighted by considering what the world would say of them. Thus does the impression which we have received from living in the world enslave our minds, that we dare not attempt to be eminent in the sight of God and holy angels, for fear of being little in the eyes of the world. Reader, how is it with thee? Art thou still hanging between God and the world? Consider for a moment, what can the world give thee in exchange for the favor of God? What can it help thee in sickness, death and judgment? Reflect seriously on this, with prayer unto God, and the snares of the world will be broken.

> Lord, save me from the fear of man,
>   Which surely brings a snare;
> And make me hear their scoffs and jests
>   With unconcerned ear.

If ye then be risen with Christ, seek those things which are above, where Christ sitteth on the right hand of God.

Set your affection on things above—not on things on the earth.

For ye are dead: and your life is hid with Christ in God.—Col. iii. 1-3.

——:o:——

My soul, wait thou only upon God: for my expectation is from Him.—Ps. lxii. 5.

———

They that wait upon the Lord shall renew their strength: they shall mount up with wings as eagles; they shall run, and not be weary; and they shall walk, and not faint.— Isa. xl. 31.

NOVEMBER 1.

At the beginning of thy supplications the commandment came forth.—Dan. ix. 23. *Continuing instant in prayer.*—Rom. xii. 12.

OH! comfortable and encouraging thought, that in the same moment the supplication ascended, the gracious answer descended. When we pray with simplicity and earnestness of soul, the return of grace and love meets our request before it hath ascended half way to heaven: and when the Lord is going to bless us, He pours out a spirit of prayer, and raises a desire for that particular blessing He is going to communicate. Therefore, when we are enabled to pray earnestly, we may be sure that blessings are coming, and that we shall certainly receive in due time a seasonable and visible help. Then let us only go on, and put, as it were, one weight of prayers after another upon the scales of the sanctuary. But it is well to be observed that we must also be watchful, and not act contrary to the intent of our prayers, which might provoke the Lord to delay His help. But when He tarries long, it is not His intention to give us a denial; but rather make us more desirous and earnest, that He may bestow the more upon us afterward. For this delay He will certainly well recompense, and grant us abundantly above all that we could ask or think.

> Lord, I will not let thee go
> Till the blessing thou bestow;
> Hear my Advocate divine;
> Lo! to His my suit I join.
>
> Joined to His it cannot fail;
> Jesus' suing must prevail.
> Friend of sinners, King of saints,
> Answer my minutest wants.
>
> All my largest thoughts require,
> Grant me all my heart's desire;
> Give me till my cup run o'er,
> Then my heart can hold no more.

NOVEMBER 2.

When the woman saw that the tree was good for food, and that it was pleasant to the eyes, and a tree to be desired to make one wise, she took of the fruit thereof, and did eat; and gave also unto her husband with her, and he did eat.—Gen. iii. 6.
Every man is tempted when he is drawn away of his own lust, and enticed. Then, when lust hath conceived, it bringeth forth sin, etc.—James i. 15.

THUS one sin always begets another: by the eyes it rushes into the heart; from the heart it proceeds into the mouth, hands and feet; from us it is transferred upon others; and thus we go on sinning, and falling deeper and deeper. Therefore we must set a strict guard over our eyes and ears; be very cautious, and resist the least beginnings of sin; not making light of any, for the least spark of worldly lust being entertained and cherished, we eat of the forbidden tree, standing every way before us, and thereby a great fire may be kindled. But having always our eyes fixed, and all our conversation upon the presence of God in Christ, so as to walk continually in the light, and directly to quell the least inward motions of evil, they will never break forth into gross outward sins, but we shall daily grow in grace. May the Lord enable me to practice this good lesson, and may He himself watch continually over my heart, eyes, lips, and all other senses and thoughts!

> With my whole heart I seek thy face,
>   Oh! let me never stray
> From thy commands. O God of grace,
>   Nor tread the sinner's way.
>
> Thy word I hide within my heart,
>   To keep my conscience clean,
> And be an everlasting guard
>   From every rising sin.

November 3.

The preaching of the cross is to us which are saved the power of God.—1 Cor. i. 18.

OH! that I might always feed upon the cross, and experience its power, till I had obtained a complete victory! Whosoever was bit by a fiery serpent, and looked upon the brazen serpent, lived (Numb. xxi. 9). Thus always to look upon Christ crucified is the one thing needful, from which all other blessings flow. "And as Moses lifted up the serpent in the wilderness, even so must the Son of Man be lifted up, that whosoever believeth in Him should not perish, but have eternal life. For God sent not His Son into the world to condemn the world, but that the world through Him might be saved" (John iii. 14, 15, 17). Oh! may the eyes of my faith be fixed immovably on thee, my crucified Saviour! for as long as I live I shall feel the biting of the old serpent, and therefore I have need to look unto thee continually; and thou, gracious Lord, afford me cure, day by day, with entire healing at last!

> So did the Hebrew prophet raise
>   The brazen serpent high;
> The wounded felt immediate ease,
>   The camp forbore to die.
>
> Look upward in the dying hour,
>   And live, the prophet cries;
> But Christ performs a nobler cure
>   When faith lifts up her eyes.
>
> High on the cross the Saviour hung,
>   High in the heavens He reigns;
> Here sinners, by th' old serpent stung,
>   Look and forget their pains.
>
> When God's own Son is lifted up,
>   A dying world revives;
> The Jew beholds his glorious hope,
>   The expiring Gentile lives.

NOVEMBER 4.

The law is not made for a righteous man, to condemn him.—1 Tim. i. 9. *For rulers are not a terror to good works, but to the evil. Wilt thou then not be afraid of the power? Do that which is good, and thou shalt have praise of the same.*—Rom. xiii. 3. See also Gal. iii. 16 to end.

THE righteous man being dead to the law by the death of Christ, and living to God in righteousness, the law can condemn him no more than a dead man, or one that liveth in heaven already, nay, Christ himself; for it condemns only the sin: but he is in Christ, without sin; for the sin being abolished, the wrath and curse of the law is also removed, and grace and blessing restored in its place. Christ has taken all his sins upon Himself, and imparted His own perfect obedience to the law to him; therefore in Christ he has fully satisfied all the demands of the law, and is entirely free from its dreadful curse in his conscience: the blood of Christ cleanseth us from all sins, and consequently from an evil conscience (Heb. ix. 9, 14; and x. 22). Being sprinkled with His blood, and graciously covered with His golden robes, the Lord is perfectly pleased, and finds no more fault with us. The atoning blood makes intercession for us with God, crying continually, "Abba, abba; mercy, mercy; peace, peace;" and obtains grace, pardon, life and salvation.

> Blood has a voice to pierce the skies;
> Revenge! the blood of Abel cries;
> But the dear stream when Christ was slain,
> Speaks peace as loud from every vein.
>
> Pardon and peace from God on high;
> Behold, He lays His vengeance by;
> And rebels, that deserve His sword,
> Become the fav'rites of the Lord.

November 5.

There is none like unto the God of Jeshurun, etc.
—Deut. xxxiii. 26.

In these last words of Moses we have the glory of God set forth. The whole universe God hath made for His own use, to be the chariot for Him to ride in, as is represented in Ezekiel's vision. In this chariot God's seat or throne is heaven. This visible universe, subject to such continual changes and revolutions, we may compare to the wheels of His chariot. God's providence is represented by the motion of the wheels; He brings to pass His own counsels in the lower world, and manages and directs all, as a man doth his chariot which he turns as it pleaseth him. How safe, then, must they be who are under the wing of the God of Jeshurun; who find Him reconciled to them by the death of His Son; and feel themselves reconciled to Him by the power of His grace! "He rideth on the heavens for their help." Verily, He it is that giveth strength and victory to His people, blessed be God. Reader, is the God of Jeshurun, the God of Israel, thy God? Is He who rideth on the heavens thy help? Does thine heart trust in Him alone, and His grace subdue thine outward iniquities, and thine inbred corruptions? Is He who rideth on the sky thine excellence? If the Lord is not thy help, alas! thou wilt prove a ruined soul. If the Lord is not thy excellence, thou art still a stranger unto God and Christ. Awake, arise, and call upon God; His ear is open unto prayer, and thou art yet on mercy's ground. Oh! call upon Him speedily, and cry unto Him earnestly, that thou perish not.

> May Christ, who ruleth in the sky,
> And is Jeshurun's God,
> My soul defend, my wants supply,
> And wash me in His blood.

NOVEMBER 6.

Let your conversation be without covetousness; and be content with such things as ye have.—Heb. xiii. 5. *For they that will be rich fall into temptation and a snare, and into many foolish and hurtful lusts, which drown men in destruction and perdition; for the love of money is the root of all evil, etc.*—1 Tim. vi. 9, 10.

A COVETOUS man is called an idolater, and has no part in the kingdom of God. But who believes that he is covetous? Now, here you see that every one is actually covetous who is not content with what he has. And what says the apostle of such as will be rich?—They fall. Not only may they fall, but they actually do fall; nor can the fall be avoided if men are determined they will be rich. O Reader! be thou frightened; get the covetous desires of thy heart subdued, and keep disentangled from worldly things; for who knows how soon you must go out of this world, and leave everything behind? Away from it with thy heart, else thy death will be very hard. The Christian's motto is, *God and enough;* for he that has God is content; and consequently always rich enough, even in poverty; and that must be a covetous man indeed, who has not enough, having God. O Lord, make me so free by faith from the love of earthly things, that I may equally praise thee, whether thou be pleased to give me something, or to take it away from me; and that I may never covetously refuse that to others or to myself which thou hast given for my own and my neighbor's comfort.

> The rich young man whom Jesus loved
>   Should warn us to forbear;
> His love of earthly treasures proved
>   A fatal golden snare.

NOVEMBER 7.

The soul of the diligent shall be made fat.—Prov. xiii. 4. *Therefore, brethren, we are debtors, not to the flesh, to live after the flesh.*—Rom. viii. 12.

You are concerned for having no more grace! What is the reason? Perhaps you are indolent, careless and unfaithful. And though you have no warrant even for an hour to live, yet unreasonably you suppose you have time enough; therefore you are not serious, diligent, and fervent in prayer for sufficient strength to be always prepared, and have boldness in death. No wonder, if you do not immediately resist sin, that it grows strong, and you always are weak and discouraged. And how can you expect to receive more grace, if you do not faithfully improve what little you have? If you would but diligently and faithfully apply yourself to the Word and prayer, God would certainly not be wanting on His part to fulfill His promises, and give you enough, but not otherwise; for it is well to be observed, that we must know it once for all, that there is no such thing as making any progress in grace, and carrying our point, unless we are mindful of ourselves; watching and praying against all sins, and whatever may be an hindrance, on the one hand; and following with all diligence that which is good, and what may be a furtherance, on the other. It is not enough to use some, but we must use all diligence; and according as our grace is increased, our diligence must increase also, since it goes against the stream.

> Well to resist the sinful power
>   Requires a strong restraint;
> We must be watchful every hour,
>   And pray, but never faint.

NOVEMBER 8.

In lowliness of mind let each esteem other better than themselves.—Phil. ii. 3. *Bear ye one another's burdens, and so fulfill the law of Christ. For if a man think himself to be something, etc. But let every man prove his own work, and then shall he have rejoicing in himself alone, and not in another.*—Gal. vi. 2-4.

IF we were truly humble, and looked upon ourselves as most miserable sinners, we should willingly submit to all adversities, and patiently bear the burdens and infirmities, considering that God has borne with us a great deal more. Observing, therefore, the faults of our neighbor, we must not forget our own. Perhaps in other things we are weaker than he. This will restrain us from judging harshly, or speaking unadvisedly to others; but, first, we should speak to God about it, and then try, with gentle means, to bring them to rights again. Nay, the best method is to consider our neighbor on the good, and ourselves on the bad side, and to see whether we can excuse him and accuse ourselves; and if his fault could not be excused in any manner, we must not suffer him to stir up our corruption, but come in with prayer between God and him, to plead his cause before the throne in hearty love. It is very easy to find fault with others; but to shew love, and restore them by prayer and brotherly correction, is quite another thing.

> Bless'd are the souls who stand afar
> From rage and passion, noise and war;
> God will secure their happy state,
> And plead their cause against the great.
>
> Though in the path of death they tread,
> With gloomy horrors overspread,
> Their steadfast heart shall fear no ill,
> For thou, O Lord, art with them still.

NOVEMBER 9.

The eyes of all wait upon thee, and thou givest them their meat in due season. Thou openest thine hand, and satisfiest the desire of every living thing. He will fulfill the desire of them that fear Him: He also will hear their cry, and will save them.—Ps. cxlv. 15, 16, 19. See also Ps. civ. 27, 28.

WHO considers these words enough! The hand of God being my chief provision and store-house, is it not a shame to be anxiously careful for anything? Has the Lord all things in His hand? then surely I shall receive what He has for me; none will be able to withhold it. Faith has always a free access to the treasures of God, who is never wanting. Christians have their chests and treasures in such a high place, even in God, that no thief can rob them, and they are sure to have enough in God; and though the Lord should try them with want a little while, yet He relieves them in due time,— their bread must rain from heaven, rather than they should be left without. You need not, says Christ, seek these other things, they shall be brought to you if ye only abide in me. If this does not comfort and strengthen us, nothing else will. Now, many rely on their full pockets and purses; but if they had true faith, it would be enough that they believed and had it in God's hand, purse and chest. If the Lord is pleased to bestow some provision on His servant, he is very thankful for it, and is careful to apply it well. But if God thinks proper to deny it him, he is content and cheerful.

> The Lord is good, the Lord is kind;
> Great is His grace, His mercy sure;
> And the whole race of man shall find
> His truth from age to age endure.

NOVEMBER 10.

They withstood Uzziah the king, and said unto him, It appertaineth not unto thee, Uzziah, to burn incense unto the Lord.—2 Chron. xxvi. 18.

HERE is the only blot we find on the name of Uzziah. As long as he sought the Lord in the right way, God made him to prosper. God helped him till he was strong; but when he was strong, his heart was lifted up to his own destruction. He was not content with the honors God had put upon him, but would usurp those that were forbidden him, like our first parents. The chief priest and other priests were ready to burn incense for the king, according to the duty of their office; and plainly acquainted him, that if, through a mistaken zeal, he offered to do it himself, he would incur the wrath of God and suffer for it; but this served only to excite his wrath, till he felt the judgment of God's hand in his punishment. Though he strove with the priests, he would not strive with his Maker, but retired as soon as he was smitten with the leprosy. Thus we see that "the God we have to deal with is a jealous God," who expects all that serve Him shall do it according to His own institutions. Do you, reader, come to Him in the way of His appointments? Take care that you come not with unhallowed fire before the Lord, lest you be also smitten. Our prayers, our graces, and our duties, must always be put by faith into the hand of our Lord Jesus, the High Priest of our profession, to be by Him presented unto God along with the sweet incense of His merits, else we shall find ourselves deceived, and have no acceptance with God.

> No strange incense let me bring
> To present unto my King;
> I renounce my own desert;
> Jesus, thou my incense art.

NOVEMBER 11.

He, the Lord, will beautify the meek with salvation. —Ps. cxlix. 4. *And if ye suffer for righteousness' sake, happy are ye.*—1 Peter iii. 14. *Lord, thou hast heard the desire of the humble: thou wilt prepare their heart, thou wilt cause thine ear to hear.*—Ps. x. 17. *The meek shall eat and be satisfied; they shall praise the Lord that seek Him: your heart shall live for ever.*—Ps. xxii. 26. *But the meek shall inherit the earth; and shall delight themselves in the abundance of peace.* —Ps. xxxvii. 11. See also Ps. xlviii. 10; Isa. liv. 11.

ALL this is for the humble and poor in spirit. How does that agree?—poor, and yet blessed! Oh! yes, poor in ourselves, but blessed and glorious in Christ. If we never experience His glory, the reason is, we are not truly sensible of our misery; but when we are come quite low, let us confidently lay hold on Christ, and we shall be blessed; for all is ours. We may say, O Lord, if thou art a glorious help to the needy, lo! here is want and misery enough! therefore, I come with all my want and poverty to the fullness of thy grace and riches, with my darkness to thy light, with my death to thy life. Grant that all my evils may be swallowed up by thy goodness and glorious deliverance! Mine innumerable wants I set before thee, as so many empty vessels, and desire to have them filled with thy spiritual and heavenly blessings.

> Oh! might I hear the heavenly tongue
>   But whisper, "Thou art mine!"
> Those gentle words should raise my song
>   To notes almost divine.
>
> How would my leaping heart rejoice,
>   And think my heaven secure;
> I trust the all-creating Voice,
>   And faith desires no more.

November 12.

Be ye renewed in the spirit of your mind. And put on the new man, which after God is created in righteousness and true holiness.—Eph. iv. 23, 24. *Therefore we are buried with Him by baptism into death; that like as Christ was raised up from the dead by the glory of the Father, even so we also should walk in newness of life.*—Rom. vi. 4.

O Lord, grant me daily repentance, and a tender feeling of my sins, that by the power of thy death the Old Man may be crucified, and by the power of thy resurrection the New Man may rise up and grow in grace, being filled and refreshed with the fruits of the Spirit! Let me ever be in earnest, and look upon every day as the very first and the very last, that with each I may, as it were, begin anew to work out my salvation with fear and trembling, and so be always prepared for death and eternity. Give me grace to surmount all difficulties, and to avoid everything that may prove a torment of conscience in the hour of death. And as there is no standing still, I humbly beseech thee to stir me up daily and hourly more and more, that I may make all haste, and "give all diligence to make my calling and election sure."

> Lord, I am vile, conceived in sin!
> And born unholy, and unclean!
> Sprung from the man whose guilty fall
> Corrupts the race, and taints us all.
>
> Soon as we draw our infant breath,
> The seeds of sin grow up for death;
> The law demands a perfect heart;
> But we're defiled in every part.
>
> Great God, create my heart anew,
> And form my spirit pure and true!
> Oh! make me wise betimes, to spy
> My danger and my remedy.

November 13.

He hath dispersed, he hath given to the poor; his righteousness endureth for ever.—Ps. cxii. 9. *In the morning sow thy seed, and in the evening withhold not thine hand.*—Eccles. xi. 6.

Those that lay up treasures on earth, suffer nothing to lie long useless, but lend out as fast as they can; and such as desire to reap soon and plentifully, are careful to sow soon and plentifully. Therefore lend and sow ye also in good time; for there may be times when you cannot shew charity, or at least not so largely. We must not pretend to pay the debt of charity with some poor mites and pence. If you will give something, give bountifully; take your hands full as if you were sowing, like the poor widow with her two mites, which she sowed out freely, though it were her whole substance. But the rich ones were not so liberal, but covetously offered only what they could spare very well. Is it not said we should sow? Now, seedsmen sow with hands full, and so should we; for God loveth a cheerful giver, and will in His turn dispense again bountifully to you, that ye should have sufficiently in all things to every good work; (but God dispensing so bountifully to you, why should you then grudge Him anything, or make only such poor returns?) for what we do to our neighbor, is the same as if it were done to God Himself, if done in faith and love.

> Awake, my zeal; awake, my love,
>   And serve my Saviour here below,
> In works which all the saints above
>   And holy angels cannot do.
>
> Awake, my charity, and feed
>   The hungry soul, and clothe the poor;
> In heaven are found no sons of need
>   There all these duties are no more.

NOVEMBER 14.

He shall redeem Israel from all his iniquities.— Ps. cxxx. 8. *O the Hope of Israel, the Saviour thereof in time of trouble.—*Jer. xiv. 8. *In wrath remember mercy.—*Hab. iii. 2.

Despair not, O my soul, in any tribulation or conflict, as if it were impossible to overcome it. The all-healing Word of God contains advice and comfort for all cases. The Lord being thy helper in all adversity, and able to turn the sharpest afflictions into the greatest blessings, He would never smite, nor withhold something from thee, if He was not willing also to heal, and give thee something better in its place. O Lord, I trust thou wilt carry me through all difficulties. Though my misery and weakness were ever so great, yet there is nothing too great for thee; it is all one to thee to help in great and little distresses; nay, the more I am surrounded with grief and weakness, the more wilt thou pity, spare and nourish me, as a tender mother does the least of all her children; and the more occasion there will be to display thy mighty salvation. The sharper and longer my distress and conflicts have been, the nearer, greater and sweeter, I trust, will also be my salvation; for the same Lord who has said I shall not be tried above measure, has also engaged to lead me on conquering, till at length all my enemies are subdued.

> There's full redemption at His throne
> For sinners long enslaved;
> The great Redeemer is His Son,
> And Israel shall be saved.
>
> A hope so great, and so divine,
> May trials well endure;
> And purge the soul from sense and sin,
> As Christ Himself is pure.

NOVEMBER 15.

There is an accursed thing in the midst of thee, O Israel: thou canst not stand before thine enemies, until ye take away the accursed thing from among you.—Joshua vii. 13. *Having escaped the corruption that is in the world through lust.*—2 Pet. i. 4. See also 2 Pet. ii. 18-22.

The entertaining of any worldly lust, and indulgence of any known willful sin, is an accursed thing, by which we are deprived of the power of God, and cannot stand before our enemies. Behold, therefore, the severity of God (Josh. vii. 21-26), and be more earnest. Make all haste to flee from the lust of the world, especially from the lust of the eye, which is the love of money. What more needful than to break off even the most subtle and specious bands of unrighteousness! Unless the splinters of the unjust Mammon be taken out, the wound cannot heal up. Nay, examine thyself closely in other things, and whatever sinful lust harbors in thy breast, be faithful to put it off, and flee from it, else you must not wonder at your being so weak in spirit. He that does not resist the sinful motions of his heart, will very easily give a loose to his hands and tongue; but he that immediately subdues the inward corruptions, will certainly be preserved from their breaking out in any sinful actions. O Lord, deliver me from all accursed things, and keep my heart always under thy closest inspection and discipline; let it not seek after the things of sin and the flesh, which thou hast called accursed; but be thou my joy and my portion. Amen.

> Why should my passions mix with earth,
> And thus debase my heavenly birth?
> Why should I cleave to things below,
> And let my God, my Saviour, go?

NOVEMBER 16.

I abhor myself, and repent in dust and ashes.—Job xlii. 6. I am meek and lowly in heart.—Matt. xi. 29. Behold, thy King cometh unto thee: He is just and lowly.—Zech. ix. 9.

My dear reader, reflect a moment who it was that made this confession, and consider the many excellencies that he had (See Job xxxi). Doubtless you will be ready to ask, Why this self-abhorrence? What did this man want? Let me give the answer for you: Before his eyes were opened he wanted humility, or the knowledge of his own vileness, the very thing that you need if not deeply humbled, and the want of which makes every man vile in the eyes of God. Elihu charges Job with an undue opinion of his own righteousness; and God, who, by stroke upon stroke, and not one too much, had brought him to the dunghill, is represented as carrying on the same accusation against him. The whole issues in Job's humiliation, and conveys a most important lesson of instruction to all mankind, never to stand upon their vindication with God. The book, in this view of it, is preparatory to the Gospel, and a striking comment upon those words of St. Paul and the Psalmist, "All have sinned, and come short of the glory of God. In thy sight shall no man living be justified." "God be merciful to me a sinner," is a prayer easy to be said, but hard to be felt. One eye upon the perfection of God's laws, and another upon your own heart, may bring you up to it. But the Spirit's light is also needful, for which you must pray earnestly.

> A sinner vile I am, O Lord,
>   A sinner day by day;
> Much cause I have to loathe myself,
>   And for thy mercy pray.

November 17.

And they sung a new song, saying, Thou art worthy to take the book, and to open the seals thereof; for thou wast slain, and hath redeemed us to God by thy blood.—Rev. v. 9.

In heaven the saints have a full sense of their great deliverance, together with a perfect knowledge of sin, far beyond anything we now conceive of it; and the glory of redeeming grace will be the eternal ground of their love and adoration. On earth, it is the great exercise and difficult work of faith, to see sin and Christ at the same time, or be penetrated with a lively sense of our desert, and absolute freedom from condemnation. But the more we know of both, the nearer approach we make to heaven; and we are our own greatest enemies if, together with the fullest comprehension of sin, and the deepest humiliation for it, we do not look steadfastly unto Jesus, and see it taken away by the Lamb of God. This, though continually repeated by the heavenly choir, is called their New Song; because it is always matter of as great joy to them, as if they had never sung it before; and because the love of God and of Christ in their redemption, is always opening upon them with new and increasing wonders. O my soul, let nothing, let not thy sin hinder thee from beginning it now!

> Saints cannot do less
> Than Jesus to bless;
> His name they rely on,
> His Godhead confess.
>
> My soul, bear a part,
> If ransom'd thou art,
> By Jesus' blood-shedding,
> His burial and smart.
>
> To Him that was slain,
> The scorn'd Nazarene,
> Be glory and honor,
> Let all say, Amen.

NOVEMBER 18.

Follow me.—Luke v. 27. *And endure hardness, as a good soldier of Jesus Christ.*—2 Tim. ii. 3.

WOULD you follow Christ? Then follow Him in self-denial, in humility, in patience, and in readiness for every good work. Follow Him with a daily cross upon your back, and look to His cross to make your burden light. Follow Him as your guide and guard, and learn to see with His eyes, and to trust in His arm for defence. Follow Him as the Friend of sinners, who healeth the broken in heart, and giveth rest to weary souls, and casteth out none that come unto Him. Follow Him with faith, resting your whole acceptance with God and your title to heaven on His meritorious blood and righteousness. Lastly, follow Him with much prayer; for though He is full of compassion, He loves to be much entreated; and when He is determined to give a blessing, you must yet wrestle with Him for it. Thus follow Jesus, and He will lead you to glory.

> Jesus, I my cross have taken,
>   All to love and follow thee;
> Naked, poor, despised, forsaken,
>   Thou from hence my all shalt be.
>
> Perish, every fond ambition,
>   All I've sought, or hoped, or known,
> Yet how rich is my condition,
>   God and heaven are still my own!
>
> Let the world despise and leave me;
>   They have left my Saviour too;
> Human hearts and looks deceive me;
>   Thou art not like them—untrue.
>
> Go then earthly fame and treasure,
>   Come disasters, scorn, and pain;
> In thy service pain is pleasure,
>   With thy favor loss is gain.
>
> I have called thee, Abba, Father,
>   I have set my heart on thee;
> Storms may howl and clouds may gather,
>   All must work for good to me.

November 19.

*The Lord is not far from every one of us; for in Him we live, and move, and have our being.—*Acts xvii. 27, 28. *Even the very hairs of your head are all numbered.—*Luke xii. 7.

OH! the close and tender love of the Lord over His people! Nothing is so mean but it is under the providence of God, since even the least things can either hurt or profit the soul. And how sweet is it to observe His footsteps even in the minutest things, and to be satisfied that we may trust our greater and lesser concerns to His care! O Lord, grant that I may never swerve from, nor do anything without thee, but that my goings in and goings out may be always done in thy presence, as if I had to do with none but thee; nay, as if we both lived together in the world. Oh! that I could transact all my affairs with thee alone, and in all places look upon thee as if thou wast only a God for me. Let me carefully mark the inward workings of thy grace, and the outward tokens of thy providence, so as daily to have a true sense of thy gracious presence in everything, more or less important; and thereby to be ever strengthened in faith, and kept in a composed state of mind; considering that nothing happens by mere chance, but all is wisely ordered by thy providential care to our good; firmly believing, if anything goes contrary to expectation, that something better will follow in its stead if we only can be quiet, and wait the time.

> God, that must stoop to view the skies,
>   And bow to see what angels do,
> Down to our earth He casts His eyes,
>   And bends His footsteps downward too.
>
> He overrules all mortal things,
>   And manages our mean affairs;
> On humble souls the King of kings
>   Bestows His counsels and His cares.

NOVEMBER 20.

Cleave to that which is good.—Rom. xii. 9. *Seek those things which are above.*—Col. iii. 1. *But lay up for yourselves treasures in heaven, where neither moth nor rust doth corrupt, and where thieves do not break through nor steal: for where your treasure is, there will your heart be also.*—Matt. vi. 20, 21.

THE manners of such things or persons as we frequently converse with cleave very easily to us. If we converse much with God and heavenly things, we shall be heavenly-minded; but if we deal much with the world and temporal things, we must be sensual and worldly-minded. Up, therefore, with thy heart to God: lift it hourly up to Him; and though it sinks down often to the earth again, yet the Lord has patience, and will as often receive it again. Therefore raise it up continually, and take great care to keep it above, that it may not sink down and be defiled with worldly things again. Thus it will be easy to abide in a spiritual frame; but without this care we cannot abide in it at all: a feather easily rises higher and higher when kept above ground, but moves very heavy upward when once fallen into the dirt. This you may take as a lively figure of an easy and heavy method in the practice of religion. Choose now which you please. Oh! that I may always choose the best, seeking the things which are above, and never plunge into the world to defile and distress my soul!

> Descend from heaven, immortal dove,
>   Stoop down and take us on thy wings,
> And mount and bear us far above
>   The reach of these inferior things.
>
> Beyond, beyond this lower sky,
>   Up where eternal ages roll,
> Where solid pleasures never die,
>   And fruits immortal feast the soul.

NOVEMBER 21.

Lord, now lettest thou thy servant depart in peace, according to thy word: for mine eyes have seen thy salvation.—Luke ii. 29, 30. *Say to them that are of a fearful heart, Be strong, fear not: behold, your God will come with vengeance, even God with a recompense: He will come and save you.*—Isa. xxxv. 4.

WILFUL unbelief only is damnable, and not the weak faith of a fearful and tempted believer. If I do not reject the ransom of Christ, my surety, but feel my utter need of it, and am heartily desirous to accept it by faith, God can no more reject me than He can reject my surety, or His own eternal decree. Yet, since I have very weak faith, and am often ready to sink into despair, it passeth my understanding to conceive how I can depart this life in peace. But as thy peace is said to pass all understanding (Phil. iv. 7), it is sufficient to keep the weakest and most fearful soul; because it is not by any power of our own, but solely by thy Divine power, that "we shall be kept through faith unto salvation." And it is equally the same to thee to carry the weakest or the strongest through the gates of death; for since thou art always the same wise, gracious, and mighty God, in all circumstances, and must do the work alone for both, I trust thou wilt lend me also, a poor weak creature, thine all-sufficient help in that time of need!

> Saints by the power of God are kept
>   Till the salvation come;
> We walk by faith as strangers here,
>   Till Christ shall call us home.
>
> Lord, at thy temple we appear,
>   As happy Simeon came,
> And hope to meet our Saviour here;
>   Oh! make our joys the same!

NOVEMBER 22.

O Lord, how manifold are thy works! in wisdom hast thou made them all: the earth is full of thy riches.—Ps. civ. 24. *Whoso is wise, and will observe these things, even they shall understand the loving-kindness of the Lord.*—Ps. cvii. 43. *Many shall be purified, and made white, and tried.*—Dan. xii. 10. *The ways of the Lord are right, and the just shall walk in them.*—Hosea xiv. 9.

O LORD, how many are thine unknown mercies! I am surrounded with them on all sides, yet how little do I observe them and acknowledge them to thy praise! If thou hast punished even the heathen for not having minded and glorified thee in thy works, what will become of me? Pardon, O Lord, this my blindness and ingratitude, and to all thy other kindness add a thankful heart, that I may joyfully praise thee for the blessing of my creation, the daily bounty of thy providence, and the adorable gift of thy Son. In all thy creatures may I see and adore thine infinite power, wisdom, and goodness, and be thereby continually strengthened in faith, and stirred up to thy praise and love. Thus let me always converse with thee, cleave to thee, and have uninterrupted communion with thee, that nothing may interfere and disturb this religious disposition of my soul in the least. Yes, O Lord, grant me this wisdom and close attention for thy glory's sake. Amen.

> The glories of my Maker, God,
>   My joyful voice shall sing,
> And call the nations to adore
>   Their Former and their King.
>
> The brightness of our Maker's name
>   The wide creation fills;
> And His unbounded grandeur flies
>   Beyond the heavenly hills.

November 23.

The sword of the Lord, and of Gideon.—Judges vii. 20. *For they are bread for us: their defence is departed from them, and the Lord is with us: fear them not.*—Numb. xiv. 9. *But my servant Caleb, because he had another spirit with him, and has followed me fully, him will I bring into the land whereunto he went.*—Verse 24. *Surely the wrath of man shall praise thee.*—Ps. lxxvi. 10.

Take care, O my soul, that there may also be another,—namely, a kingly spirit with thee, as there was with Joshua and Caleb, not to be discouraged on account of thy weakness, and great number of frailties and enemies, as if it were impossible to live holily and get the victory. Behold Christ, the true and great Joshua and Caleb, marches out before thee, to make war Himself against thine enemies, and who can conquer Him? He is unchangeable, His spirit now is as mighty as ever, and His word as powerful and sharper than a two-edged sword. Against thy various infirmities He offers also a variety of Divine strength; and against each of thine enemies He holds forth to thee a particular sword in His word, and abiding in His word thou shalt surely conquer. Though the enemy should raise thine inward and outward calamities to the highest degree, as so many strong walls, yet he must fall; one single word will strike him down.

> Let troubles rise, and terrors frown,
>   And days of darkness fall,
> Through Him all dangers we'll defy,
>   And more than conquer all.
>
> Nor death nor life, nor earth nor hell,
>   Nor time's destroying sway,
> Can e'er efface us from His heart,
>   Or make His love decay.

November 24.

Hearken unto me, ye stout-hearted, that are far from righteousness: I bring near my righteousness, it shall not be far off; and my salvation shall not tarry. We are all as an unclean thing, and all our righteousnesses are as filthy rags.—Isa. xlvi. 12, 13; and lxiv. 6.

TRUE religion is founded upon the knowledge of the true God. Sinners are apt to think they have a high opinion of God, because they think highly of His mercy; whereas God is as holy and just as He is merciful; and He will as certainly punish the guilty, as He will pardon the penitent and believing soul. "God, I thank thee I am not as other men are," says every self-righteous sinner; not considering that if God were extreme to mark what is amiss, no flesh living could be justified. "God be merciful to me, a sinner," says every true Christian and real believer. Till this be thy language, O my soul; till thou feelest thyself a lost, ruined and helpless sinner; till thou art brought to acknowledge the justice of God in thy condemnation; till thou art driven to Christ as thy only refuge and hope of salvation, thou art "ignorant of God's righteousness, art going about to establish thine own righteousness, and thou dost not submit to the righteousness of Christ."

> I am, saith Christ, the Way;
>   Now, if we credit Him,
> All other paths must lead astray,
>   How fair soe'er they seem.
>
> I am, saith Christ, the Truth;
>   Then, all that lack this test,
> Proceed it from an angel's mouth,
>   Is but a lie at best.
>
> I am, saith Christ, the Life:
>   Let this be seen by faith;
> It follows without further strife,
>   That all beside is death.

November 25.

Thou therefore endure hardness, as a good soldier of Jesus Christ.—2 Tim. ii. 3. *This charge I commit unto thee, son Timothy, according to the prophecies which went before on thee, that thou by them mightest war a good warfare.*—1 Tim. i. 18. *Watch thou, endure afflictions.*—2 Tim. iv. 5.

Princes combat with flesh and blood, Christians wrestle with principalities and powers. Their wars give days of truce, ours not a minute's rest. Conditions of peace there may cause retreat; nothing but death here can raise the siege. Kings, if overcome, may save themselves by flight; but Christians may as soon fly from themselves as from their enemies. The soldier of Christ is in a field of continued conflict; he cannot let fall his hands but Amalek prevails. Not to be a conqueror, is to be a prisoner: not to win the field, is to lose the soul; security wounds thee, yielding kills thee, but victory crowns thee. Therefore watch as for thy life; fight as for thy soul; the time will come when "these enemies thou seest to-day thou shalt see them no more for ever!" Then thou shalt lay down thy sword and take up thy crown, and sing, "Victory, victory," for ever, through the blood of the Lamb! Let, then, the prospect of heavenly glory fire thee. Though thine enemies be powerful, yet remember to go forth against them in the strength of the Captain of thy salvation; though assaults be many and my enemies mighty, if God strengthen me, I have enough to comfort me; for the greater my enemy, the more glorious my victory; and the more glorious my victory, the more triumphant my glory.

> Lord, let me spare no inbred foes,
> But fight them well by faith;
> Be daily dealing mortal blows,
> And triumph at my death.

November 26.

I will heal your backslidings.—Jer. iii. 22. *He will heal us; He will bind us up.*—Hosea vi. 1. *It is God who worketh in you, both to will and to do of His good pleasure.*—Phil. ii. 13.

O MY dear Saviour, I would fain believe in thee, be faithful, obedient, and work always that which is good. And since this is also thy will, I trust it shall be done; for if thou wilt and I will, who can hinder it? True it is, that sin, flesh, the world, and devils, are against it; but shall these enemies be stronger than thou, the mighty God? Shall their opposition be able to quell thy work in me, if I do not consent to it? That can never be. The more violence they use upon me, the more earnest may I be with thee in prayer; and the more I pray, the more glorious will thine assistance be; the more they hinder, the more thou wilt further, that all their hindrances may be swallowed up by thy furtherances, as the serpents of the sorcerers in Egypt were swallowed up by the serpent of Moses. The enemy will fall by his own sword; and the greatest opposition will turn to my good, and to the promoting of thy work. Everything, indeed, can overcome me if I do not abide in Christ by a continual acting of faith and prayer; but by thus abiding in Him, all opposition proves not only weak itself, but profitable to my soul.

> We honor our exalted King!
>   How sweet are His commands!
> He guards our souls from hell and sin
>   By His almighty hands.
>
> Fearless of hell and ghastly death,
>   We'll break through ev'ry foe;
> The wings of love and arms of faith
>   Shall bear us conquerors through.

November 27.

I am like a green fir-tree; from me is thy fruit found.—Hosea xiv. 8. *I will rebuke the devourer for your sakes, and he shall not destroy the fruits of your gound.*—Mal. iii. 11. *In that day sing ye unto her, A vineyard of red wine. He shall cause them that come of Jacob to take root; Israel shall blossom and bud, and fill the face of the world with fruit.*—Isa. xxvii. 2, 6.

Is it not a disagreeable thing for a gardener to see the finest blossoms and fruits destroyed by the caterpillars? Doth it not rejoice him to see all the branches bow with ripe fruits? Oh! my heavenly Lord, grant that I may not displease, but rejoice thy heart also. Let me abide in Christ my true vine, and always bring forth good fruits. But since every fruit has its enemies, and thou hast no sooner worked anything, than the insects of sin endeavor to destroy it, I beseech thee to make me watchful of these insects, and diligent in every good work. Rebuke the devourer presently, and preserve me as a branch of Christ, night and day, as thou hast promised, that my fruits may endure to eternity. Doth a diligent gardener dress and cultivate his garden as well as he can,—why shouldst not thou cultivate my heart also, since thou art honored by my fruits! Oh! yes; I trust the crystal stream of thy throne will water me, that I may bring forth greater plenty of fruit.

> Like trees of myrrh and spice we stand
> Planted by God the Father's hand;
> And all His springs in Zion flow,
> To make the young plantation grow.
>
> Let my Beloved come and taste
> His pleasant fruits at His own feast.
> "I come, my spouse, I come," He cries,
> With love and pleasure in His eyes.

NOVEMBER 28.

I will do it.—John xiv. 14. And what is that? Whatsoever thou desirest. For the Lord *will fulfill the desire of them that fear Him.*—Ps. cxlv. 19.

YEA, He does "exceeding abundantly above all that we ask or think;" granting not only according to the notion of our narrow hearts, but according to the riches of His glory, as becomes His majesty. Christ delights in great petitions; for He is a great Lord, and is rich unto all that call upon Him. He has all the riches of His merits and gifts, not for himself (since being the very God, He wanted nothing for himself), but only for us, even the rebellious, who sincerely call upon Him. Therefore what He has as Mediator, all belongs to me, if I do but call upon Him faithfully. O my soul, pray to Him; nay, be much in prayer; and as often as thou pourest out thy soul before Him in prayer, let nothing resound in thy heart but these words: "I will; I will do it." As God can never lie, there is not one single groan lost; but every one will be found to be a jewel in the life to come: by which thy riches are increased, and one treasure put to another. Oh! how much is there neglected in this already! why shouldst thou not be earnest now to redeem that little remaining part of thy time, by prayer for eternity, to lay up there many treasures, and richly adorn thy crown? O Lord, grant that this may be done!

> Now is the time, He lends His ear,
>   And waits for your request;
> Come, lest He rouse His wrath, and swear
>   "Ye shall not see my rest!"
>
> Come, then, O house of Jacob! come
>   To worship at His shrine;
> And, walking in the light of God,
>   With holy beauties shine.

November 29.

Joshua drew not his hand back, wherewith he stretched out the spear, until he had utterly destroyed all the inhabitants of Ai.—Joshua viii. 26. *For this purpose the Son of God was manifested, that He might destroy the works of the devil.*—1 John iii. 8.

A WILLING subjection to any one sin is not consistent with the grace of God, and true saving faith (Rom. iv. 14); for though wicked inhabitants will abide in the heart, and sometimes prevail over the believer, they must not reign there, nor should be suffered to stir without resistance; since we may be utterly ruined by the dominion of a single sin,—that is, by a single subjection to it, as by the dominion of a thousand, just as a bird is caught in one single snare; and though you are actually converted, and have gained the dominion over your sins, yet you must not draw back your hand, and lay the spear and the sword of the Spirit aside. There is no truce in this war, nor any rest found but in fighting; for if you beat not your enemies, they beat you. Therefore the Christian soldier's watchword is, Fight on, looking to Jesus. Satan left Christ only for a time; much more will he renew his assaults upon us again and again. But if the conflict lasteth long, remember that is also the case of others; and even the ancient fathers have gone under it till they were gray; at last the victory will be the more sweet and glorious. Only, above all things, take the shield of faith; for faith alone triumphs: by which we are in covenant with Christ, and He makes one cause with us.

> 'Tis faith that conquers earth and hell
>   By a celestial power;
> That is the grace that shall prevail
>   In the decisive hour.

NOVEMBER 30.

Ho, every one that thirsteth, come ye to the waters, and he that hath no money; come ye, buy and eat; yea, come, buy wine and milk without money, and without price.—Isa. lv. 1. *Come, for all things are now ready.*—Luke xiv. 17. *Him* (be it who it will) *that cometh to me I will in no wise cast out.*—John vi. 37.

How could a tender mother's heart cast out her sick child, calling for help! Come, my poor soul, come only as well as thou canst. Better to come in a cold, fearful, miserable condition, than not at all; for if we cannot come boldly to Christ with a strong faith, we must even come trembling, just as we are; nor will such coming be offensive to Christ; for He says, "Him that cometh," come how he will, "I will in no wise cast out." A feeling of joy is not needful to bring us to Christ, but a feeling of our wants; for it is not required to bring any money of our own worthiness, but only the whole heap of our misery along with us, and desire grace. God does not look upon the sensible joy of faith (for this is His particular gift, which He could soon give if need was), but upon the sincerity, application, and earnestness of a poor sinner. John Bunyan fitly compares such a one to a man who would fain ride a full gallop, whose horse is hardly able to go a good trot. In this instance, the intention of the rider is not to be judged by the slow pace of his horse (which resembles our corrupt and unwilling nature), but by his whippings, spurrings, and beatings of the beast.

> See, dearest Lord, our willing souls
>   Accept thine offered grace;
> We bless the great Redeemer's love
>   And give the Father praise.

Jesus said: Whosoever drinketh of this water shall thirst again: but whosoever drinketh of the water that I shall give him shall never thirst; but the water that I shall give him shall be in him a well of water springing up into everlasting life.—John iv. 13, 14.

In the last day, that great day of the Feast, Jesus stood and cried, saying: If any man thirst, let him come unto Me, and drink.—John vii. 37.

—:o:—

So is the will of God, that with well-doing ye may put to silence the ignorance of foolish men.—1 Peter ii. 15.

Not rendering evil for evil, or railing for railing; but contrariwise, blessing: knowing that ye are thereunto called, that ye should inherit a blessing.—1 Peter iii. 9.

December 1.

Be not overcome of evil, but overcome evil with good.
—Rom. xii. 21. *For who is he that will harm you, if ye be followers of that which is good?*—
1 Peter iii. 13. *All things work together for good to them that love God.*—Rom. viii. 28.

THE Christian life is a warfare, and the conflict between sin and holiness, and between sorrow and comfort, is often very violent. The child of God has many evils to encounter with. Sin, Satan, self, and the world, are daily enemies. He is also exposed oft to poverty, affliction, reproaches, and persecution. Oh! my Saviour, help me to overcome all evil in the strength of thy grace; give me a heart to do good to all who may seek to hurt me. Who is he that will harm you, if ye be followers of that which is good? Not the Father, for He loves you; not Jesus, for He died for you; not the Spirit, His work is to comfort you; not good men, they love those who follow that which is good; not wicked men nor devils, for though enemies, they are confined, and cannot stir one step beyond what thy God and Saviour permits them. When you meet with a trial, look not to men, but to Jesus. Pray for patience to bear it, and look up for a blessing upon it. Then all things shall work together for thy good (Rom. viii. 28). Let every temptation make you more careful, and put you on closer watching against the enemy. Cleave to Jesus by faith and prayer, like a child to its parent, when it sees an enemy coming toward it. Behold Him, flee to Him, rest upon Him, and then you will rejoice in Him.

> How glorious, Lord, thy wisdom shines,
> And baffles Satan's deep designs!
> Thy power is sov'reign to fulfill
> The noblest counsels of thy will.

December 2.

Prayer shall be made for Him continually; and daily shall He be praised.—Ps. lxxii. 15. *Thy kingdom come.*—Matt. vi. 10. *Pour out your heart before Him.*—Ps. lxii. 8.

Oh! what a condescending King we have, who may always be approached! Who would not pray? You say, Oh! that my coldness and indifference would permit me to do it. But are you not sensible of your wants and miseries? Is not this coldness and backwardness misery enough? Therefore you ought also to pray, and to pray most when you are so dull and drowsy, else it will never be better with you. Arise, therefore, and pray; the good Spirit of God will assist you in it. "Encouraged by the promises of a prayer-hearing God, and a special assistance of the Holy Spirit in this work, we must, even in the greatest conflicts, not omit to resist the temptations of the devil. And though we have sinned, not defer it long; but pray directly, and say, The Lord is merciful, and I am unworthy and unable to pray! But, alas! what shall I do? Shall I wait till I am worthy and able? Oh! no; perhaps that time will never come; for I am always a great, miserable sinner. A Christian stands always in need of prayer; for since the sense of sin does not leave him, he must not leave off prayer." Lord, grant me more of the spirit of prayer, and let it never be extinguished in my heart!

> Arise, my soul, from deep distress,
>   And banish every fear;
> God calls thee to His throne of grace,
>   To spread thy sorrows there.
>
> Go then, my soul, and talk with God,
>   By Christ who'd thee redeem;
> In mercy oft He lifts the rod,
>   To bring thee back to Him.

DECEMBER 3.

What doest thou here, Elijah?—1 Kings xix. 13.

LET this question be supposed as addressed to us: What dost thou here in this world? Art thou "working the work of Him that sent thee," or standing all the day idle? Art thou in the post assigned thee by Heaven, truly called, and properly qualified for it, and faithfully discharging the duties of it? or hast thou thrust thyself into it without warrant or invitation; and therefore hast no cause to expect success? What dost thou here in this retirement? Is the world shut out of thy thoughts, and are the visits of the blessed Spirit invited! What dost thou here, if thy peace with an offended God is not already made, or most earnestly desired and sought after? If thou really wantest peace and safety, plead the blood of Jesus, flee to the city of refuge. What dost thou here in times of trial and temptation? Art thou flying from the danger, or boldly facing it in the name and strength of the Lord? Art thou ashamed of the cross, or dost thou willingly take it upon thee? Elijah failed here; he fled from Jezebel. And did such an one as Elijah fear? Then howl, ye fir-trees, if the cedars be thus shaken! hold fast by Christ, ye weak ones, if the strong fall! What dost thou here below? Art thou not pitching thy tent on this side Jordan, satisfied with thy present portion? or art thou "looking to a better country, to a city that hath foundations, whose builder and maker is God?" Life is uncertain, death approaches, the Judge is at the door, then "prepare to meet thy God."

> Arm me with a jealous care,
>   As in thy sight to live;
> And thy weak servant, Lord, prepare
>   A good account to give!

December 4.

Mine eyes are ever toward the Lord; for He shall pluck my feet out of the net.—Ps. xxv. 15. *Happy is the man that feareth alway.*—Prov. xxviii. 14.

OH! how long can some enemies hide themselves with their nets before our eyes, and draw in all on a sudden! It is unspeakable how cunning and powerful our enemies are,—how they lie in wait everywhere, so that in all places, and at all times, we are surrounded with many cruel murderers of souls! Blessed is he that keeps clear from self-confidence, and, fearing always, says within himself, as soon as he awakes in the morning, Who knows what temptations I may meet with to-day? Perhaps when I arise, by the first step my feet may be entangled in dangerous snares and nets. And as self-confidence ever will be ashamed, and a firm confidence in the Lord never shall (Rom. ix. 33), grant, O Lord, I beseech thee, that, distrusting myself, I may fully put my trust in thee, watching evermore in all things, and looking cautiously in all places about me, where there is any fear of danger. Whatever I am about to do or to speak, let me first converse with thee by prayer; that keeping always close to thee, I may be preserved against the power and craft of mine enemies, as in a stronghold; and confidently say, according to thy own pattern given (Ps. xvi. 8), "I have set the Lord before me: because He is at my right hand, I shall not be moved."

> God is my portion and my joy;
> His counsels are my light,
> He gives me sweet advice by day,
> And gentle hints by night.
>
> My soul would all her thoughts approve
> To His all-seeing eye;
> Nor death nor hell my hope shall move,
> While such a friend is nigh.

DECEMBER 5.

My Father worketh hitherto, and I work, (as also the Holy Spirit). *For as the Father raiseth up the dead, and quickeneth them; even so the Son quickeneth whom He will.*—John v. 17, 21. See also John ix. 4, and xiv. 10.

O MY poor soul! is not the blessed Trinity thy God, in three Persons, able to destroy the works of the devil, and fulfill His good-will in thee? Oh! yes, He works both to will and to do; and that very thing which is above your own power, He works, and nothing else. If you can do little, He works much; if nothing at all, so much the better, then He works all; for He is our all, since we are nothing, and can do nothing. And happy are we that we can have Him for our support in all things; and that the children of God are not required to direct their own steps, but shall be led by their heavenly Father. Now, O Lord, since by the will, guidings, and workings of my own heart, I throw only so many hindrances and blocks in my way, grant, I beseech thee, that, in true dependence on thee, I may venture everything; and, despairing of my own sufficiency, may always abide in thee, draw all necessary strength from thee by prayer, and bring forth many good fruits which may last to eternity! For thy work in true believers, weak as it may seem now, will last for ever, and none shall be able to destroy it.

> Lord, let thy counsels guide my feet
>   Through this dark wilderness;
> Thy hand conduct me near thy seat,
>   To dwell before thy face!
>
> Then, if the springs of life were broke,
>   And flesh and heart should faint,
> God is my soul's eternal rock,
>   The strength of every saint.

December 6.

Draw nigh to God, and He will draw nigh to you. Resist the devil, and he will flee from you.—James iv. 7, 8. *The effectual fervent prayer of a righteous man availeth much.*—Chap. v. 16.

O my dear soul! draw nigh to God in prayer, and He will draw nigh to thee; be instant in it, and the devil cannot stand against thee; for prayers will drive away sin and Satan, as the wind drives the smoke before it; prayer works wonderful great things, and will make possible what seemeth impossible. If God has given thee some spiritual blessings already, this is an encouragement to hope also for that which thou lackest yet; therefore only pray confidently, and you shall receive evermore; for unbelief is the only reason that God cannot work wonders for us. Pour out upon my soul, thou living and wonder-working God, the spirit of prayer; let me pray and strive, pray in faith, and pour out my whole heart before thee (Ps. lxii. 8). Let me strive in faith that the Lord may impart the blessing and draw nigh to me; for without thee to be with me, all my prayers and all my strivings are in vain.

> My God, I bow before thy feet;
> When shall my soul get near thy seat?
> When shall I see thy glorious face,
> With mingled majesty and grace?
>
> How should I love thee and adore,
> With hopes and joys unknown before!
> And bid this trifling world begone;
> Nor tease my heart so near thy throne.
>
> Creatures with all their charms should fly
> The presence of a God so nigh;
> My darling sins should lose their name,
> And grow my hatred and my shame.
>
> My soul should pour out all her cares,
> In flowing words, or flowing tears;
> Thy smiles should ease my sharpest pain,
> Nor shall I seek my God in vain.

DECEMBER 7.

I am crucified with Christ: nevertheless I live; yet not I, but Christ liveth in me: and the life which I now live in the flesh I live by the faith of the Son of God, who loved me, and gave Himself for me.—Gal. ii. 20.

IN spiritual things we are too often living upon self. We seek in frames, forms, creatures, and animal life, that inward peace and stability of mind which is only to be found in the Redeemer. Outward duties are well in their place; but they have no divine life in themselves, or to give. They are to be performed, but not trusted in; to be used with grace, but cannot buy grace. They are as the scaffold of the building,—a means for carrying on the work, but not the end of the great design. In the power of Christ they are blessings; without it they have no power. The whole trust must be in Jesus. He is the way, the truth, and the life: without Him prayers, praises, rites, and ordinances, are carcasses without a soul. Every performance of outward worship is so, unless the Saviour fills it with His Divine Spirit. Then it is we experience a communion of heart, a reviving of the soul after the adorable Jesus, and a delightful view behind the veil of outward ordinances (such as no carnal eye can behold), manifesting the Lord in His goodness, beauty, grandeur, blessedness and glory.

> The faith and hope of things unseen
>   My best affections move;
> Thy light, thy favor, and thy smiles,
>   Thine everlasting love.
>
> These are the blessings I desire;
>   Lord, be these blessings mine,
> And all the glories of the world
>   I cheerfully resign.

December 8.

Take this child away, and nurse it for me, and I will give thee thy wages.—Exod. ii. 9.

As Moses was ordered to be saved by the most cruel enemy's daughter, so Satan himself, even when he meditates our destruction, must be a means of our life. So also Matt. xii. 48, *Who is my mother?* etc. (Isa. viii. 10, and ix. 6). O Lord Jesus, if thou art a child born unto me, and I am willing to receive thee as my Immanuel, thou wilt be my shield and exceeding great reward, and defend me powerfully against all my enemies. O my dear Saviour, if thou art mine, all is mine, even thy Father, thy Spirit, and thy heavenly glory,— all accidents, all enemies must work for my good, and be instruments and ministers of my salvation. Oh! that I may, trusting in thee, never fear anything; but thinking directly it is mine, may only make good use of everything. Thus even the very worst would turn to my greatest blessing; and without it perhaps I should want as needful a thing as a mill or a ship does when destitute of wind and water.

> My soul, survey thy happiness,
> If thou art found a child of grace;
> How richly is the Gospel stored!
> What joy the promises afford!
>
> All things are now the gift of God,
> And purchased with our Saviour's blood,
> While the good Spirit shews us how
> To use and to enjoy them too.
>
> If peace and plenty crown my days,
> Then help me, Lord, to speak thy praise;
> If bread of sorrows be my food,
> Those sorrows work my real good.
>
> Whatever fills my temporal cup,
> Make me with gratitude to sup,
> And trust the faithful promise given,
> That I shall dwell with thee in heaven.

DECEMBER 9.

Speaking to yourselves in psalms, and hymns, and spiritual songs, singing and making melody in your heart to the Lord.—Eph. v. 19. *Teaching and admonishing one another in psalms and hymns.*—Col. iii. 16. *Paul and Silas prayed, and sang praises unto God.*—Acts xvi. 25.

If we are obliged to promote the temporal good of our neighbor, how much more the spiritual, by edifying discourses! But how is it? The children of God, when a person visits them, (says a certain divine), are sometimes troubled, and know not what discourse to enter upon: at last they begin an unprofitable discourse, or at least they suffer others to do it, and are silent at it. I will tell you what I have done in such cases: I first prayed to God, saying, "O good God, here I receive a guest, and have nothing to set before and treat him with; I pray thee to give me the right bread for him;" which the Lord was pleased to hear in such a gracious manner, that I could sooner enter into an edifying discourse. And thus keep our conscience clean; and though perhaps the lips were frozen up at first, they are thawed and opened by prayer. Some foolish philosophers, to the great offence of others, mock at divine things, and even at prayer; as if we needed no other help than our own depraved reason and will. But what St. Paul says (Rom. i. 22) is fulfilled in them:—"Professing themselves to be wise, they became fools." What will become of these poor scoffers upon their dying beds, and at the day of judgment? Oh! that they would take warning while it is time.

> Now if some proper hour appear,
>   Let none be overawed;
> But let the scoffing sinners hear
>   That we can speak for God.

DECEMBER 10.

Tell his disciples, and Peter (who was deeply fallen) *especially.*—Mark xvi. 7. *If any man sin, we have an advocate with the Father, Jesus Christ the righteous: and He is the propitiation for our sins; and not for ours only, but also for the sins of the whole world.*—1 John ii. 1, 2. *Wherefore lift up the hands which hang down, and strengthen the feeble knees.*—Heb. xii. 12.

HAST thou been slack, unfaithful and fallen away? Oh! poor soul, thou art not to make light of it; but why wilt thou continue in thy fallen condition any longer, and complain? Get thee up and ask pardon of Christ; He is ready to forgive and receive thee again, like Peter, "having received gifts for the rebellious." Delay not to lay hold of thy ransom, which is greater than all the sins of the world; nay, the ransom is paid for this very sin, and a pardon purchased by it already. Therefore sue it out, and be not discouraged, nor listen to the temptation of giving up hope, and turning back to the world. The Lord even now reaches forth His hands to thee anew by this very word; come, lift thyself up at it, and be careful for the time to come to be so much more cautious, humble and gentle toward others; for a Christian's foot may trip; but when recovered, it slides deeper into humility.

> Salvation! oh! the joyful sound,
>   'Tis pleasure to mine ears;
> A sov'reign balm for every wound,
>   A cordial for my fears.
>
> Buried in sorrow and in sin,
>   At hell's dark door I lay;
> But I arise, by grace divine.
>   To see a heavenly day

December 11.

Behold, we come unto thee,—Jer. iii. 22,—(and) *I will come to you.*—John xiv. 18. A lively representation of this happy meeting, see Luke xix. 4-6.—*Zaccheus ran before and climbed up into a sycamore-tree to see Him: for He was to pass that way. And Christ said unto him, Make haste, and come down; for to-day I must abide at thy house.*

O my dear Saviour, since I come to thee, and thou to me, we shall certainly meet one another. Who will oppose and obstruct it? The devil and sin? Oh! no; this wall of separation is pulled down. Christ says, "Come unto me; I am not an angry judge, but a loving Mediator between God and thy frightened conscience: keep to me, and fear no wrath. I sit here, that, believing in me to make intercession for thee with God, no wrath or disgrace can befall thee. Should wrath and punishment come upon thee, it must first come upon me: wrath is quite impossible." Yes, O my soul, it is indeed impossible; for thy Jesus is the dear Son of God, in whom dwells all the fullness of grace; and the Father, looking upon Him, His wrath must vanish away, and everything in heaven and earth be changed into smiles of love and grace (Eph. i. 6). Dangers and conflicts being hot, God hastens with His assistance. At other times He tarries, and the work of our whole renovation goes on by little and little, that, improving in the exercise of patience and faith, we may also bear with others, and learn not only to quicken our diligence, but also to wait for Him.

> In thine own ways, O God of love,
>   We wait the visits of thy grace;
> Our soul's desire is to thy name,
>   And the remembrance of thy face.

DECEMBER 12.

Mine iniquities are gone over my head; as an heavy burden, they are too heavy for me.—Ps. xxxviii. 4. *Come unto me, all ye that labor and are heavy laden, and I will give you rest.*— Matt. xi. 28.

It is a sure sign that a man is awakened out of his sleep, when he discovers the error of his dream. In the drawing up of water out of a deep well, so long as the bucket is under water, we feel not the weight of it; but as soon as it comes above water, it begins to hang heavy on the hand. When a man dives under water, he feels no weight of the water, though there may be many tons of it over his head; whereas a tub half full of the same water, taken out of the river, and set upon the same man's head, would be very burdensome to him, and make him soon grow weary of it. In like manner, so long as a man is over head in sin, he is not sensible of the weight of sin, it is not troublesome to him; but when he begins once to come out of that state of sin wherein he lay and lived before, then beginneth sin to hang heavy upon him, and he groans under the weight thereof. So long as sin is in the will, the proper seat of sin, a man feels not the weight of it, but, like a fool, it is sport and pastime to him to do evil. It is therefore a good sign that sin is removed out of its seat, out of its chair of state, when it becomes burdensome to us; and such a sense of sin may well be considered as an entrance into a state of grace. Give me, O Lord, a true sense of my sin, and an apprehension of the mercy of God in Christ, and ability to embrace Him as my Redeemer and Saviour.

> Give me, O Lord, the broken heart,
> Which mourns for sin with inward smart,
> And will to thy dear cross repair,
> And seek and find its healing there.

December 13.

Return, ye backsliding children, and I will heal your backslidings.—Jer. iii. 22. *When he was yet a great way off, his father saw him, and had compassion, and ran, and fell on his neck, and kissed him. And said, Bring forth the best robe, and put it on him; and put a ring on his hand, and shoes on his feet, etc.*—Luke xv. 20-23.

HEAR, therefore, the voice of thy loving Father and Shepherd, O thou backsliding child and lost sheep, crying earnestly, Return, return! Do not run on in the broad way with the world any longer. Are you not tired yet of the husks of the world? Do you feel no troubles in your soul? Shall not these drive thee to God? Lo! thy Father and Shepherd seeks thee. He is gone forth to call and meet thee already. He will receive thee willingly and joyfully. Come, only praying as the prodigal son, and He will freely forgive thee all, though thou hadst sinned ever so much. He is also able to heal and correct the most desperate corruptions of thy heart; He can deliver thee from the very jaws of hell and the devil; nay, if thou even wast possessed with more than seven devils, He can still cast them out. Begin to call upon Him earnestly in prayer, and, poor and wretched as thou art, come to Him as the physician of thy soul; for the physician and the sick, a rich Saviour and a poor sinner, are the best suited to one another. He healeth all our diseases, and can make possible what seems most impossible to thee.

> Come, all ye vilest sinners, come,
>   He'll form your souls anew;
> His Gospel and His heart have room
>   For rebels such as you.

December 14.

Watch ye therefore, and pray always.—Luke xxi. 36. *Let us lay aside every weight, and the sin which doth so easily beset us.*—Heb. xii. 1. *Watch, for ye know not what hour your Lord doth come.*—Matt. xxiv. 42. *Take ye heed, watch and pray.*—Mark xiii. 43.

THE hearts of men are not like unto clocks, which only want to be wound up once a day; oh! no; the dullness and distraction is too great and dangerous. We must lift them up many times a day; yea, watch continually to lay aside every weight. Our going out and coming in, nay, all things, even the very least, we must do with prayer, always strictly examining what is the will of the Lord; else, if they are done after our own will, they do not tend to the glory of God, and cannot be attended with His blessing. But if we earnestly strive against our own will in prayer, patiently suffering every hour what the Lord thinks proper to lay upon us, and will be ruled by His hints and slight strokes of His rod, many heavy afflictions, and scourges, and whips, may be avoided; for the burdens which we bring upon ourselves by our own will and impatience, are always the heaviest. A Christian has daily his proper burden, like a clock its weights, by which the flesh is kept under, so that the spirit can rise up; therefore, when anything comes cross, he looks upon it as his weight for the day, to stir him up to the exercise of prayer and meditation in the Word of God. O Lord, grant that I may always bear thy easy yoke, and never be the cause of my own distress and dullness!

> Wait on the Lord, ye trembling saints,
> And keep your courage up;
> He'll raise your spirit when it faints,
> And far exceed your hope.

DECEMBER 15.

Give an account of thy stewardship.—Luke xvi. 2.
God shall bring every work into judgment, with every secret thing, whether it be good, or whether it be evil.—Eccl. xii. 14. *For we must all appear before the judgment seat of Christ; that every one may receive the things done in his body, according to that he hath done, whether it be good or bad.*—2 Cor. v. 10.

O LORD, how have I wasted my time, goods, and faculties! O pardon me for thine infinite mercy's sake, blot out my debt by thy blood; and grant, that henceforth, keeping a daily good account, and acting more prudently, faithfully, and diligently, my reckoning may not be false at last. But preserve me also from all needless cares, since the care to get something is not the steward's business, but only to husband everything faithfully. "Teach me, O Lord, and give me wisdom and grace to govern my house, and manage all my affairs rightly. Be thou the principal governor and father of my family. I would be nothing but thy servant; direct me only in all things, that I may not suffer or do any harm." He that does not expostulate with God, but accuses himself as guilty in all things, even his best performances, and flies to Christ as his only refuge, will be justified of God through the righteousness of His dear Son. And being thus adopted of God, he is ready and willing to be governed and directed by him in all things as a child.

> That awful day will surely come,
>   Th' appointed hour makes haste,
> When I must stand before my Judge,
>   And pass the solemn test.
>
> Thou lovely chief of all my joys,
>   Thou sov'reign of my heart!
> How could I bear to hear thy voice
>   Pronounce the sound, Depart!

December 16.

Examine yourselves, whether ye be in the faith.—
2. Cor. xiii. 5.

Many might be induced to pray for faith if they did not presumptuously pretend to it; for such as have actually faith, often doubt whether they have any or not; and those that are without, imagine they have enough. But faith is only wrought in the souls of those who are deeply humbled by a thorough conviction of the greatness and heinousness of their sins, confessing themselves not only with their lips, but with a true sense of their hearts, to be the chief of sinners. Without this repentance we do not enter through the right gate, and our faith is only fancy; for faith is the greatest and most difficult thing even to a child of God; it receives Christ into the heart, and overcomes the devil, world, and all sins, which is not easily done. Therefore, if the generality of people had true faith, nothing were easier to believe; for what can be easier than to give a mere assent to the Bible as true, which is all that Christians mean by faith in general. The wicked, therefore, who live in sin, deceive themselves in thinking they have faith; for faith giveth victory over the world. And all who trust in their own works, deceive themselves too; for the prayer of faith is, "God be merciful to me a sinner!" "Lord, save, or I perish!" If, then, the first Christians had need to examine themselves, how much more have we! Therefore, the best and safest way is, to pray earnestly for that faith which has boldness, and triumphs even in death.

O Lord, thy power and grace display,
   Let guilt and death no longer reign,
Save me in thine appointed way,
   Nor let my humble faith be vain.

December 17.

For thy name's sake, lead me, and guide me. Pull me out of the net that they have laid privily for me; for thou art my strength. Into thine hand I commit my spirit: thou hast redeemed me, O Lord God of truth.—Ps. xxxi. 3-5. *When the ark set forward, Moses said, Rise up, Lord, and let thine enemies be scattered; and let them that hate thee flee before thee.*—Numb. x. 35.

Every one having his own particular gift, has also his own particular enemies, who lay various nets and hindrances in his way. But as everybody must clear the way for a king when he travels, much more so our enemies, when the King of kings guides us and goes before us. Grant, O Lord, that all my goings and restings may be done at thy will! (Numb. iv. 17, 23). Be gloriously pleased to go always before me, and to make room, that mine enemies may be scattered, and fall into their own nets; for thou, who dwellest in heaven, laughest at all, even mine inward spiritual enemies; and art able to confound their deepest craft, and strongest power. Enlighten my darkness, blessed Jesus, that I may see my enemies distinctly; and strengthen my faith in thee, that I may not fear them. Be the Captain of my salvation; lead me on praying and believing; and do thou fight all my battles for me. So shall I come off conqueror through thy love, and will give to thee eternal praise.

> Great God, preserve my conscience clean;
> Wash me from guilt, subdue my sin;
> Thy love shall guard me from surprise,
> Though threatening dangers round me rise.
>
> My faith would seize some promise, Lord;
> There's power and safety in thy Word;
> Not all that earth and hell can say,
> Shall tempt to drive my soul away.

December 18.

And Moses said unto them, This is the bread which the Lord hath given you to eat.—Exod. xvi. 15.
See also 1 Cor. x. 3, 4.

This manna was entirely different from common manna, which is shook from the leaves of trees, and used only in medicine; this dropped down from the clouds, and was truly a miraculous production, as is evident from the following circumstances: that it fell but six days in the week; that it fell in such prodigious quantity as sustained almost three millions of souls; that a double portion of it fell the day before the Sabbath, and none on that day, etc. This manna is called "spiritual meat," because it signified spiritual blessings in heavenly things. Christ Himself is the true manna, the bread of life, of which that was a figure (John vi. 49-51). The Word of God is a manna too, by which our souls are nourished (Matt. iv. 4). The comforts of the Spirit are also a "hidden manna" (Rev. ii. 17). These come down from heaven, as the manna did,—are the support and comfort of the divine life in the soul while we are in the wilderness of this world. The manna gathered in the wilderness was not to be hoarded up, but eaten; so they that have received Christ, must live upon Him daily by faith, and not think of laying up a stock to-day to serve them to-morrow. They that did eat manna in the wilderness hungered again; whereas they that feed on Christ by faith shall never hunger. "Lord, evermore give us this bread!"

> Whilst in the wilderness I stray,
> Thy manna, Lord, I need,
> And fresh bestow it every day,
> Or I shall faint indeed.

DECEMBER 19.

What wilt thou, Queen Esther? and what is thy request? It shall be even given thee to the half of the kingdom.—Esther v. 3.

Dost thou want nothing, O poor soul? Hast thou nothing to ask? Oh! yes, you say, a great deal. Well, then, draw near to thy gracious King and Bridegroom without fear. Lo! He holds out His golden sceptre to thee, saying, Only ask; not the half, but the whole of my kingdom shall be granted; nay, I will give myself unto thee. O dear soul, pray and tell Him everything that is wanting, be it ever so great or ever so small! His loving-kindness will hear even the least petition; nay, He will seem to be ignorant of what thou dost not tell Him. But whatever is poured out before Him is actually addressed and lodged in its proper place, and does not lie upon thy heart any longer, but upon His heart, which cannot rest till you are relieved. And if you have experienced His help aforetime, in great or small things, you may depend on His readiness to help you out of troubles hereafter; only be earnest in prayer for His help. We often imagined we were willing and drawing near to Him, but He was unwilling, and refused our request; but it is not so: He rather draws us, and desires our relief more than we do; for it is He that works even this willing mind.

> Are those the happy persons here
>   Who dwell the nearest to their God?
> Has God invited sinners near,
>   And Jesus bought this grace with blood?
>
> Go then, my soul, address the Son
>   To lead thee near the Father's face
> Gaze on His glories yet unknown,
>   And taste the blessings of His grace.

DECEMBER 20.

What wilt thou that I shall do unto thee?—Luke xviii. 41. *Thou shalt love the Lord thy God, etc.*—Matt. xxii. 37-39.

O LORD, dost thou also ask me this question? Oh! yes. Well, then, I answer, That I may see how gracious thou art; that, knowing thy love in thy light, I may love thee again. This is the sum and substance of all my prayer; because thou requirest it so seriously of me. "If any man love not the Lord Jesus Christ, let him be Anathema Maranatha" (1 Cor. xvi. 22), But thou dost not require it as of myself, well knowing that I can do nothing; but signifieth only what I am to ask of thee, and what thou art willing to give and to work; for thou dost not require anything but what thou workest thyself, and workest everything that thou requirest; therefore faith and love being required by thee, I require the same from thee first. Grant, oh! grant them to me, that I may return them to thee again. And since nothing is pleasing to thee but what is thy own gift, I trust that thou wilt certainly hear and fulfill this my request. However, as my salvation is not grounded on my own, but on thine and thy Father's love and counsel, save me by free grace through thy merits, and let me go on covered all over with grace and pardon. This is treasure enough, by which my heart can be well satisfied.

> He that can shake the worlds He made,
>   Or with His word, or with His rod;
> His goodness, how amazing great!
>   And what a condescending God!
>
> Our sorrows and our tears we pour
>   Into the bosom of our God;
> He hears us in the mournful hour,
>   And helps to bear the heavy load.

December 21.

In returning and rest shall ye be saved; in quietness and in confidence shall be your strength.—Isa. xxx. 15. *In your patience possess ye your souls.*—Luke xxi. 19. *Take heed, and be quiet; fear not, neither be faint-hearted.*—Isa. vii. 4.

CHRISTIANS must suffer patiently, and patience is their armor, while God is fighting for them. But when we are unwilling to suffer, going about to make complaints everywhere, and to seek human comfort, or to rid ourselves, by our own contrivances, we lose the comfort of the Lord's help, we are stirring up the wasp-nest of our unruly thoughts, and bring more trouble upon ourselves and others; nay, we are fighting against God, who thereby intends to cure our impatience, pride and anger; for the more peevish and wild we are, the more desperate is our disease; and consequently, we have so much more need of such sharp but wholesome trials of affliction to mortify these bad passions of the flesh. Therefore we must not presume to murmur or complain, which will only make bad worse; for he who, through impatience, will flee from one trouble, may run into ten others; and though it is possible sometimes to rid ourselves out of trouble, yet the help is not so glorious and blessed as if we had waited for the help of the Lord. Grant me to wait always on thy help; for the Lord's good time will come, though He tarry long.

> Sure I must bear if I would reign;
> Increase my courage, Lord!
> I'll bear the toil, endure the pain,
> Supported by thy Word.
>
> Must I be carried to the skies
> On flowery beds of ease,
> While others suffered for the prize,
> And sailed through bloody seas?

December 22.

Whoso loveth instruction loveth knowledge; but he that hateth reproof is brutish.—Prov. xii. 1.

NOTHING can be said so bad of us which we have not the root of in our heart; and though we are convinced of and strive against our own weakness, yet we may not strive so earnestly as to conquer. Therefore God comes to our assistance in a sharp reproof from others; for He knows how to use even the faults of others to our good. And if we receive everything as from Him alone, striving so much against this our frailty, that we may not be offensive to our neighbor any more, we certainly gain a great victory and blessing. But if we grow impatient and make many excuses, being unwilling to put up with anything, we make evil worse, and neglect the amendment of ourselves and others. O Lord, make us better, and give us patience!

> How should the sons of Adam's race
>   Be pure before their God!
> If He contend in righteousness,
>   We fall beneath His rod.
>
> To vindicate my words and thoughts
>   I'll make no more pretence;
> Not one of all my thousand faults
>   Can bear a just defence.
>
> Then seek the Lord while yet His ear
>   Is open to your call;
> While offered mercy still is near,
>   Before His footstool fall.
>
> Let sinners quit their evil ways,
>   Their evil thoughts forego,
> And God, when they to Him return,
>   Returning grace will shew.
>
> He pardons with o'erflowing love;
>   For, hear the voice Divine:
> My nature is not like to yours,
>   Nor like your ways are mine.

DECEMBER 23.

Therefore we conclude, that a man is justified by faith without the deeds of the law.—Rom. iii. 28.
Ye see then how that by works a man is justified, and not by faith only.—James ii. 24.

BOTH these Apostles wrote by inspiration. St. Paul answers this question both affirmatively and negatively: That a man is justified before God by faith, without the deeds of the law; and in the 20th verse positively affirms, "That by the deeds of the law shall no flesh be justified." St. James asserts, that "by works a man is justified, and not by faith only." St. Paul speaks of a justification before God: James, of a justification before men. St. Paul speaks of the justification of penitent sinners before God: James, of the justification of saints before men. St. Paul, of the justification of sinners believing in the righteousness of the Lord Jesus Christ for pardon and life: James, of the works of righteousness after justification by faith in Christ. Paul speaks of faith touching its office in the article of justification before God: James, of faith in its fruits and effects. Whenever there is a true faith, it must fix on Jesus Christ alone for salvation;—that is its principal act. This same faith unites to Christ; and where there is union, there must be love; and where there is love there must be obedience; and where obedience is, there will be a reward of grace; and when the reward is acknowledged to be of grace, and not of merit, God will have all the glory in time and eternity.

> Let all who hold this faith and hope
>   In holy deeds abound;
> Thus faith approves itself sincere,
>   By active virtue crowned.

DECEMBER 24.

For wherein shall it be known here that I and thy people have found grace in thy sight? Is it not in that thou goest with us? So shall we be separated, I and thy people, from all the people that are upon the face of the earth.—Exod. xxxiii. 16.

READER, do you adopt the language of Moses, and request with him that, in all your removals, God's presence may go with you?—that you be not permitted to stir without this distinguishing testimony, that you are in the path of duty? Are you waiting upon the Lord, earnest to serve Him in sincerity and truth,—"not being conformed to this world, but transformed by the renewing of your mind," and desirous to be numbered with His separate people? Then you may expect the Divine blessing, and your way to be prosperous. It was a distinguished privilege of the Israelites, that they were to dwell alone, and not to be reckoned among the nations; and it is the privilege and duty of the spiritual Israel to be separate and distinct from the world; they are a separate people in the love of God; in their election in Christ; in the covenant of grace made with them in Him; in effectual vocation; in their being seated with Him to all eternity. Nor are they reckoned among the nations; but as they are called out of them, and generally treated as the refuse and offscouring of all things, they do not reckon themselves to be of the world, but as pilgrims and strangers in it. Lord, let my lot be among thy separate people, the righteous, both here and for evermore!

> Among the righteous let me dwell,
>   And cast my lot with them;
> Be dead to pleasure, dead to wealth,
>   And to the world's esteem.

December 25.

And thou shalt call His name Jesus; for He shall save His people from their sins.—Matt. i. 21.

Sin is the deadliest foe we have; it cast our first parents out of Paradise; it defaced God's image in man; it brought pain, sickness, and death into the world, and a spiritual death into the soul; it causes a distance from God, and a dislike to His holy ways; it exposes body and soul to the last judgment of a holy God, and will sink every unpardoned offender into everlasting destruction. How is this deadly foe to be conquered? Reader, be careful in this matter, and seek after a remedy that will be lasting and efficacious. Duties, prayers, tears, sacrifices, morality, and partial reformations, avail nothing in this case; all below Christ Jesus will prove physicians of no value. Jesus is the only Saviour; His blood is the only atonement for sin; this sprinkled upon the heart by the Spirit, and apprehended by faith, removes the guilt and curse of sin, and speaks pardon and peace; His grace breaks the power of sin and makes us hate it: thus is holiness secured in the heart and walk, as well as peace in the conscience. His people are all that believe in Him, and depend upon Him for pardon, peace, and everlasting salvation. In that happy number, reader, may thou and I be found! may we be enabled to look to Him, to receive Him as our Lord Jesus, able and willing to save to the very uttermost! And may we walk as the redeemed of the Lord, in righteousness and true holiness all the days of our life! Amen.

> He died to bear the guilt of men,
>   That sin might be forgiven.
> He lives to bless them and defend,
>   And plead their cause in heaven.

December 26.

Pour out your heart before God.—Ps. lxii. 8.

What a different view does this lively text give of praying, when opposed to the usual expression of *saying our prayers*,—saying what our books or our parents teach us. To pour out our hearts, is like emptying a vessel of all its contents, so that nothing remains; and, oh! what a pleasing, awful, important thing must this be! Whatever is in my heart, my guilt or fears, my sins or sorrows, my cares and crosses, my wants, my dangers, my weaknesses, temptations, darkness, and ignorance, my doubts and anxieties respecting both body and soul, myself and others, the Church and the world; every thought that arises, relating either to past, present, or future,—I have leave to empty myself of, to pour out by drops, or in a copious stream, till not one burden remains; and this before God, who is a prayer-hearing God. He can send a Hannah away no longer sad,—can say, "Son or daughter, be of good cheer, thy sins are forgiven thee." No wonder, then, that real prayer is so much unknown, or is such a cordial when it is made before Him who is a refuge for us. Away, then, for ever with the prayer of the formalist; may I learn fervency of devotion from my heavenly Master, who, in His agony, prayed till drops of blood fell down! To a suffering Jesus I look for pardon and cleansing. Oh! let me be accepted in the Beloved, and purged daily from my defilements, and so become a vessel to honor, sanctified for the Master's use for ever. Amen.

> Oh! let my earnest pray'r and cry
>   Come near before thee, Lord;
> Give understanding unto me,
>   According to thy word.

December 27.

By the grace of God I am what I am.—1 Cor. xv. 10. *Born again, not of corruptible seed, but of incorruptible, by the word of God. As new-born babes, desire the sincere milk of the word, that ye may grow thereby.*—1 Peter i. 23, and ii. 2.

What made the wonderful difference between Saul the Pharisee, and Paul the Christian?—Grace. What made him trample upon his former legal righteousness, and desire to be found in the righteousness of Christ?—Grace, enlightening grace. Wherein consists the difference between the mere moralist and the real Christian? There may be a moral conduct where there is no grace—no principle of saving divine faith; there may be the fear of the Lord, taught by the precept of men, and not by the Spirit of God. One may attend the ordinances of religion; have a regard to outward decency; may have a name to live, while dead; be high in profession, and, at the same time, a stranger to the power of godliness. Have I this principle, called Grace, in my soul? Have I been born of the incorruptible seed? Have I tasted that the Lord is gracious? Then shall I desire the sincere milk of the word; and thence will draw comfort and nourishment for my soul. Redeeming love shall be my delightful subject; it will sweeten everything in the service of Jesus, will constrain to extensive usefulness in my track of life; the grace of God in Christ Jesus will enlarge my views, keep me humble in heart, and give the praise where alone it is due. Through the sincere milk of the Word, may I grow daily, and be nourished up to eternal life!

> Whate'er I am, I am by grace;
> And unto God be all the praise!
> Grace turns the water into wine,
> And makes the human heart divine.

December 28.

We must all appear before the judgment-seat of Christ.—2 Cor. v. 10.

And are there scoffers, who madly question the coming of the Lord? The hour hastens when infidelity shall doubt no more (1 Thes. iv. 16). How will sinners fade away when, visible to all, the Judge shall appear on His great white throne? Before Him shall stand the whole race of men, small and great; and by the testimony of God and their own consciences, it shall be fully proved and openly declared, what they have been, and what they have done. Then sentence, most righteous, irrevocable, and big with eternity, shall be pronounced. On the wicked everlasting punishment; on the righteous, life eternal! Oh! think what destruction is hanging over your heads, ye obstinate transgressors; for, "Behold, He cometh with clouds, and every eye shall see Him; they also which pierced Him, and all the wicked kindreds of the earth shall wail because of Him. Now is the accepted time,—the day of salvation;" now embrace Him, as your offered, your all-sufficient Saviour; so shall you be for ever delivered from Him as your angry Judge. If this you neglect, how shall you abide the day of His coming in flaming fire? Lift up thy head, my soul, none else is Judge but Christ! Will He, who bore my sins, plead against me in judgment? No; I know in whom I have believed; and that He is able to keep that good thing, my soul, which I have committed to Him, against that day.

> An awful day is drawing near,
>   When Christ will judge the quick and dead!
> Ah! sinner, how wilt thou appear,
>   With all thy sins upon thy head!
> Now mercy seek which may be found;
> For yet you stand on praying ground.

DECEMBER 29.

We, being many, are one body in Christ, and every one members one of another.—Rom. xii. 5. *But now are they many members, yet but one body. And now ye are the body of Christ, and members in particular.*—1 Cor. xii. 20, 27. *Behold, how good and how pleasant it is for brethren to dwell together in unity!*—Ps. cxxxiii. 1.

OH! the blessed communion of saints; one member has the benefit of all the other members' gifts, prayers, and ministrations. One prays for all, and all pray for one. What one has, the other enjoys also. It may be truly said of them, All is yours. There is no envy, no haughtiness, no strife or harm among real saints; for why should I envy that which is my own? Why should I despise that which serves for my necessary assistance?—and why should I strive against and hurt him whose hurt is my own? Is there any strife between the members of our natural body? By no means; they all serve, help, and assist one another; and if one be injured and suffers, all the rest run to its relief, and are neither tired nor angry, if the healing does not follow immediately. O Lord, unite us all in hearty fellowship and tender feelings for each other; and stop all open and subtile divisions which are fermented by lofty spirits, who always boast of mighty things, and to be wise above the rest. Suffer not a self-conceited and a party spirit, which is the spirit of the world, to influence the members of thy body; but bless and grace them all with true humility; then we shall live in a solid union and uninterrupted harmony.

> Oh! glorious portion of the saints!
> Let love suppress our sore complaints,
> And tune our hearts and tongues to sing,
> "All glory to our Sovereign King!"

DECEMBER 30.

Ye are the epistle of Christ, etc.—2 Cor. iii. 3.

THE image is beautiful and instructing:—"The epistle of Christ, written, not in tables of stone," —not on a stony heart, but on a heart of flesh; a heart softened by grace, and made capable of good impressions; the heart, the seat of vital religion. So runs the gracious promise (Jer. xxxi. 33). The Word read and preached is not effectual without the operation of the Spirit of God. By the Spirit, Christians are cast into the Gospel mould; thereby get evangelical, spiritual, and heavenly dispositions; their resemblance to Christ is gradually increased; they have the witness in themselves—have the comfortable experience that they are Christ's, when they can read His image on their hearts. They are manifestly declared to others, that they are the epistle of Christ, by their good conversation and conduct in the world, confessing Him before men, and speaking forth His praise. "Holiness to the Lord" is written with lovely characters on this epistle. Am I the epistle of Christ? Do I read the epistles of Christ in my Bible; and find them written on my heart? Do I read the mind of God there, and heartily approve of His mind? Oh! blessed discovery! What condescending grace! The great God, by His Spirit, to dictate epistles so loving and kind! the great God, whom I have offended, to send me a pardon, not only in His Word, but by His Son also. I would read this epistle from heaven over and over again. Oh! how much do I find in it, while the Spirit opens my understanding to understand the Scriptures!

> Lord, write thy law upon my heart,
>   For thine epistle I would be;
> But write it well on every part,
>   And make me all resemble thee.

DECEMBER 31.

ALLELUIA.—Rev. xix. 1.

Thou began the year, O my soul, with a Hosannah, imploring the Lord's blessing, canst thou now conclude it with an Alleluia? Surely thou canst celebrate the praise of a gracious and loving God. Take a review of the past year; hast thou not had many mercies? Have not the eyes of the Lord been upon thee for good? Hath He not conducted thee through many dangers? Canst thou not, with truth as well as gratitude, set up thine Ebenezer, saying, "Hitherto the Lord hath helped me!" (1 Sam. vii. 12). If thou hast not been fruitful in good works, is thy Lord to blame or thyself? Whatever good has been done in thee or by thee, surely belongs to the favor of God; and whatever has caused shame or humiliation is nowhere chargeable but upon thyself. "Praise the Lord, then, O my soul, and all that is within me praise His holy name; forget not all His benefits" (Ps. ciii. 2-4). Thou wilt soon, O my soul, enter upon another year: let dear-bought experience teach thee to avoid all occasions of evil, and keep thee close to thy God. If thou livest to see another day, set out afresh, and remember to offer thy daily sacrifice of obedience as well as of praise to thy gracious God. Let every revolving day remind thee of thy approaching last day, and daily be thou preparing to meet thy God, that so when thy days are ended, thou mayest sing Alleluias before the throne of God and the Lamb for ever and ever.

> 'Tis Jesus, the First and the Last,
>   Whose spirit shall guide us safe home;
> We'll praise Him for all that is past,
>   And trust Him for all that's to come.